Ebenezer W. Warren

**Nellie Norton**

or, Southern slavery and the Bible

Ebenezer W. Warren

**Nellie Norton**
*or, Southern slavery and the Bible*

ISBN/EAN: 9783744737890

Printed in Europe, USA, Canada, Australia, Japan

Cover: Foto ©Lupo / pixelio.de

More available books at **www.hansebooks.com**

# NELLIE NORTON:

OR,

## SOUTHERN SLAVERY AND THE BIBLE.

A SCRIPTURAL REFUTATION

OF THE

PRINCIPAL ARGUMENTS UPON WHICH THE ABOLITIONISTS RELY.

A VINDICATION OF SOUTHERN SLAVERY FROM THE OLD AND NEW TESTAMENTS.

BY

REV. E. W. WARREN.

MACON, GA.:
BURKE, BOYKIN & COMPANY.
1864.

MANY books have been written in favor of slavery; but few of them have been generally read. This little volume claims no superiority over any of them. It was thought that a reply to abolition objections, based upon the Divine argument, might satisfy many minds who had not the time to devote to a thorough investigation of the subject, and, perhaps, set the question, as to its moral aspect, forever at rest.

It is presented in popular form, because that was thought to be the surest way to place the argument before the public mind. The author is deeply impressed with the fact that *slavery is of God*, and, desiring others to embrace the same truth, has here presented the scriptural arguments by means of which his own conclusions have been formed.

The author asks the indulgence of the critic into whose hands this little volume may fall. In the daily press of pastoral engagements, which were of paramount importance, he has given his weary evenings, when not otherwise occupied, to the composition of this book; and, therefore, he feels that it has many imperfections.

An humble volume, whose aim is the vindication of the Divine economy, and the establishment of Bible truth in the popular mind, and with the earnest prayer that the Author of all good, may bestow upon it His blessing to the accomplishment of these ends, the work is sent forth with feelings of diffidence by

THE AUTHOR.

MACON, GA., MAY 4, 1864.

## CHAPTER I.

*Anxiety to see a Slave—The Welcome—Kindly Greetings—Family Prayer—The Higher Law—Discussion.*

"Mother do show me a slave as soon as the steamer gets near enough."

This request was made by a beautiful young lady, as she stood on the deck of a large steamer that was nearing the port of Savannah. It was her first trip South. The fulfillment of a promise of long standing, made to a dear uncle, that when her education was completed she would pay him a visit. He had left New England when quite young, and having married a Southern lady, seldom returned except on business, or to spend a few weeks with his aged parents.

In contemplating this visit there was but one thing that marred the anticipated pleasure of the mother and daughter, that was the idea of seeing the poor slave in chains, of listening to his groans of anguish, while they were powerless to free him from his bondage.

They had been led to regard as real, all the tales of woe, all the horrible tragedies, of which they had so often read in speeches, sermons, books or newspapers. They were sincere in believing slavery to be the "sum of all villanies;" and they had mutually agreed to give their influence to the cause of "human liberty and equal rights," in other words, to abolitionism.

Fully expecting to see the negroes chained together and bearing heavy iron weights, the curiosity of Miss Nellie Norton was fully awake to catch the first glimpse of a slave.

The steamer having reached the wharf, the passengers came thronging to the shore, some after long absence eager to receive the affectionate greeting of their friends, some in search of pleasure, while others, with pallid cheeks and wasted forms, have come to seek new life and strength from the balmy breezes of a more Southern clime.

"And sure enough you've come, sister; welcome to our Southern soil and home. I am so happy to see you." Mrs. Norton threw her arms around the neck of her brother, and for a moment both shed tears of joy at meeting again after so long an absence. "And Nellie, dear Nellie, is this——! Surely this is not my little Nellie whom I last saw eight years ago in New England! Why how you have grown! No, this is my niece, Miss Norton. Come let me seat you in my carriage, then I will see to your baggage."

As Mr. Thompson led the way to the carriage, Nellie, still on the qui vive to see a slave, could not longer restrain her curiosity.

"Uncle, do show me a slave if there is one here."

"Jack, come here," cried Mr. T. The carriage driver promptly obeyed his master's call, advancing with hat in hand. Jack was a fine looking mulatto, neatly dressed in a suit of broad cloth, his hat being tidily bound with crape. "Here is a slave, Nellie," said Mr. T.

"Oh no,.uncle, you jest, do you not? That cannot be a slave. I thought you Southerners kept your slaves chained lest they should run away from you."

"Pshaw, Nellie, you have certainly been to Brooklyn and heard that villainous hypocrite Henry Ward Beecher. But here we are at the carriage. Jack remain here until I go and have the baggage put in the wagon."

"Yes, sir," said Jack with a quick and emphatic voice.

The ladies being seated, concluded that while they were waiting they would begin to acquaint themselves with slavery by obtaining information from one of the sufferers. Nellie, who felt her superiority as an educated young lady, over the ignorant people of the South, as she imagined them to be, began the conversation with Jack, the negro carriage driver.

Hesitating for a moment as to whether she should address him as Mr. or Sir, as a free man or as a servant, she finally began without either. "Are you in my Uncle's service?"

"Yes'm, I b'longs to mas' George."

"How do you like him?"

"I likes him fust rate; "he's mighty good to us, feeds us well, gives us plenty of close and is good all de time."

"But would you not rather be free, as we are, so that you could go where you please, and when you please?"

"Don't know, Missus, color'd folks han't got white folk's ways, no how; we wouldn't know how to 'have ourselves; we too ignunt."

"Suppose I were to buy you and carry you home with me, and set you free, so that you could work for yourself and have everything you made, would you like that?"

"Ef you'd carry mas' George and miss Penny and the child'ens wid you, and let me stay with dem; not 'thout."

" Why would you rather live with Uncle and be a slave than to go with me and be free ?"

" I couldn't quit mas' George, no how ; he's mighty good man, and den Miss Penny she's monstrous kind, and when we get sick she 'tends to us and nusses us so good, and gives us such nice fixin's to eat, and has us 'tended to mighty kind."

" What a stupid dolt," said Nellie, softly to her mother. " Poor fellow he loves his chains."

Mr. Thompson having arranged the baggage, came and took his seat in the carriage with his sister and niece. Jack was ordered to drive forward, and while they were going to Mr. T's residence they conversed on family matters, Southern scenery, society, &c.

After a ride of several hours, they approached the elegant home of their relative. The house stood on a slight elevation, surrounded by exquisite shrubbery, tastefully arranged and trimmed, while at the distance of a few hundred yards could be seen two rows of neatly painted negro cabins.

Mrs. Thompson, meeting them at the gate with the true grace and cordial affection of a cultivated Southern lady, extended to them a most hearty welcome. The children, too, of whom there were five, were all eager to see cousin Nellie and aunt Julia, of whose coming they had heard so much. They were each embraced in turn, and seemed delighted to see their Northern relatives.

They entered the richly furnished dwelling just as the sun sank to his evening repose, charming the visitors with his gorgeous coloring of the Western sky. After arranging their toilet, the ladies were invited in to tea. Having spent some time in social conversation around the table, all were assembled for family prayer. At the sound of a bell the house servants came in and seated themselves near the door. One of them handed Mr. Thompson a Testament from which he read a chapter, occasionally stopping to make explanations. When the chapter was finished, they all knelt and he prayed, while an occasional response in the way of an audible groan proceeded from some of his colored auditors. This was an unusual scene to the new comers, who were totally ignorant of Southern life and negro character, no remarks, however, were made, for they feared to speak, lest they might wound the feelings of their deluded relatives, who ignorantly imagined it was right to hold human beings in slavery.

" Well, Nellie, you have now seen several of my slaves, what do you think of them and slavery?" said Mr. Thompson, after they were all seated in the parlor.

"Do you ask me for the *truth*, uncle?"

"Certainly I do, my dear, I would not have you speak an untruth."

"I think well of your *slaves*, as you are pleased to term them, but I abominate the laws and public sentiment which doom them to a life of servitude."

"Then, my dear niece, you abominate the law of God, and the sentiments inculcated by his holy prophets and apostles. I do not feel reproached by your remark, but I would kindly suggest the propriety of an investigation from the Bible, of the origin and perpetuity of slavery, at some convenient time while you are here."

"Uncle, slavery shocks *humanity*, how could it then be taught by the Divine Being? I cannot believe it, and if I did, I do not think I could confide in the justice and goodness of such a Being."

"Why, Nellie, you shock me, if God is not such a one as you would have Him to be, you will not worship Him. If he does not come up to *your* standard of what he ought to be; if He dares to teach what does not accord with *your* views, then you reject Him. Consider, my dear niece, of what presumption you are guilty."

"But, uncle, there is a law of the human mind higher than all other laws, having its own intuitive perceptions of what is right and wrong: this law of the mind is *above all other laws*, and is at liberty to accept or reject any proposition, as it may accord with or differ from this intuitive moral consciousness. Slavery comes in direct antagonism with this law of my mind, and hence I reject either the interpretation or the authority of any and every standard which favors slavery."

"These 'laws of the human mind,' these 'intuitive perceptions,' this 'moral consciousness,' were given you by your gracious Creator. Then they are creatures of His. Now shall the Creator become subordinate to the creature? 'Shall the thing formed, say to Him who formed it, Why hast thou made me thus?' But from what did you learn your ethics, or metaphysics, or rather infidelity, I ought to call it, for it is really worse than the system either of Paine, or Hume? I am more and more astonished at you. I was not aware that abolitionism had resorted to such desperate ends to sustain itself. I knew that Theodore Parker had rejected the Bible because it was a pro-slavery book, but I did not know that the sentiment had taken possession of the pulpit, the press and the schools, so thoroughly that a girl just from her alma mater should be so well versed in the whole argument. But I did know that this would be the last and only successful point from which abolitionism could be defended. The North *must* give up the Bible and religion, or adopt our views of slavery."

" Not so fast, uncle, I have not admitted that the Bible is a pro-slavery book, nor do I believe it. Upon the contrary, I have been taught to believe in its Divine origin, to reverence its holy truths, and to obey its heavenly precepts. I only said what would be the case in the event it did teach slavery."

" I am glad, dear Nellie, you have been so piously taught; I only regret that this religious education has taken such slight hold upon your reverence; for with your firm belief in the Divine origin of the Bible, you reverence the higher law more than you do its heavenly instructions. You will believe the Bible is from God, a holy book, worthy of the heart obedience of all, unless it teaches slavery, in which event it is ' *sans Dieu.*' Well, I see you are afraid of the Bible, the only revelation from heaven, the only sure unerring source of information. So you must be left to 'the law in your members which wars against the law of your mind, and *brings you into captivity to the law of sin.*'"

" No, uncle, I am not afraid of the Bible, nor do I fear to investigate the subject of slavery as revealed in it. I am only surprised that you should have been so deluded as to believe the institution can find any favor with a holy God. I am willing at any time to begin the investigation with you."

" Very well, then, the arrangement is understood. When you have had sufficient time to rest, and look at slavery a little in its practical workings, say one week from the present time, our investigation shall begin."

The remainder of the evening was spent most pleasantly in conversation upon other matters, and at a late hour all retired.

The succeeding week passed most agreeably to all the members of the household.

The flowers and shrubbery, of which there was a great variety, covered a large and beautiful plat of ground in front of the house. Thither Nellie resorted some portion of every day, with her young cousins, and delighted them no little with her ana'ysis of many of the flowers. Several times during the week she strolled down to the negro cabins, with one of her little cousins. She desired to look into the treatment of her uncle's slaves, and read, if possible, in their faces, and hear from their half concealed expressions, which she supposed would almost involuntarily escape from their lips, the evidence of their misery occasioned by the bondage. At every visit her surprise was increased, to find them so entirely free from all care, and manifesting so contented, cheerful and happy a spirit.

## THE DISCUSSION.

Agreeably to the understanding of the week before, the family assembled in the parlor after tea, with a view to the anticipated discussion. The two elder ladies being seated on the sofa, Mr. T. invited his niece to draw near the centre table, upon which lay a large Bible. Taking in his hand a concordance, for more convenient reference to any text bearing upon the subject, he seated himself opposite to her. Both of them felt confident of being able to maintain the positions which they were about to assume. Nellie was but little versed in the teaching of the Bible, but she had selected from her uncle's library "Wayland's Moral Science," and that was as good authority as she wanted. Dr. Wayland was a wise and learned man; too much so, in her opinion, to make a mistake, and too good to misrepresent the doctrines of the Bible. She was familiar with his opinions on this subject, for they had been taught her with great care.

Mr. Thompson had come South with the usual prejudices against slavery which Northern birth and education instil. He had not consented to become the owner of slaves from mercenary motives. At first his conscience forbade the idea of holding a fellow being in servitude, and he did not do so until as a conscientious seeker after truth, he had carefully investigated the subject from the Scriptures. He was therefore familiar with the subject in all its bearings.

" 'The Bible is the sufficient rule of faith and practice,' was a dogma taught by the great reformer, Martin Luther, and one to which all protestants have given their most hearty assent," said Mr. Thompson, as he took the Bible into his hands and opened it without reference to book or chapter. As he did so he kept his eyes on Nellie all the time, to catch, if possible, her expression of assent to this truth. But she had carefully guarded herself against any admission which might be afterwards used to her disadvantage in the argument. . She felt herself to be the representative of abolitionism, and she was determined it should not suffer on account of the unwariness of its advocate—the ground must be maintained, the point carried at all hazards. So she was silent.

"Hear, O Heavens, give ear, O Earth, for it is the Lord that speaketh." This quotation was made by Mr. T. with solemn emphasis, then turning to Genesis ix: 25, he read, "Cursed be Canaan; a servant of servants shall he be unto his brethren, and he said Blessed be the Lord God of Shem, and Canaan shall be his servant. God shall enlarge Japhet and he shall dwell in the tents of Shem: and Canaan shall be his servant." Here, Nellie, is the origin of slavery, it comes directly from God through His servant Noah."

"Excuse me uncle, for the comparison, I intend no personal disrespect to you, but you really remind me of Rip Van Winkle searching for the flag of George the III, after the Independence of the American Colonies was gained, and acknowledged by Great Britain. To go back to the flood, to an old man just aroused from the stupor of drunkenness, in order to justify American, or I should say, Southern slavery. Let the odium rest upon those who foster the wicked institution. Really, uncle, you must be hard pressed for a scriptural argument."

"You speak lightly of the 'preacher of righteousness,' as Noah is called in the sacred word. He alone was found worthy of deliverance from the deluge, and to become the second father of the human family, from whom descended the Son of God, the world's Redeemer. It is written, '*Honor* thy father.' But to the argument. I thought you were too well versed in logic to object to tracing effects back to their causes; and that you were too fond of looking through a subject, to be desirous of commencing short of the beginning, or to stop short of the ending. My purpose is, according to the agreement, to investigate the subject as taught in the Bible. I am beginning at the fountain, and shall trace the stream through all its meanderings, showing its origin, regulation and perpetuity."

"Do not be on the opposite extreme of Rip Van Winkle, and run too fast to read, nor despise things because they are old."

"Truth loses none of its value by age, nor is error entitled to respect on account of its later origin. If you will not accept the Bible as authority, why the discussion is at an end."

"Oh! no uncle, proceed. I only objected to your going back so far to vindicate slavery in its present revolting aspect."

"And I only went back to show that this revolting institution, as you are pleased to call it, was ordained by God, and was therefore right, for God can do no wrong."

"I remember," said Nellie, "to have heard one of our preachers giving an account of slavery, and I think it was from the Scripture

B

you have just read. He said the poor Israelite who became hopelessly indebted, was sold, that the debt might be paid; but at the end of seven years he was by law released. So I don't think you will prove perpetual servitude from this law."

"Your preacher thought this poor Israelite descended from Canaan, did he? It might be well for him to study genealogy. There is a law regulating the slavery of the poor Hebrews, found in Exodus xxi: 2-6, 'If thou buy an Hebrew servant, six years he shall serve, and in the seventh he shall go out free for nothing. If he came in by himself he shall go out by himself: if he were married then his wife shall go out with him. If his master have given him a wife, and she have borne him sons or daughters; the wife and her children shall be her masters', and he shall go out by himself. And if the servant plainly say, 'I love my master, my wife and my children, I will not go out free, then his master shall bring him unto the door, or unto the door post: and his master shall bore his ear through with an awl, and he shall serve him forever.' This law is also repeated in Deut. xv: 16, 17. The law here enacted was a *necessity* growing out of the nature of things. I mean, the organization of human society, and the dependences of the poor classes upon the rich. This form of slavery exists to a greater or less extent in all countries, where African slavery does not. At the North, you make slaves of the poor people, instead of supporting them voluntarily, as we do. You enslave your unfortunate kindred who become dependent upon you for support. The truth is, the world never has, and never can exist without slavery in some form. T. R. R. Cobb, an able writer on this subject says: 'In every organized community there must be a laboring class to execute the plans devised by wiser heads; to till the ground, and to perform the menial offices necessarily connected with social life.' It therefore follows, as a consequence, that where negro slavery does not exist, the rich will enslave the poor of their own race.

"The curse pronounced by God, through Noah, upon Ham and his descendants, is subject to no such restrictions and limitations as governed enslaved Hebrews. It was to extend from generation to generation, to be perpetual. Hence you see Abraham 'the father of the faithful, the friend of God,' was the owner of a large number of slaves. Some were 'born in his house,' and some were 'bought with his money.' So it is evident that slavery was common in those days; and the domestic slave trade, so much abhorred by the abolitionists, and which affords themes of such bitter denunciations against the South, was also practised, even by the very best men.

"*Abraham trafficked in human flesh*, when he bought servants with his money."

"My dear uncle, you shock me, you horrify me, when you say that Abraham, 'in whom all the families of the earth were to be blest,' bought human beings for the purpose of enslaving them. Surely this cannot be true; but, if it is, I apprehend, the reason is to be found in the fact, that in the dark age in which Abraham lived, the people were not civilized and enlightened as they are now. They saw through a glass darkly, that was but the misty twilight of our day."

"But Nelly, it was so ordained of God, and He was not less wise and good then than now. The advancement of the world has not enlightened the mind, nor refined the sensibilities of deity. I think your sensibilities are morbid, when they revolt at that which God has done. Your sympathy for the slave is, I fear, quite above your reverence for Deity. Be careful, lest in avoiding Scylla you are wrecked in Charybdis."

"As much as I love you, my dearest uncle, and much as I confide in your honesty and intelligence, you must excuse me for not taking your *ipse dixit* as to the *perpetuity* of slavery. That Abraham bought and held them is certainly true, and that Canaan was to be a 'servant of servants,' and was to serve his brethren, is also true; but it does not therefore follow that the institution was to be perpetual. I cannot believe it. *I do not wish to believe it.*"

Nellie's cheek flushed, and she grew animated as she emphasized the closing sentence: "Your proofs are insufficient; they want point and force. Your quotation is irrelevant; the phrase 'servant of servants,' does not mean perpetual servitude," she replied.

"Then," continued her uncle, "they shall be strong enough for you, if you will take divine testimony. Will you be kind enough to open the Bible and read Leviticus xxv : 44–46 ?"

Nellie took the Bible and opening to the chapter and verses, reluctantly read:

"Both thy bondmen and thy bondmaids which thou shalt have, shalt be of the heathen that are round about you; of them *shall ye buy* bondmen and bondmaids. Moreover, of the children of the strangers that do sojourn among you, of them shall ye buy, and of their families that are with you, which they begat in your land, and they shall be your *possession*. And ye shall take them *as an inheritance* for your children after you, to inherit them after you; they shall be your *bondmen forever*. But over your brethren, the

children of Israel, ye shall not rule one over another with rigor."
Nellie closed the book and sat silently, while a shade of discontent rested upon her usually bright face. She felt no disposition to speak, for she knew not what to say, and yet silence was painful, for her uncle might construe it into acquiescence. Her suspense was short, however, for the mother and aunt, at the other side of the room, had found it most difficult to interest themselves, so as to forget what was going on, and had therefore by tacit consent, suspended their conversation in order to hear Nellie read what the Lord had said by Moses, on the perpetuity of slavery; and seeing her embarrassment her aunt broke the silence. "I think your discussion had better be suspended for the present; we will grant, if you ask it, that you are both erudite and intellectual; can you not give us some proof of your superior social powers? Don't you think you can afford to play the agreeable for the balance of the evening?"

"Then in one minute we will join you," said Mr. T., and turning to Nellie, he said, "As we will not have another opportunity for several evenings, to converse on this subject again, I wish to mention a few of the points contained in the quotation you have just read, that you may consider them at your leisure.

1st. It establishes the domestic slave trade: 'ye shall buy bondmen and bondmaids.' 2d. They were permitted to buy children from their parents: 'Of the children of the strangers that do sojourn among you, of them shall ye buy.' 3d. They were the property, or chattel, of the owner: 'And they shall be your possession.' 4th. There was no limit to their servitude, it was to be made perpetual: 'An inheritance for your children, your *bondmen forever.*' Here you have divine proof that a holy and just God did perpetuate slavery.

"To-morrow evening my young friend and neighbor, Mr. Mortimer, is to pay you a visit; on the next, Saturday evening, Jacob and Phebe are to be married, and on Sabbath afternoon it is our custom to attend the religious services of the colored people. In the mean time you may be able to give a few leisure hours to considering the subject of this evening's conversation and see what the 'law and the testimony' say."

Nellie's mind was not at rest. The Bible certainly did teach that slavery was a perpetual institution. Its chains were forged in heaven, by God himself, and so fastened, that no power could sunder them but His. Here were the words, she had read them herself, she could not be mistaken; and yet she had repeatedly heard the contrary asserted, by ministers in whom she had the utmost confidence. Her Sabbath School teachers had taught her that slavery was inhuman, iniquitous, the sum of all villainies, that there was no authority whatever for it in the word of God, that Southern cupidity had forged its chains, and Northern philanthropy *must* break them; that it was the peculiar mission of the more enlighted and christianised people of the North to 'break every yoke' and set every bondman free, and with these sentiments even the great Dr. Wayland certainly agreed. "How can it be? certainly the Bible is not a pro-slavery book. Surely! God is not a pro-slavery God. Impossible!! but here is *His* word. If it should be true, (and how am I to doubt it? have I not been taught to *believe*, to reverence, to obey it?) what am I to do? Give into the idea of slavery? Never, *never*. But can I give up my God and my Bible? Never, no NEVER—*perish the thought*. O God help me, for I know not what to do. O God, I cleave to thee! 'Let God be true, but every man a liar.'"

Poor Nellie, there was an invisible struggle going on, of which none dreamed but herself. All her efforts to dispel her troubles and engage pleasantly in the conversation were fruitless. She finally arose, and bidding them good night retired to her room, not however to sleep, but to wrestle in agony as to whether she should cling to the prejudices of her early education and still advocate abolitionism, and in that event to reject the Bible as a revelation from God; or in humble confidence in the justice and immutable righteousness of its great author, accept the Bible with all its teachings. Finally she caught the idea, that Southern slavery could not be defended from the sacred volume, and laying the flattering unction to her heart, quieted her nerves and fell asleep.

## CHAPTER II.

*Visit of Mr. Mortimer—Negro Wedding—Sabbath School—Prayer Meeting.*

Nellie did not awake the next morning till the sun had ascended high up into the heavens, and covered the earth with his golden light.

Amy, the chamber maid, had the room well warmed, and had been long waiting impatiently for the young sleeper to awake.

"Missus, time to git up, breafus' ready, been waiton long time for you."

Nellie opened her eyes upon the Ethiopian maid, and beholding her bright countenance, her smiling face and ivory teeth, was reminded of the fact that she was in the land of slavery. When she stepped upon the thick warm carpet and advanced to the fire, and gazed around upon the many comforts that met her view, and became cognizant of the dusky Amy's attentions, having, for their object, *her comfort*, her convictions of Southern life and manners were materially modified. She had not yet discovered that *blight* she expected to behold imprinted by slavery upon everything, animate and inanimate, on manners, customs and habits. She had expected to see a cold remorseless tyranny, a grinding aristocracy; and a dumb, despairing, revengeful slave population. She had expected proud hauteur, overbearing and heartless despotism on the one hand, and cringing servility, composed of hopeless fear and smothered wrath, on the other. She had expected to see moss-grown decay, and evidences of an effeminate civilization, instead of warm, genial comfort, general satisfaction and happiness, and universal signs of confidence, love and prosperity.

Nellie had been accustomed to wait entirely on herself at home. Here she finds a chair placed by the fire for her, polite hands warm her shoes and stockings and hand them to her. Her garments are likewise warmed and handed to her. Nimble fingers aid in adjusting her attire, the water is poured into the bowl for her, and a towel is extended to her, and when the last touch of arrangement has been given to her hair, skilful hands slip her morning dress over her head, and with a few expert manipulations, complete her attire, and leave her ready to descend to the breakfast table.

"You looks mighty nice dis mornin' Miss, I bound Mas' George 'praise you, and think you mighty sweet when he sees you. Dis dress mighty purty, I 'specks you gib it to me when you go home.

Gwine to have big weddin' to-morrow night ma'am, Misses been busy 'bout it all de mornin'. Jacob and Phebe gwine to marry, and uncle Jesse gwine to 'form de sarimony, and me and Elsey gwine to be de tendunts wid Sam and Guss," &c. Thus the jubilant girl ran on in a strain of intelligence to the surprise and pleasure of Nellie, till she descended to the dining room.

> "Her world was ever joyous—
> She thought of grief and pain
> As giants in the olden time,
> That ne'er would come again."

After breakfast, Nellie and her young cousin, Alice Thompson, walked to the front porch. The day was one of those rich, hazy autumnal days, all flooded with glorious sunshine, and mellowed by a soft Southern breeze so common to our Southern climate. They then walked to the back door, and gazed for a while on the magnificent live oaks, and majestic magnolias, that shaded the back yard.

On all sides, elegance, comfort and plenty were visible, accompanied with contentment, peace and happiness. Nellie's eye, with a delight bordering on rapture, took in the glories of the whole scene: its fields, its fences, its trees, its shrubs, its houses, its gardens, its evidences of solid prosperity and comfort; and she mentally contrasted it with her own prim, precise, economical home. She contrasted the cold calculating manners of the North, with the open, warm, genial habits of the South. She arrayed the hired indifferent services of "white helps," with their frequent "warnings," with the confiding filial obedience of Southern slaves, jumping with a smile to perform a behest. She could not help comparing the cold, selfish relations existing between mistress and servant in New England, and the open, warm, friendly, confiding feeling manifested between the slaves and their owners. Here was a master and mistress engaged in preparations at considerable trouble and expense, to furnish a sumptuous supper and appropriate dressing to gratify two slaves who were going to be married. Nellie was surprised, but could not be blind to these things.

She and Alice took a walk among the negro cabins, and the ebony damsels crowded around and followed them with the greatest glee imaginable, now and then one venturing a remark at which all the rest would giggle immoderately; and when Nellie thought proper to engage in some slight badinage, the universal merriment seemed to reach its utmost hight. Nellie had never seen such merry servants.

Not one seemed borne down with that mighty incubus of care and oppression she had expected; but decked out in bright colors, and new shoes, and flaming "head handkerchers," they followed her as entirely free from care and liberty-longing as school children upon any academy lawn.

"You Jim! aint you comin' along wid dem chips?" Thus resounded from the vicinago of her huge pot, the voice of "Aunt Fanny." It was "Aunt Fanny's" business to cook for the "chilern," and take care of them, the latter she did most effectually by ruling them with a rod of birch. Her large pot is filled with meat, greens and "dumplings," and the "taters" are wrapped in the ashes. When at twelve o'clock, all are ready, she deals out to all according to her "resarved rights," that is to say, she has a half dozen or more large trays and basins, filled with the contents of the pot, around which gather from three to five of the little Africans, and seating themselves, eat till they are all satisfied.

"You, Jim," says Aunt Fanny, as she saw Nellie approaching, "aint you comin' long wid dem chips? I see you foolin' long dar, sir; never mind, I whip you for dat sho's you born; you see if I don't now." While "Aunt Fanny" is very good naturedly explaining to Nellie how she cooks for and takes care of "de chilern," and was very proud of being so honored by the attention of "young miss," Jim approaches the pot with his basket of chips, wholly unobserved by "Aunt Fanny," whose kind heart has already forgotten the threat, and getting on his knees, throws the chips somewhere near about the fire, while he gazes all the time, with open mouth, into the face of Nellie.

Twenty or thirty little darkies gather around her, all fat and saucy, jolly and lively, and not in the least disconcerted, they gaze into her face, and laugh and stare, with the whites of their eyes upturned and their mouths spread from— side to side.

"Do they get enough to eat, aunty?"

"God bless your soul, chile, plenty; I stuffs 'em, see how fat dey is."

"Where do you get the food?"

"I gits it from de smoke-house every mornin'. Boss weighs it out, and I biles de middlin', and greens, and dumplins for 'em in de pot, and cooks de taters in de ashes. Plenty, dey gets nuff, sho."

Thus pleasantly and swiftly the time glided away with Nellie. Late in the afternoon Mr. Mortimer came over to take tea and make the acquaintance of Mrs. Norton and her daughter. He was the friend and neighbor, and intimate associate of Mr. Thompson, and was always a welcome guest in his family. He was of medium height, and very graceful, with an intellectual cast of features. He was intelligent and agreeable, commanding fine conversational powers, and a high-toned gentleman of unexceptional moral character. The elegance, courteousness and affability displayed by Mr. M. during the evening, made time pass in the family circle with unwonted celerity, and all seemed disappointed when the hour of eleven arrived and their young friend took his leave.

After his departure no remarks were made as to the young visitor. Mr. and Mrs. T. waited for their relatives to say how they were pleased, and Mrs. Norton waited for Nellie; she from choice, or design, was silent. To tell the whole truth, she was very favorably impressed, but would not commit herself till a better and more thorough acquaintance with his true character. " Make haste to be slow in forming your opinion of young men," was her father's favorite proverb, and she believed it was correct and acted upon it.

Saturday, the wedding day, dawned upon the world in cloudless glory. It was a jubilant holiday for all the servants on the plantation of Mr. Thompson.

The bride-groom expectant was Jacob, now foreman of the plantation. He had been promoted to the important post of "driver" for his fidelity and honesty. He was about twenty-five, of a yellow complexion, and as dashing and good humored a fellow as you find in a day's drive. He devotedly loved his master and mistress, and would have died for Miss Alice. Phebe was about twenty-six, and was Mrs. T.'s house-maid, a quiet, respectful woman, who knew her duty and always did it well. Her complexion was dark.

They were about to consummate a long cherished attachment, and both the master and mistress thought fit to grace the occasion with their presence, and invited their guests also to enjoy this, to them, novel scene.

Mr. Mortimer, having come over by special invitation, joined the party, who proceeded to the neat double cabin whose larger room had been cleanly swept and neatly arranged, and on whose wide hearth a bright fire was blazing.

Negro weddings are more stately and solemn than one would naturally suppose. Negroes are impressible creatures, and are easily affected by aught of the august.

The whites stopped in front of the door, rather than crowd through the anxious mass of lookers-on, but they enjoyed a tolerable view, and heard all that was said.

The door of the little room was thrown open, and one couple elegantly dressed, entered, ranging themselves on the right; then another couple, ranging themselves towards the left; these were followed by Jacob and Phebe. Each female attendant wore a white muslin dress, with white flowers in their hair, all tidily arranged by Mrs. Thompson, Alice and Nellie. Each male was dressed in broadcloth, with shining boots, ruffled shirts, standing collars and white gloves, with their pocket handkerchiefs but half concealed in their breast pockets. Phebe was tastefully dressed in white, with slippers and a long white veil; altogether she presented an elegant appearance. Jacob was done up in a new suit of broad cloth, a present, for the occasion from his master; he wore a white vest, gloves and cravat, and with a fair personal appearance, was the *ne plus ultra* of negro elegance.

Not a sound was heard, all were silent and still as the grave. "Uncle Jesse" advanced, with book in hand; there was a solemnity of appearance about his face and demeanor highly instructive and impressive. After a moment's pause, to collect his thoughts and appear dignified, he began:

"God made Adam fust, he staid long time in the garden 'thout a wife, but he wan't satisfied and happy, though he have every other thing he want. Then God say, it no good for the man that he be alone, I make a help meet for him, to comfort him in sickness and nus him in trouble, and to talk to him when he lonesome. So God make Eve outen Adam's rib, and say, she bone of your bone and flesh of your flesh, and for this cause a man shall quit be father and mother, and stay with his wife. Any body present got any objections to this lady and gentleman bein' married into holy matrimony, so they now make it known or hold their peace forevermore. Once, twice, thrice—no objection.

"Jacob, take Phebe by the hand. Do you brother Jacob take Phebe to be your lovin' and true wife? Will you love her like Abraham loved Sarah, treat her kind like Isaac did Rebecca, be faithful to her like Zacharias was to Elizabeth, and not cleave to no other woman but her, till she die—do you?" A graceful bow and a scrape of the foot, was the affirmative response.

"Do you, sister Phebe, take brother Jacob to be your lone husband. To honor him as Sarah did Abraham, and obey him as Rebecca did Isaac, and nus him, and comfort him as Elizabeth did

Zacharias, and always cleave to no other man till he dead—do you?" A quick courtesy was the response. "Then I pronounce you husband and wife, with the blessing of God to live together forever. Amen."

Great confusion followed as each one pressed forward to wish the newly married couple "much joy." Many efforts at wit were made, and a general scene of hilarity ensued, which was kept up till supper was announced. The repast was not less sumptuous than elegant. The "bride's cake" was exquisitely beautiful.

"Uncle Jesse" asked a blessing at the table, at the conclusion of which each bowed his head and scraped his foot. It was interesting to see the young "gen'men," waiting on the "ladies," as they handed round the table first one dish and then another.

But the scene after supper, far surpassed anything which had preceded it. The "playing songs," and kissing, the joyous peels of laughter, the continuous gleeful mirth, the "uproarious," outbursts of merriment, beggar all description. I therefore lay down my pen, and leave the reader to imagine, what must have been the impressions on the mind of Miss Nellie Norton, just from New England.

If you have never witnessed one of these scenes, be assured, kind reader, it is good for dyspepsia, a certain cure for the "blues," and will make a preacher laugh.

But we leave the negroes to play and sing what they please, and as long as they please, to fiddle, "pat Juba," and dance and have a merry time generally, if they like. The hour is late and we must prepare for the Sabbath, when we are again to meet some of these happy Ethiopians, but under different circumstances.

On arriving at the house, Mr. Thompson opened his mail, which pressing engagements since its arrival at sun down, had prevented. "A letter for Nellie," he exclaimed. She came bounding to his side, and opened and read with great eagerness, the following note:

PULASKI HOUSE, Sav., Nov. 23d, 18—.

*Miss Nellie Norton:* Dear Young Friend—You will doubtless be surprised to receive this from me, bearing date at this place. My health suddenly failed, my symptoms became alarming, and my physicians recommended a trip South, to which my parishioners generously consented.

It would afford me pleasure to come out and spend a few days with you and your good mother, which I contemplate doing at my earliest convenience.

What a beautiful land is this, how sweet its breezes, how balmy its

air. What a paradise it would be but for the curse of slavery
But O the groaning of the oppressed! May the time be hastened
when every yoke shall be broken

   In haste,    Your affectionate Pastor,
                DANIEL B. PRATT.

"O Mother, it's from Mr. Pratt, and he is in Savannah, come because his health failed, and wants to come out and see us. Uncle, can't you send for him in the morning, and let him come out to-morrow?"

"Shall I send for him on *Sabbath*, Nellie?"

"O yes, uncle, it's no harm *under the circumstances* to send for a poor sick preacher to get out and enjoy a little fresh country air, is it?"

"Well, just as you say. I don't think you would survive till Monday, so I will have the carriage off early. Write him a note, that we will expect him early to dinner; a cold dinner, enjoyed by warm hearted friends." Nellie tripped away to pen the note, while Mr. Thompson went to inform Jack that he must go up to the city early in the morning, with the carriage, to bring out a gentleman who was at the Pulaski House.

At one o'clock, on Sabbath, Dr Pratt arrived. He was met at the carriage by Nellie, and her mother, and Mr. Thompson. Mr. T. extended to him a cordial welcome, and invited him to make his house his home while at the South. In this invitation, Mrs. T., after being introduced to the Doctor, cordially united. Dr. Pratt was surprised at the open hearted frankness and generosity of his new friend. It was his first trip South, and he was not prepared to believe there was anywhere to be found such whole souled generosity, much less among the slaveocracy.

If the reader desires a description of Daniel B. Pratt, D. D., they can just imagine a short, stout man, with large blue eyes, a bald head, a fair skin, and a large roman nose, with a polite and easy address, and a real "down Easter's" brogue, compressed lips, erect head, rather inclined to throw it back, with a large natural protuberance on the top of the head. He was phrenologically a man of self-will, self-esteem, and great firmness, amounting to stubbornness.

At three o'clock Mr. Thompson asked Dr. Pratt if he would accompany him and Nellie to the negro church to witness a negro Sunday School and Prayer meeting. He readily consented. A walk of near a half mile brought them to a neat little painted house with glass windows, and a bell. On entering they found about thirty negro children, all in clean clothes, some with hats and some with bonnets, and some bare headed, seated on the front benches.

A white lady was sitting near. She was a worthy young lady, and I must honor my readers with an introduction to her.

Miss Kate Nelson was the governess in the family of Mr. Thompson. She was "to the manor born," a true Georgian lady. She was thoroughly educated, graceful, dignified and intelligent, modest and retiring, but not bashful. She knew her duty, and as a conscientious christian, was always found laboring to discharge it. It was her custom, at Mr. T.'s request, to teach his young negroes, orally, every Sabbath afternoon, and learn them to sing. In catechising them, she asked the question and then answered it, and made all the pupils repeat it after her two or three times till they could remember it. They displayed an accurate knowledge of the creation, flood, calling of Abraham, the ten commandments, &c. In learning them to sing, it was her custom to read the first line of the verse, then have them all repeat it, then read the other in like manner, then repeat both together, and so through the song, singing each verse as soon as they could repeat it. I observed that Miss Nelson seemed partial to those songs which had a chorous, and the school seemed to sing them with greater zeal.

The little ones all sang with open mouths and extended voices. It was really refreshing to see and hear them. They were always delighted with the exercises, and engaged in them with their whole soul and mind. They felt complimented when honored with the presence of "Mas' George," which was not unfrequent.

The New England clergyman was surprised, but was evidently reluctant to believe that any "good thing could come out of Nazareth." He expressed no approbation, for the sin of slavery could not be atoned for, in his estimation, by anything which the master could do. Nellie was delighted, "enthused," carried away with the scene. She was extravagant in her praise, and her generous young heart felt the impulses she so eloquently expressed.

Before the exercises closed, the house was moderately filled with adult people, who had come in to attend the prayer meeting.

As soon as the Sabbath School exercises were concluded, the children were dismissed, to go home or remain as they pleased. Many of them moved to seats a little in the rear, and soon all was still and quiet.

Dick, the chorister, lined out and led in singing—

"When I can read my title clear."

All joined in swelling the strain, and many made "melody in their hearts unto the Lord." Negroes love to sing, and never drawl out their words into discordant sounds. There is no dragging in their voice, never a nasal sound. The lips apart, the head thrown back, the chest expanded, the eyes generally closed, and a full, round, sonorous voice is uttered forth by each; the commingling of which charms and thrills the heart of the listener.

At the conclusion of the song, one of the colored brethren, at the request of "uncle Jesse," led in prayer. Brother Jesse arose and addressed Dr Pratt, as the "visiting brother," and invited him to conduct the meeting, but the Doctor declined, rendering as an excuse, ill health, and fatigue, but promised to do so at some future day, if he could.

"Uncle Jesse" then read the 14th Chapter of John, one so interesting to every christian heart. He paused and gave a short comment on the first of the chapter, reminding them of the blessed mansions in their Father's house; and the coming of the Savior for them, when all was completed for their comfort; concluding his address with many earnest words of exhortation, and then closing by prayer. He asked as was his custom, if any other brother had anything to say. Brother Gabriel, a tall black, middle aged man arose and said:

"My bredren, I's happy on dis nospicious occasion to 'zort you on in de pilgrimage. Abraham, he set one foot fore de tudder in gwine to Canaan, but he met de lion in de den, and he squash him to de ground, and vociferate him to death. Dat was a solemngizin' sight, 'twixt Abraham an' de lion. He growl and turn he hair de wrong way, and grin and show he long sharp teeth, and Abraham, he no staggulated in de least, but only de more violenter; he put forth he hand and wench him into nothin'. Den Joshua, he start to de promised land, and he meet de blazin sarpent, but he no go back. No, he say, Ef you no git out'n my way, I bruise you head. And good as he word, he smash he head wid he rod o' blossoms, what he walk wid; and de sarpent he dead quicker. Now bredren, what you do ef you be dar, I feard you run, you go back, you no go ober de lion an' de blazin' sarpent. But ef you see Abraham standin' on Nebo lookin' over into de promised land, and see him die a shoutin', case he so happy, den you want to smash de lion too. And ef you see Joshua standin' on Mount Zion, talkin' wid de Lord face to face, for forty days, and see he face shine bright as de moon, clear as de sun and terrible as an army wid banters, den you be willin' to meet the 'noxious warment, and distribute he head from be body.

"My bredren, we hab de lion ob dis world, and de sarpent ob de debil to meet ebry day. De one got he den ebry where, de udder kindle her fire under you' feet. Watch all de day long, and pray de night tru' my bredren and sisters. Watch all de year, and all de life long. Don't be onconsiderate, but 'joice all de way, and let de anxiety ab de heart be above, and run de way wid laquity an' light. Ef you fight de lion, like Abraham, an' 'molish de sarpent like Joshua, den when you comes down to de dark waters of Jubilee, you will mount de milk white hos', and fly away to Gallilee. Amen"

During this short, pathetic address, many "Amen's," "dat's so," "bless God," and "I feels 'em," were uttered by the colored auditory.

In conclusion they sang on "Jordan's stormy banks I stand," with the chorus, "I am bound for the promised land." Beginning with the last speaker, all moved round, indiscriminately shaking hands, swaying to and fro, keeping time with the music. When they reached the little circle of whites the scene became affecting in the highest degree. "God bless you master," "God bless you, mistis." "We'll meet in heaven," "O sweet Jesus," and similar expressions were uttered by most of them, while the big tears that rolled down their faces and the powerful grasp of the hand, manifested the sincerity of the ardent impulses which were so apparent.

Nellie wept great tears of joyous sympathy, and so did Mr. T., Alice and Miss Nelson. Dr. Pratt alone remained unmoved, untouched by the happy scene before him. He seemed as emotionless as a statue of marble.

With the exception of Gabriel's speech, everything connected with the meeting was solemn and deeply affecting, well calculated to leave the heart with better feelings and desires. But Dr. Pratt was greatly disgusted with slavery when he heard the ignorance of Gabriel. He did not remember that some white ministers had displayed as great a want of divine knowledge, only they had clothed their ignorance in better language. For instance: one white minister pronounced Leper *Leaper*, and said, "The Leaprosy made persons leap like a frog." Another said "there was sixteen other young men rared up in and around and about me, but now where is 'um? They is scattered to and here and fro and there, and I is left a loneful watcher upon the hill-tops of Zion." Another said, "the Savior put fur skins in the water to turn it to wine." Another examined to see if Jonas, Simon Peter's father, "was the same who swallowed the whale."

But I must leave my readers to their own conclusions. It is for me to state facts, and for you to draw whatever deductions you may please. It may be well to premise, however, that we should be guarded never to identify an institution with its abuses. Every blessing of heaven is abused, more or less, in the hands of sinful men.

Nor should we judge of a people by a single man of the race, who is not a *representative character*. It would be unjust to judge the American people by such a baboon as Abraham Lincoln, or the South by such a traitorous blackguard as Brownlow. Nor should negro intelligence be adjudged by the standard of Gabriel.

As they walked back to the house, Mr. Thompson turned aside to a negro cabin to see a sick servant, while the doctor and Nellie walked on.

With eyes yet red with weeping, Nellie turned to the doctor and said: "That was a melting sight; the simple-hearted, sincere piety of these poor negroes, is perfectly fascinating to me. The perfect freedom from all ostentation and formalism, the unrestrained and unaffected fervor of impulse, the big tears, the hearty grasp of the hand, the honest, heartfelt "God bless you," is really refreshing to me. This must be primitive christianity, unadulterated by the spirit of the world. I thank God their masters feel so pious an interest in their souls, and that their efforts at evangelizing them have met with such signal success. *They are the happiest people I ever saw.*"

Without raising his head, the doctor replied morosely: "They are the most miserable wretches unhung. To play the hypocrite as they did to-day, just to please and obey a tyrant whom they call 'master' There was no religion in it. The whole form and pretensions were enacted in obedience to your uncle's behests. It is the deepest and most fearful form of hypocrisy, thus to tamper with the solemnities of religion. Your tears surprised me, I would as soon think of weeping in a bedlam."

They had arrived at the house, and the conversation ceased. Poor Nellie felt mortified and disappointed in the severe censoriousness and mistaken views of her pastor. She knew he was mistaken, but could only wish and pray that future developments might remove his false impressions.

## CHAPTER III.

*Nellie Retires from the Discussion—Dr. Pratt takes her Place—Perpetuity of Slavery—An ancient Slave's Opinion—Slavery in the Decalogue.*

Mrs. Norton and Nellie were delighted to see their pastor. It was really refreshing to see a Northern face in their temporary Southern home, and to meet one congenial spirit, who could enter into all their feelings, and with whom they could converse freely on the subject of slavery. Mr. and Mrs. Thompson, too, were glad to receive and entertain the pastor of their relatives, and finding him an educated gentleman of extensive and varied information, he was a most welcome guest.

He frequently rode with Mr. T. over his farm and saw his negroes at their work. He saw their toil and sweat, and heard their cheerful songs and merry laughter. He asked a great number of questions as to their dispositions, contentment, subordination, morals, &c.

Turning to Mr. Thompson, one day, as they rode along, he said, "I am surprised to find a man of Northern birth and education holding men, women and children in involuntary servitude." "Why?" said Mr. T. "Because Solomon said, 'train up a child in the way he should go, and when he is old he will not depart from it,' and I know you were trained differently from your present practice." "True," said Mr. T., "but Solomon did not say, train up a child in the way he should *not* go, and when he is old he will not depart from it. If he is trained rightly he will not depart from it, but if wrongly, he may be led by a kind Providence to discover his error and abandon it. My early education on the subject of slavery was all wrong. I have by the goodness of an all-wise Providence been led to discover and abandon the error."

"You do not pretend to defend slavery as right, do you?"

"If I did not, I should abandon it before another day."

"Well, I suppose I need not be surprised, for there is no telling what an influence prejudice, or cupidity, may exert in forming the conclusions of the human mind."

"Nor early education and fanaticism," said Mr. T. They had both arrived at the gate, and alighting from their horses, the conversation ceased.

After a moment's absence in his room, Mr. Pratt took his seat in the parlor. Nellie was just finishing a very difficult piece of music on the piano, and was soon seated near her pastor.

"You have had a pleasant ride this morning, I hope," she said as she drew near him.

"The ride was pleasant, but I have brought all my sympathy for the poor suffering negro with me, and find it is going to be a 'thorn in the flesh,' a 'body of death,' clinging to me. It will greatly mar, if not entirely destroy, the pleasure of my visit South."

"Do you think the negroes here are as unhappy as you expected to find them, before you came?" said Nellie.

"They do not seem to be so, but it may be they are too well trained to show their discontent before strangers. They seem as cheerful as laborers in wheat harvest. They talk, and laugh, and sing, and pat, and dance, and appear not to feel their bondage, but this cannot be possible. The bare idea that they are slaves fills me with horror."

"But do you think them capable of doing as well for themselves, if they were free, as they are now doing in a state of slavery? To test the matter, how do they compare, in prosperity and happiness, with the free negroes in New England?"

"Very favorably, I must confess. No doubt but they are better fed and clothed, and are less liable to temptation and vicious habits. But they are slaves and have no rights. The system of bondage has taken away from them the heritage bequeathed to them by their Creator. All men are born free and equal, and no one should dare infringe upon the universal rights of man."

"But," said Nellie, "as you seem to think the infringement of these rights 'feeds and clothes' them better than freedom does, and that 'they are less liable to temptation and vicious habits'—in a word, makes their condition better than it otherwise could be, is it not a mercy, rather than an injustice, to hold them in such servitude?"

"What do you mean, Nellie? Has your short stay already poisoned your mind with abominable pro-slavery sentiments? You talk like a Southern slaveholder."

"O, no," said Nellie, "these were impressions made upon my mind by observing uncle's servants, and I wanted an answer to the argument. I have observed them in their domestic duties, in their festivals, in their sports and past times, and in their religious devotions, and I am sure I never saw a laboring class at the North so happy, so uniformly cheerful, or more 'fervent in spirit, serving the Lord,' and the suggestion has occurred to me, that after all, bondage may be the condition assigned them by Providence."

"You astonish me, Nellie! God is a holy, just and merciful being, and could never, either by His word or providence, sanction so unholy a thing as slavery. The Bible teaches no such thing, and if it did—well I think I should have to appeal to the higher law of conscience."

Nellie looked thoughtfully at him for a moment, and then asked with much seriousness, " Mr. Pratt, is the authority of conscience superior to the authority of the Bible ?"

"That is a theologico-metaphysical question, the discussion of which we will defer to another time," was Mr. P.'s reply.

Nellie manifested no further surprise at this ignoring of the word of God as supreme authority on all moral subjects. She had heard it often before, and had been pretty well educated in the same views; but the struggles she had recently experienced had made too deep an impression on her mind to be soon forgotten. She thought it best to give a slight turn to the conversation, and so remarked, " Uncle and I have agreed to investigate the subject of slavery from the Bible; we have had one evening's conversation, and I must confess some surprise at the plausibility of his arguments. The truth is, I am unable to meet the question upon scriptural grounds, though I am certainly not so well versed in the Bible as I ought to be. As you are to spend several days with us, by your permission, I will turn over my part of the discussion to you. I am sure you are a whole hearted abolitionist, and certainly will be an overmatch for my pro-slavery uncle. Will you thus relieve me, and permit me to sit by as an interested listener ?"

" Certainly, if your uncle has no objection. And who knows but I may be sent here by Providence to convince a christian slave holder of his error; and that he, by liberating his slaves may rebuke this "sum of villainies," and set his neighbors a worthy example. If he is not lost to all reason, I shall be able to convince him, I am sure. Argument, sarcasm and ridicule, have great power. Then he can not stand before such men as Wayland, and against the moral rebuke of the civilized world. I am ready at once, to enter upon the discussion."

Mr. Thompson entered just as the clergyman ceased speaking.

Nellie lost no time in introducing the subject. " Well, uncle, I have engaged Mr. Pratt as my representative in our Bible discussions on slavery. He has consented to take my place, if you have no objection, and as you are so confident of your ability to justify slavery from the Bible, I feel sure you will consent to the arrangement. Your Southern chivalry will naturally desire a foeman worthy of your steel."

"Thank you, Nellie. I am pleased with the arrangement. I shall have a double advantage in Mr. Pratt. A scholar fully able to understand the meaning of the Divine word, and a christian with moral honesty enough always to concede a point when fairly established from the infallible source of truth. I can only express surprise that a student of the Bible should not already have so far satisfied himself on the subject as to admit without further investigation, that slavery is a divine institution, that it is of God."

"So far from this, sir," said Mr. Pratt, "I believe it is the institution of Satan, and only permitted to exist for a short time, like other sins which are forbidden, as a scourge to our race, as a trial to us, to prove man, and see what are the depths of depravity which exist in his heart. I am only surprised to see a man of your intelligence and professed piety, holding slaves. To see you guilty of such injustice to your fellow beings as to hold them in bondage, forging chains and riveting them upon them, and crushing out their manhood with the "weight of servitude.'"

"Do you believe," said Mr. T., "that the negro is less a man in his southern bondage, than he is in his African idolatry and superstition? Do you believe his contact with the social and religious elements of southern society, though restricted by slavery, has degraded him beneath the Bushman, the Hottentot, the Cannibal, or even below the somewhat more elevated Central Africans, who bow down daily to their household gods, and who in their superstition, lay on the funeral pile, the surviving widow to be consumed with the body of her deceased husband? Do you think the enlightened and christian slave, is less happy, less contented, less elevated in the scale of moral existence, than his ancestors were in the dark land of Ham? Your familiarity with ethnology, has long since taught you that southern slaves are the happiest of all their race, and approximate more nearly the great object for which God has created man. This being undeniably true, then where is the injustice of which you speak? Is it doing a man injustice to enlighten his ignorance, to teach him how to enjoy the social relations of life, to deliver him out of barbarism and introduce him into civilized life, to break the fetters of idolatry and superstition, and teach him the knowledge of the true God, to take his being and fill it with all those holier purposes, desires and aspirations, which have been so long exiled by the reigning demon of darkness? If this be injustice, then sir, do we plead guilty to the charge, not otherwise."

"Injustice is done a man," said Mr. Pratt, "when his natural or acquired rights are taken from him, no matter what these rights are, or whether he uses them or abuses them; if he should misuse them; the wrong is to himself."

"I suppose then," said Mr. Thompson, "if a man purchase a gun to shoot himself, and I knowing that fact, take it away, I do him an act of injustice, by taking away from him the power to commit suicide. If a man threatens the life of another, the officer who arrests and imprisons him, thereby preventing murder, does injustice by stopping the abuse of physical liberty; or if a woman, in a violent passion is about to beat her child to death, and I seize hold of her, and by constraint dispossess her of the freedom to kill her child, I do her injustice. Or to put a very plain case, when a man becomes so depraved that he is not restrained from the violation of law, and a court imprisons him as a felon. it does him injustice. Or if an individual refuses to pay his just debts, and his creditors by due process of law, imprison him, they do him an act of legal injustice. Sir, is this your sense of justice? You cannot deny that these are legitimate deductions from your premises."

"O, that is not what he meant, uncle," said Nellie, rather impatiently, as she saw her representative had committed himself too far, and that her uncle was making him appear the advocate of a most licentious and wicked freedom, and taking from society all lawful means of self-protection.

"I mean, sir, that God has made 'all men free and equal,' and any infringement of this freedom and equality, except for the maintenance of law and order, is an act of injustice, and one at which a pious man should shudder."

"You take for granted the very point in issue, and quote from the Declaration of Independence instead of the Bible. God did not make all men free and equal. He has enslaved some by placing them in bondage to others. Ham manifested the wicked traits which afterwards developed themselves in his descendants. and on this account Heaven forged the chains of slavery and placed them upon him, using his father, Noah, as His agent. Hear Him: 'Cursed be Canaan, a servant of servants shall he be to his brethren. And he said, blessed be the Lord God of Shem. And Canaan shall be his servant. God shall enlarge Japhet and he shall dwell in the tents of Shem, and Canaan shall be his servant' Thus when there was but one family on earth, a portion of it was doomed to servitude. A 'servant of servants,' the menial, the slave of servants. Now, was this slavery? If so, was it of Satan or of God? If of God, has he made all men free and equal? Were Ham and Japhet made equal, when one was placed over the other? Were both made free when one was put under slavery to the other? There is a great deal of prating nonsense in the world claiming very high and respectable paternity."

"But let us take a step further, and see how the *Divine institution of slavery* was afterwards regulated under 'father Abraham,' who owned perhaps a thousand slaves. When the covenant of circumcision was instituted, God told him, 'He that is born in thy house, and he that is bought with thy money, must needs be circumcised.' Here was a recognition and a ceremonial regulation of the institution. One of the servants of this 'father of the faithful,' afterwards recognized slavery as the ordination of God, although himself being in bondage under the divine decree. He said, 'And the Lord hath blessed my master greatly, he is become great; and He hath given him flocks and herds, and silver and gold, and man servants and maid servants.' They were not hired servants, for they were born in his house and bought with his money, just as Southerners hold slaves. This honored slave of Abraham did not look upon the institution which held him in bondage as an evil, but a blessing, 'the Lord hath blessed my Master greatly.' But again look at the light in which the law recognized it. In Exodus it is said, 'If a man smite his servant or his maid with a rod, and he die under his hand, he shall be surely punished; notwithstanding if he continue a day or two, he shall not be punished, for *he is his money.*' Now if such a law as this were found upon a Southern statute book, the world would be filled with holy horror, at its inhumanity; yet such is the enactment of Him who doeth all things well. Here too is a recognition by the divine law, of the property of one man in another, one man is the *money*, the chattel of another. Again the sickly sensibilities of erring man, are shocked at the revealed will of the King of all the earth. Uzza feared to trust the tottering ark to the Lord, and put forth his hand to save it, but his presumption was punished by instant death. Let us take timely warning. What God gives we will receive, what he commands, we will obey, what he withholds we will not covet. We are always safe under the guidance of unerring wisdom. 'It is the Lord, let him do what seemeth good unto him.'"

At this stage of the argument, the parties were interrupted by a summons to dinner. Nellie and the parson both felt relieved at the prospect of having time for reflection before being compelled to reply to the proofs presented by Mr. T.

Dinner being over, the parties retired to their several apartments, and, at five o'clock, all re-assembled in the parlor, feeling the more cheerful for having enjoyed a refreshing nap.

"Mr. Thompson," said Mr. Pratt, "I discover you are a strict constructionist. I do not adhere so much to the letter, as to the spirit of the Bible. The letter killeth, but the spirit maketh alive. I do not attach so much importance to detached portions of revelation, as I do to the character and attributes of its Great Author. He is too holy to authorise sin ; too merciful to place one man in the power of another; too just to discriminate so widely between the privileges he confers upon his intelligent creatures. He will never give to one people the right to place the galling yoke of slavery upon the necks of another. He will never place one tribe or nation under the feet of another to be trod upon. He will never appoint an institution, which crushes out the manhood, and effaces the human feelings of any race, reducing them to the level of beasts. This is not in accordance with the Divine character. I honor and reverence the Divine name too much to admit any such thing. 'Justice and judgment are the habitation of his throne,' but there is neither justice nor mercy in slavery."

"You decide what the Bible *ought* to teach," said Mr. T., "by your knowledge of the character of Deity, and not by what He has really said. Pray, from what source do you derive your knowledge of Him, if not from the Bible, and how do you know anything of his character from this source, only as you believe what it says? Then you admit, that the Bible as a whole is true; and if so, its detached portions are also true. You must either admit that the quotations made are interpolations, or they are the words of God. If the former, then the '*onus probandi*' rests upon you, and I am ready to hear your proof. If they be the words of God, you must admit that slavery is taught in the Bible, and instituted in Heaven. In your sermons at home, you urge upon your congregation the necessity of repentance, and to prove its importance you quote detached portions of the word of God, and so of every other truth, however important, which is taught in the Bible. I have heard ministers say, (and you may have done the same,) that to ascertain with certainty the meaning of any given text in the Scriptures, it is best to consult all the parallel passages. This fact attests the truth well known and acknowledged by all Bible students, that the Scriptures do not exhaust any subject in any one given verse, chapter or book. It is one of the evidences of the inspiration of the Bible, that a most beautiful and striking harmony is maintained by the writers of the various books of the Bible, when treating of the same subject. But with this fact, you are more familiar than I, as you are professionally a theologian. Your proposition to judge what God will teach by his character, and not by his word, reminds me of a little private discussion to which I once listened. It was between a minister and an infidel. The former was affectionately urging upon the latter the importance of personal religion, as necessary to his happiness here and hereafter, and quoted the Scripture, 'Godliness is profitable unto all things, having promise of the life that now is, and of that which is to come,' and then added, 'He that hath the Son hath life, but he that hath not the Son of God, hath not life.' The infidel replied: 'I do not wish to hear anything from the Bible. God has given me reason, and my reason tells me that God is too great and good a Being to doom a soul to perdition just because he refuses to believe on his Son.'"

"Your premises lead to the infidel's conclusion, and I must confess profound astonishment at its enunciation by a religious teacher. If the Book of God is taken at all, it must all be taken; for 'all Scripture is given by inspiration of God, and is profitable for doctrine, for reproof, for correction, for instructions in righteousness.' Permit me to suggest, that the passages referred to, may have been given for the 'correction' of the errors of abolitionists, and for their 'instruction in righteousness,' since their tendency to depart from truth certainly needs a counteracting influence.

"Peter, speaking of the olden time, seems to have apprehended a disbelief in those, or some other portions of the old Scripture, and, therefore, under the direction of inspiration, says: 'For the prophecy came not in old time by the will of man: but holy men of God spake as they were moved by the Holy Ghost.' You will have, my dear sir, to admit slavery, or reject the Bible—which horn of the dilemma will you take?"

"Neither, sir," said the minister, "I will reject slavery and take the Bible. I will, however, admit, for the sake of argument, that in those dark ages, God permitted it on account of the hardness of the people's hearts, as he did divorces and other wrongs, which were to be of temporary duration, and which were to give way before the progressive civilization of the world, as the darkness is dispersed before the sun, and heathenism before the gospel of Christ."

Nellie did not like the answer of her representative; she could not exactly see how it was, "for the sake of argument," to make any such admission. If it were true, he ought to have said so; if not, he should have withheld the admission. As to slavery being only temporary, the Scripture on that point, quoted by her uncle, had given her no little trouble. She did not see how her pastor, a conscientious man, could withhold his assent from the truths proven; but if he admitted them, then it was impossible for him to escape the next argument, which she foresaw her uncle would adduce.

"Slavery," said Mr. T., "was not only permitted, but absolutely decreed, as I have abundantly shown from Scripture. You admit, 'for the sake of argument,' not for truth's sake, that it was permitted. I must confess, sir, with your Dr. Wayland, that 'I wonder that any one should have had the hardihood to deny so plain a matter of record. I should almost as soon deny the delivery of the Ten Commandments to Moses.' I have a single quotation which I made to my niece a few days ago, to prove that it was not the Divine purpose that slavery 'was to be of temporary duration, and to give way before the progressive civilization of the world,' but that it was to be a perpetual institution, 'forever.' I refer to Leviticus xxv: 44–46. Nellie, will you please read the paragraph."

"Before she reads," said Mr. Pratt, "I desire to say, that when I said 'I admit for the sake of the argument,' I did not intend to be understood as denying that the Scriptures did authorize slavery, but that I did not admit all your conclusions. I do not think it either wise or honest to deny a fact which is clearly proven."

"Then you admit slavery is of Divine origin?" said Mr. Thompson.

"Well, yes, I cannot truthfully deny it, and I intend to meet the question fairly," said Mr. Pratt.

Nellie smiled approvingly, as she opened the Bible and read: "Both thy bondmen and thy bondmaids, which thou shalt have, shall be of the heathen that are round about you, of them shall ye buy bondmen and bondmaids. Moreover of the children of the strangers that sojourn among you, of them shall ye buy, and of their families that are among you, which they begat in your land: and they shall be your possession. And ye shall take them as an inheritance for your children after you, to inherit them for a possession. They shall be your bondmen forever."

"Now," said Mr. Thompson. "let us look at this Scripture as Christian men, in search of Divine truth. 1st. Here is slavery, 'they shall be your bondmen and bondmaids.' They were to be held in servitude, 'obliging them to labor for the benefit of others, without their contract or consent.' 2d. Here is traffic in human flesh, in living men, human beings; 'of them shall ye buy bondmen and bondmaids.' I am certain that the word 'shall' in this connection, *enjoins* it as a duty upon the Israelites to enslave, these heathens. 3d Here is vested property in human beings: 'they shall be your possession.' 4th. They were to be bequeathed by parents to their children, just as any other article of property: 'Ye shall take them as an inheritance for your children' Lastly, its perpetuity. This slavery was not to be limited by the intervening of the year of Jubilee, or release, but it was to endure without end: 'they shall be your bondmen *forever*.'

"As you have quoted Dr. Wayland," said the Elder, "my reply shall be that which he made to your Dr. Fuller on this very subject: 'I believe slavery, then, as now, to have been wrong, a violation of our obligations to man, and at variance with the moral laws of God. But I believe that God did not see fit to reveal His will on this subject, nor indeed on many others, to the ancient Hebrews. He made known to them just so much of His moral law as He chose, and the law on this subject belonged to the part which he did not choose to make known. Hence, although they did, what in itself was *wrong*, yet God not having made known to them His will, they were not guilty.'

"You have admitted," said Mr. T., "that slavery was appointed by God, yet you contend that it was "wrong, a violation of our obligations to man, and at variance with the moral law of God," but that God concealed the evil of it from the ancient Hebrews. You make God commit a wrong by appointing a wicked institution, and then, whether from benevolent motives, to screen from punishment, those upon whom the wrong was entailed, or to prevent censure resting upon the Divine purity, you do not say. He conceals the wrong from His chosen people. I will not presume, sir, that either you or Dr. Wayland intend all your language expresses; it would be too presumptuous, too impious; it would be a worm arraigning the holy and just One, and rejecting as wrong, what He did, simply because it did not agree with his own standard of right. Dr. Wayland has long enjoyed an enviable reputation as a learned and pious man, but when writing on the subject of slavery, he uses some language bordering on blasphemy, e. g.: "If the religion of Christ allows us to take such license from such precepts as these, the New Testament would be the greatest curse that ever was inflicted on our race." Presumptuous man! to bring a railing accusation against His maker. I would rather adopt the saying originated by the Bishop of Norwich, that the Scriptures have an "expansion of sense and meaning," or that by the Bishop of London, that they have a "prudent and accommodating elasticity." The latter, to say the least, are more polite and courteous attacks upon the Divine wisdom and goodness. If the view of Dr. Wayland, which you have endorsed, be correct, it amounts to this: "The Almighty has said to His people, you may commit "a sin of appalling magnitude;" you may perpetrate "as great an evil as can be conceived;" you may persist in a practice which consists in "outraging the rights" of your fellow beings, and in "crushing their intellectual and moral nature." You may perpetuate a "wrong;" you may violate your "obligations to man;" you may violate the "moral laws of God." You may enslave those who have an inherent, natural and inalienable right to freedom, reducing them to bondmen and bondwomen. You may take away their manhood, and reduce them to a level with brutes. And although I know it is wrong, I will not hold you guilty, because I have not chosen to reveal my will on this subject. Now, sir, a cause which must be sustained by a resort to such subterfuges must be "pronounced desperate indeed, and unspeakably forlorn." Let us once permit ourselves to call in question the perfections of Deity, or the plenary inspiration of His word, to doubt His infallible veracity, or to form our opinions on moral subjects from principles independent of the Divine word, and we have no centripetal force attracting us to Truth, but we will be led astray by every ignis fatuus in the religious, scientific or social world. Once unsettle the public confidence in the fundamental truths of the Bible, in its reliability and safety as a standard, and you open the door to a flood of evils which no man can number, and the wicked consequences of which the most astute cannot anticipate.

"But to advert once more to your hypothesis, you say slavery is at variance with our obligations to man, and a violation of the moral law of God. My reply is simply this: 1. God has ordained slavery; this has been proven by the law and the testimony, and you have admitted it. 2. God has never ordained an institution in obedience to which man violates His moral law, or infringes the rights of his fellow-beings. But He did ordain slavery, therefore slavery does neither the one nor the other. To deny this, is to charge God with worse than folly.

"To make assurance doubly sure, we will again refer to the Divine testimony on this subject. You will admit that both tables of the commandments given to Moses contain at least the elements of God's moral law, and that they have not been abrogated, that they still are and will be to the end of time, of full force and effect. Do you admit this?"

"Certainly I do," said Mr. Pratt, "for while the ceremonial law, consisting of types and shadows, has past away, because fulfilled, the moral law contained in the Decalogue, is for all time and every dispensation."

"Very true," said Mr. T., "and these commandments regulate: 1st, our duty to God; this is called the first Table; and 2d, our duty to man, and this is called the second Table. Now, then, if slavery interfered with our duty to God, or is a violation of His moral law, here is the place to ascertain that fact. He is not silent; let us hear Him. He *recognizes* slavery in our duty to Him. "The seventh day is the Sabbath of the Lord God, in it thou shalt not do any work, thou nor thy son, nor thy daughter, thy *man-servant* nor thy *maid-servant*, nor thy cattle, nor thy stranger that is in thy gates" Now, if slavery had been wrong, this would certainly have been a fit occasion for God to have said so. He was giving a law for all time, for every age of the world's advancement, and for every condition of its religious and social being. If it had been offensive to Him, is it not marvelous that He did not say "Liberate," instead of "do no work on the seventh day." But it was the labor of the seventh day, and not the slavery that was displeasing to Him. "If it be wrong, as you assert, and if He instituted it, as you admit, then, as the laws say, He is *particeps criminis*, a party to the crime. But let us look at the second table, which regulates the relations of men to one another, and prescribes their rights. "Thou shalt not covet thy neighbor's house, thou shalt not covet thy neighbor's wife, nor his man-servant nor his maid-servant, nor his ox, nor his ass, nor anything that is thy neighbor's." The Lord here establishes the exclusive and uninterrupted ownership in slaves as much as in houses or cattle; the right in them is as much a vested one as in his wife or children, the relation being different. Now, is it not wonderful that our All-Wise Creator did not see it was "at variance with the rights of man" and take this opportunity to prohibit it, instead of putting slaves in the catalogue with other property which it was sinful to covet. How completely He could have settled this question by saying "Thou shalt not hold thy fellow-men in bondage." Why did He not thus speak? Abolitionism would, and does say so. The civilized world say so. Only God and the South say otherwise. With profound respect for the clerical vocation of yourself and Dr. Wayland, I must suggest that you are rapidly tending to that point of advancement when you will be "wise above what is written." Indeed, even now you prefer to judge of what God ought to do and say, by your knowledge of His character, rather than to let Him speak for himself, and accuse Him of reticence in matters of such solemn moment that duty commands you and him to cry aloud and spare not. You have declared an eternal war with heaven's institution, you denounce what God permitted, you would extirpate what He perpetuated, and anathmatise what He has blessed.

"You have said you will meet the question fairly. I shall, therefore, expect that none of the tergiversations which have so often characterized Northern fanatics in their denunciations of slavery. A subject that cannot be established by a fair, honest and manly discussion, does not deserve an advocate; whatever a christian cannot prove from the teachings and spirit of the Bible, he ought to abandon, and whatever he finds clearly taught there, he should fear to condemn and cease to oppose. Like Moses before the burning bush, he should in humility take off his shoes, for he stands on holy ground. "He that teacheth man knowledge, shall not he know? The King of all the earth will do right."

"Visitors entering, to call on Mrs. Norton and her daughter, the conversation was suspended and the gentlemen took a walk into that part of the farm adjacent to the house. Mr. Pratt was solemn and thoughtful. His mind was evidently laboring to call up some almost forgotten argument, to use in reply to what had been said. Finally his mental abstraction passed away, and he engaged in agreeable conversation, exhibiting his usual amiable temper and social qualities.

After tea, Mr. Pratt was requested to lead the devotions of the evening, and being furnished with a Bible, Mr. T. requested the servants to sing a song of their own selecting. Dick, the ostler, was a pious old servant, never absent from prayers, unless providentially detained, and he usually led the singing on such occasions, and, to tell the truth, he was rather proud of his musical abilities, and had not quite prudence enough to conceal it. As it was the first time he had been called on to sing, since Mr. Pratt's arrival, he felt some pride in making a good selection, and executing the performance, *secundum artem*. So after rubbing his eyebrows for a moment, and uttering some inaudible words to one who sat next to him, he sat erect, and began in a full, but soft and melodious strain, in which all the other servants united:

> " Amazing grace, how sweet the sound,
> That saved a wretch like me;
> I once was lost, but now I m found,
> Was blind, but now I see."

When they came to the verse—

> " The Lord hath promised good to me,
> His word my hope secures,
> He will my shield and portion be
> As long as life endures."

Dick's eyes were closed, his hands clasped across his bosom, and the big tears chasing each other down his rough cheek. Mr. Pratt's religious feelings were deeply touched at the melody and pathos with which the negroes sung. Nothing was more evident than that they sung with the spirit, and with the understanding also. In his prayer, the elder returned thanks in a most fervent and eloquent manner, that these poor Ethiopians were ever brought from the superstition and idolatry of their fathers, to know and worship the only living and true God; and that as they had been torn away from their native homes, their lots had been cast among those who "cared for their souls," and that though they were in physical bondage, they were spiritually free; and that though they were servants of an earthly master, they were the children of God. With feelings more than ever softened towards those who were guilty of the "sum of all villainies" and a deep sense of God's goodness to man, the Elder with the family left the table.

## CHAPTER IV.

*The two Matrons' opinions of the discussion—Nellie anxious for it to proceed—Moses an Abolitionist, how proven, how disproven—The Angel and Hagar—Poligamy and Divorce—Dr. Wayland—Reply to his Argument—Sumner proven in a falsehood.*

Nellie took her seat at the piano and played Home, Sweet Home, with the variations, in exquisite style. Mr. Pratt then requested her to sing one of their favorite congregational hymns, which she did quite to the taste and satisfaction of all present. Her mother took silent pleasure in the scientific performance of her accomplished daughter, while the uncle and aunt freely expressed their admiration for the accomplishments of their loved relative.

The two matrons, the mother and aunt of Nellie, would have been pleased to lead the conversation of the evening, and engage the attention of those present on the various styles of music, and the new improvements which had been made in singing, &c., since their day. They would have greatly enjoyed a suspension of the discussion of slavery, and given themselves up to a social converse. Neither saw any probability of an early termination of the engagement, or that either was open to conviction by the other. But they did not feel that it would be very polite in them to assume the prominence of leading the conversation of the evening.

Mrs. Norton wanted her brother convinced of his error, if he were in one. She had always heard that slavery was wrong, and had taken it for granted, as she had never before heard it denied, but she had never investigated it. Her pastor, she supposed, had done so, and she believed he had talents enough to understand the subject, and honesty sufficient to tell the truth, and she therefore believed what he had always preached on the subject, without giving herself any further trouble. If he were wrong, the sin was upon him. He was paid to teach, and it was his business to know that all he taught was true; her business was to listen, receive and practice. On moral and religious subjects he was employed to do her thinking, and it was not her business to call in question whether it was correctly done or not. Thus have many good souls been led into a thousand snares by the ignorance, prejudice or bigotry of others. If the blind lead the blind, both shall fall into the ditch.

Mrs. Thompson having been raised to slavery, and being a conscientious, intelligent woman, felt no doubt whatever that her husband would be able to vindicate slavery from the Bible, against all attacks that could be made on it. She had gone through all the scriptural proofs with her husband years before, and as new abolition arguments were brought out it was their custom to carry them to the Bible and see if they would stand before its light. She therefore felt sure that her husband would be able to justify slavery before any one whose eyes were not blinded, and whose heart was not hardened against the holy revelation of the King of heaven on this subject. But as she saw no prospect of convincing Mr. Pratt that slavery was right, she could conceive of no real good that would come of the discussion; but as a good wife she held her peace. Nellie, however, was anxious for the discussion to continue. She began to doubt whether slavery was a "sin of such appalling magnitude." She did not see from her stand-point of observation that it "crushed the moral and intellectual natures" of the negroes: but she believed the reverse to be true. It elevated, it lifted up, it expanded the intellect and refined the moral sensibilities of these children of Canaan. She had seen some very intelligent and sensible ones among them, and bright exemplars of the principles of our holy religion, and she could not devise how an evil tree could bear such good fruit, how a bitter fountain could send forth such sweet waters, how an institution cursed of God and man, could prove such a blessing. Besides, in her struggles of conscience, she had determined to commit her faith to the Bible and cleave to it as the only anchor of safety, and unfailing and immutable source of truth. She still sympathized with her pastor, and could not yet say that slavery was right. Her early education had made such strong impressions on her mind that they clung to her with wonderful tenacity, and she entertained an undefined hope that her pastor would find some *scriptural* escape from those texts referred to by her uncle.

"Moses, the great Jewish law-giver, was an abolitionist," said Mr Pratt.

All present were startled at the announcement, and looked the surprise they felt. He continued: "If he had not have intended to abolish it, he would not have enunciated this law, which is found in Deut. xxiii: 15, 16—'Thou shalt not deliver unto his master, the servant that is escaped from his master unto thee; he shall dwell with thee, even among you in that place which he shall choose, in one of the gates where it liketh him best; thou shalt not oppress him.' How could slavery long exist where escapes were frequent and recovery by the master forbidden by law, and that law strictly enforced by the people as their law-giver required? This, sir, is not the language of a pro-slavery man. You Southerners never use it; you hate the men that do. This is an anti-fugitive law, enacted for the gradual and peaceable extirpation of slavery. Here, also, is a Divine justification for the Northern States, which have enacted laws against the return of fugitive slaves to their Southern masters. Then call us no more a lawless horde, a mobocratic people, for resisting laws which contravene the enactments of heaven. It is a violation of the revealed will of God, to return a fugitive slave; and a constitution and laws which require it are iniquitous and ought to be resisted. It is demanded by humanity, by religion, by all that is holy, that they should be resisted. A government which enforces by law a violation of the Divine will, has forfeited its right to national existence. An institution which requires for its perpetuity a conflict with the revealed law of God, should never for one moment be tolerated among an enlightened and civilized, much less a christian people. The institution is unjust, ungodly, diabolical, and deserves the perpetual anathemas of every philanthropist upon the face of the earth. Why does God stay his vengeance from the implacable and unmitigated oppressions and iniquities of the South?"

Mr. T. smiled at the ardor of the parson, and felt that he had often heard at the North as high sounding words with as little truth, and had frequently before listened, unmoved, to as eloquent nonsense.

Such exhibitions of "zeal without knowledge" were common occurrences "beyond the line." As Mr. P. seemed to have exhausted his vocabulary, Nellie turned to her uncle to see if he was not overwhelmed with the argument. He replied:

"God has either enacted slavery, or He has not. He either countenances the institution, or He does not. He is not on both sides of the question, as you seem to think. He has not said and unsaid, done and undone. He has not given slavery to his people and then ordered its abolition. He is not so changeable, so fickle as that. 'I am God, and I change not.'

"Let us, however, consider this celebrated text, upon which you base your triumphant vindication of the fanaticism of the North. *Of* whom was it spoken, and *to* whom?

"Evidently of the heathen, and to the Israelites. God was giving them a diversity of rules of conduct for their government, in their social and national relations to the tribes who were the original inhabitants of Canaan. Hence his instructions to the Hebrews not to

F

return a fugitive slave to his heathen master. The Israelites could not have been commanded to detain a slave who had run away from themselves; to withhold their own property from their own use. This would seem unreasonable; indeed, it would be preposterous. But if a slave ran away from his *heathen* master for cruel treatment, he being innocent, and having sought refuge among the Israelites, from an unjust and cruel master, whose right it was by the custom of heathen nations at that time, to maim or murder him, then were the humane and merciful Hebrews to offer him such protection as *justice* and *mercy* required.

"This you will find, upon investigation, to be the opinion of our oldest and best commentators upon this subject. But to say that the Hebrews must detain the property of the Hebrews, that the Israelites must be a refuge for the slaves of the Israelites, is simply nonsense.

"Every man would draw his sword against his neighbor, and, instead of obeying the paternal injunction of Joseph : 'See that ye fall not out by the way,' there would have been endless civil wars ; they would have been like the wicked, to whom ' there is no peace.'

"There may have been three reasons for this law against the return of fugitive slaves. 1. The heathen had no divine right for holding slaves, as the Hebrews did. They had made slaves of prisoners taken in war ; ' might was right' with them. 2. They were a wicked and cruel people; slavery with them was connected with, and subject to the very worst developments of cruelty and inhumanity, and the masters being in the ' deep, dark, death-damps' of heathenism, there was no possibility of any knowledge of the true God being imparted to them. 3. As the Hebrews understood the rights of masters over their slaves, they would never have interfered, even with this cruel form of vassalage, without a divine injunction, specially given, requiring it. Even to this day, you find no abolitionists among the more learned and intelligent Hebrews. Now, if we admit your interpretation to be correct, we are required to believe that one passage of Scripture authorizes us to hold slaves, and another takes it away ; that the Divine Being who authorizes his people in one statute to purchase and hold bondmen ' forever,' in another place denies the existence of any such right. Indeed, that Moses intended in the same code of laws to establish and abolish slavery ; with one hand to set up, and with the other to strike down the institution; to say and unsay; to enact and repeal ; to enforce and revoke; to grant rights and then destroy them. Now it is easy enough to see how Sumner or Channing, Parker or Beecher, would dispose of this difficulty, by an appeal to the higher law of conscience, or by a total rejection of the Bible and its great Author, on account of abolition sentiments and precepts, but you take the Bible, the whole Bible, as true, and as consistent with itself, you do not believe it is self-contradictory. How you can dispose of it, I am at a loss to know, if you attempt to harmonize your construction with the Scriptures I have quoted, and with your own and Dr. Wayland's admissions. If your construction is right, why did the angel say, 'Hagar, Sarah's maid, whence comest thou, and whither wilt thou go?' And when she said, 'I flee from the face of my mistress, Sarai,' why did he say 'Return to thy mistress, and submit thyself under her hands?' Had he who had been in the presence of the Holy and Just One, taught by infinite wisdom, sent on a mission of love, mercy and justice, been kept ignorant of the fact that slavery was iniquitous, and that fugitives should be detained from their master's? Or did he commit a blunder and do his errand badly? Or was he unfaithful to his Divine Master? Or must you not admit that he was sent for the very purpose of reclaiming this runaway slave, and sending her back to her lawful mistress. The latter alone can be true.

"Then if an angel of God, a messenger of heaven, did right in returning one, you would do wrong in retaining the other, unless, indeed, you of the North are the Israelites, and we of the South the heathens—you alone possessing the knowledge of the true God, and we in the 'death of damps' of idolatry—you the merciful, and we the unjust, iniquitous murderers of our slaves. Perhaps abolitionists 'are the people, and wisdom will die with them.' Perhaps they are the christians, and the only humane and philanthropic people in the universe. If one should listen at their unmeasured denunciations against us, their unsparing abuse, and consummate dictation, he would hardly conclude otherwise than that they thought themselves infallible in judgment, unerring in their conclusions, without sin in their lives, and surrounded by a heaven of purity at home where no more righteousness was needed; that slavery was indeed 'the sum of all villainies,' the sin of the age and the crime of the earth, and they were responsible, physically, morally and politically, for its extinction, and that nothing else was to be done until this was accomplished. This great revolution is to be brought about, not by the power of moral suasion, not by the melting appeals of the Gospel of love, not by the 'spirit of meekness,' not by any of the means used by the great Redeemer to reclaim man from his errors, but rather as Rehoboam would enforce the subjection of the tribes of Israel, with a whip of scorpions."

"Perhaps," said Mr. Pratt, "I indulged a little too much of Northern feeling and sentiment for a Southern parlor. 'The wrath of man worketh not the righteousness of God.' I shall endeavor to be more guarded in the future, lest we both should imitate what you call the 'unholy spirit of Northern fanaticism.' Greater seriousness and less declamation comport with the investigation of Scriptural truth."

"Thank you, sir." said Mr. T., "I will endeavor to follow the worthy example which you will doubtless set me."

"I think," said Mr. P., "your mistake grows out of your interpretation of this isolated text. It was undoubtedly spoken of the servants of heathen masters, and your argument has some plausibility; indeed, I am not prepared, just now, to refute it, if it be incorrect. But your construction of all those passages you have quoted, is certainly erroneous. I have admitted that God sanctioned slavery—I do not mean in the sense of approval. His sanction of this institution was no more than His sanction of poligamy or divorce; they all stand upon the same footing—were all evils, and only permitted for the time being, and were not designed to be perpetually inflicted as evils upon society. The Canaanites were idolatrous, and perhaps it was a mercy to enslave them to a religious people, as this was the only means of bringing them to a knowledge of the true God, and with this merciful purpose, it was temporarily permitted."

"If it were a mercy," said Mr. T., "to enslave the idolatrous Canaanites, that they might be brought to a knowledge of God, it is no less a mercy to enslave other descendants of Ham, who are likewise in idolatry, and place them where the rays of the Son of Righteousness may fill them with holy light and saving knowledge. The same reason that made it a mercy then, makes it a mercy now, only with this difference in favor of modern slavery: that the Christian dispensation affords multiplied facilities for their Evangelization, and has so far softened the hearts of masters generally, that the rigors of ancient slavery have entirely disappeared.

"I wonder you have not detected the fallacy of your proposition, 'that slavery has no more divine sanction than poligamy or divorce.' God did permit the two latter, but where do you find for them an expressed sanction? It is no where to be found. Christ said it was not so from the beginning. 'Have ye not read that He which made them at the beginning, made them male and female, and said for this cause shall a man leave father and mother, and cleave to his wife, and they twain shall become one flesh." The only sanction you can find for divorce, except for whoredom, is in the regulation of the evil as Moses found it. If you call this a sanction, I am sure you ought never again to deny that the Bible sanctions slavery. Poligamy, as well as divorce, was forbidden in the above quotation from the Savior: 'Shall cleave to his wife,' not wives, 'they twain (two,) shall be one flesh.' But Jacob, and David, and Solomon, and perhaps other good men practiced poligamy in violation of the original law of marriage I plead no justification for it; Moses made none. He dealt with an intractable people, of perverse disposition: and while he enunciated the original law to stand as a perpetual rebuke to them for this evil practice, he regulated it, i. e., put bounds to it beyond which it dare not go, and thus greatly lessened the evils which it was impossible for him to reform. These evils are only *malum prohibitum*, i. e., they are sins, because prohibited, not otherwise; they were not in conflict with the immutable principles of right, but they were opposed to the relations which were designed to exist among the sexes—and would not therefore have been wrong, if they had not been forbidden. God might, then, without any violation of the immutable principles of right, permit them, and this permission, in a theocracy, might be a tacit revocation of his original law forbidding them. But you say that slavery is *malum in se*—evil in itself—a violation of the immutable principles of justice and right. If so, any sanction of it, however short, is a sanction of that which violates the 'unchangeable principles of right.' Therefore, according to your admission, God sanctions a violation of a righteous principle.

"In the beginning God forbade poligamy and divorce. When introduced and practiced for a time on account of man's depravity, the Saviour revokes the regulation of Moses, telling why it had been *permitted*, and forbids absolutely the practice of them forever afterwards. But not *one word* is said by prophets, apostles, or the holy Redeemer, against slavery. (*I challenge the world to disprove this assertion.*) This, to my mind, is a most significant and convincing fact." Mr. T. ceased speaking. A distressing silence reigned for a moment, Nellie, the meantime, looking first at her uncle, and then at Mr. Pratt, wishing some one would break the silence. She felt, if what her uncle said was true, her pastor ought to yield and confess that he was in error, as she now was pretty well satisfied he was. The pastor soon rallied, however, and with some warmth, replied: "Mr. Thompson! I tell you slavery is wrong, I care not what you say; my *humanity* tells me it is *wrong*, and all the argument and sophistry in the world can't convince me it is right. My *conscience* and my *feelings* guide me and teach me; and I am satisfied the poet described you masters of the South when he said:

'Man's inhumanity to man, makes countless thousands mourn'

Is inhumanity right? is it right to cause human suffering? If not, then tell me not that slavery is right."

"Pardon me, sir," said Mr. T., "you take me quite by surprise. I expected a reply to the argument. But I need not be astonished, for you Northern people never have given, and never can give the subject of slavery a fair and impartial investigation. The time has past for that. Prejudice against the institution has so preoccupied the mind, as positively to incapacitate it for the task. Many at the South once believed it was wrong, and they owe the correction of the error somewhat to the fanaticism of the Abolitionists. When you began to denounce it as a great sin, and to petition Congress for its abolition, and to form your emancipation societies, our people cautiously began to investigate the morality of the institution. Knowing that the Bible alone was infallible on moral subjects, they began to 'search the scriptures.' The consequence is, that all intelligent Southerners are now convinced that slavery is right, and they never will abandon the institution, nor can they be driven from it. The Northern people never discovered the evil till they had *sold* their slaves and pocketed the proceeds. Suddenly they were aroused to the fact that slavery was wrong. They did not go to the Bible to prove its error, but to humanity. From this source they drew their principles, and then went to the Bible to torture it into a support of their preconceived opinions. This enabled them to see a great many things which were not there, and to place constructions upon the Divine word wholly at variance with its meaning. They have so long dallied with their Delilah that they are shorn of their manhood The power of prejudice, in the hands of political demagogues, sensationalists, press and pulpit, have completely bound them. Opposition to slavery has become much the larger portion of their religion. It has pervaded society to such an extent, and taken such powerful hold upon public sentiment, that but few men have moral courage enough to doubt the *ipse dixit* of the veriest political tyro that prates from the rostrum against the South. There are more sermons preached against slavery than against drunkenness, theft, debauchery, or any other sin to which fallen humanity is heir. A Sabbath School book cannot be written in a style acceptable to to the Northern mind, unless it condemns it in some part. No doubt but there are more prayers made for the cessation of slavery than for the discontinuance of idolatry among the heathens; indeed, it is considered a crime of the 'darkest malignity,' notwithstanding the sanction it receives from Divine Revelation."

"I have determined," said Mr. Pratt, "to adhere to the question of moral wrong in slavery. I am not at all convinced by anything you have said or proven from the Scriptures, that slavery does not involve moral guilt. I will again avail myself of the very accurate definition and conclusive argument of Dr. Wayland. Slavery is the 'right to oblige another to labor for me without his contract or consent, with the additional right to use all the means necessary to insure the exercise of the original right. I suppose God made of one blood all men that dwell upon the earth, that we are all partakers of the same nature, as we are all the children of one common parent. I suppose that this *common nature* is not affected in any respect by the color of the skin, the difference of the hair, or by any other variety of physical formation. * * * I believe that every individual is endowed with an immortal soul, and that he is placed in the present state of probation, a candidate for everlasting happiness or everlasting woe. He has an intellect capable of endless progression in knowledge, and is animated with a desire to improve that intellect to the utmost. God has given him a right to improve it to whatever extent he pleases. He is endowed with a conscience which renders him susceptible of obligations both to God and to man. In virtue of this endowment, it is his imperative duty to seek, by all the means in his power, to know the will of God; and it is his inalienable right to serve God in the manner which he believes will be most pleasing to the Creator. He has powers of external action, and by means of his intellect he may use these powers for the improvement of his own condition; and provided he uses them not in violation of the equal rights of his brethren, he may employ them as he will, and the result of this employment is strictly and exclusively his own.' Now, Mr. Thompson, look at slavery in connection with these views, as a candid man, as a philanthropist. Slavery denies, in spirit, that 'God of one blood made all men that dwell upon the earth.' It abrogates the one '*common nature*' derived from one common parent. It annuls the religious rights of the enslaved, and denies to them the privilege of moral and intellectual culture. It restrains them from the employment of their own time for their own benefit. Now, sir, can a system be right which must necessarily involve such injustice? *Can it?*"

"You are an admirable tactician," said Mr. T. "Having found the Bible a pro-slavery book, you resort to Dr. Wayland. Divine truth being against you, you seek help from what the Abolitionists have decided to be 'the most simple and conclusive argument they have read.' Now, as you have left the Bible because it is against you, and gone to the 'Author of the Moral Science' as the best authority to which you can appeal, what will be your next step if he should prove insufficient? I ask this question in time, that you may be casting about in your mind beforehand. A good general is always prepared for a retreat, in the event of a reverse. But I am under no obligations to reply to your article from Dr. Wayland. Our proposition was to discuss slavery from the Bible. I will, however, notice the views, if for nothing else, just to show the sophistry of your celebrated author. 'Slavery,' you say, 'denies, in spirit, that God of one blood made all men that dwell upon the earth.' How slavery denies its announcement you did not say. We find it in the same book in which we find 'thou shalt buy bondmen and bondmaids.' We have the same authority for the belief of the one that we have for the practice of the other. God is the author of both—we then are free. Your charge falls (whether with becoming humility you must decide,) upon the author of the Bible. If we held slaves without any Divine authority, your charge would at least possess some plausibility; but you left the Bible without showing it to be anti-slavery. It is not very courteous to that volume to call it in as a witness against us, when you have tacitly denied the credibility of its testimony. Again, you say, 'It abrogates the common nature derived from one common parent.' How so? Have we ever denied that negroes were descended from Adam and from Noah; that we have one common Father? Have we ever denied that they were totally depraved, fallen sinners? Have we ever denied that they are immortal beings, or withheld from them the Gospel? Have we denied that they were flesh and blood and bones; were subject like ourselves to joys and sorrows, health and sickness, life and death? Does slavery deny the common humanity of bondmen in any respect?

'Is he not man, by sin and suffering tried;
Is he not man, for whom a Saviour died?'

You assert what cannot be proven, and take for granted the very point in issue. Do you hold that the obligation of a child to obey the parent 'abrogates' the 'common nature,' because children are bound to 'obey their parents?' Is an apprentice bound to his principal for a term of years thereby removed beyond the pale of our common brotherhood? If so, every pupil at school, every young man in College, every operative in the workshops and factories, is for the time being excluded from participation in the 'common nature' inherited from one common parent? I think you mean more than you have said. You doubtless had in your mind the *ad captandum* saying of Dr. Channing: 'The consciousness of our humanity involves the persuasion that we cannot be owned as a tree or a brute.'

"Thank you for the quotation," said Mr. Pratt, "I was not able to call it up, but the idea was in my mind; I only wanted the words."

"You suppose, then," said Mr. Thompson, "or rather Dr. Channing supposes that slavery makes trees and brutes out of negroes. We burn trees for firewood very frequently, but I have never known a slave thus burned. We build houses and fences, and bridges, and Railroad cars and steamships, and masts out of trees, but we have never as yet appropriated our negroes to such purposes. We will leave to Yankee ingenuity, that can make nutmegs and hams out of wood, or sell a flask of liquor for a Bible, so complete being the imitation, I say we will leave it to them to teach us how to convert a negro into the uses of a tree. As yet we have more trees than negroes, and we are satisfied for each to occupy its appropriate place.

"But again, you say it makes 'brutes' of them. We use our brutes here to ride, to pull the plough, to draw the wagon and carriage; but we have not yet learned that our slaves are able to perform such services. It remains for some Yankee in the future to ride to town on the back of a negro fellow, or to invent the yoke or harness to pull the wagon, or to be drawn to the city by four of them. Yankee ingenuity has never yet failed in accomplishing its purpose, and we can't say, but that a man who has found out that slavery makes trees and brutes of negroes, may yet, if he can only get legal possession of them, appropriate them to these purposes. Now, sir, I have answered your Dr. Channing in strict accordance with Prov. xxvi: 5. Answer a fool according to his folly.

"God says 'buy bondmen and bondmaids.' You say, Oh, no! that would be, in spirit, to deny that God of one blood made all men that dwell upon the earth. God says 'Canaan shall be a servant of

servants to his brethren.' You shrink back with horror and say
'forbear, for that would abrogate the common humanity derived from
one common parent.' God says 'they shall be your possessions,
your money.' 'Never, no never,' you say, 'may humanity forbid,
for this would be to make them as trees and brutes.' Now, sir, who
is to be believed and who obeyed, you or your Maker?"

"But you do not say," said Mr. Pratt, 'that in law you consider
your slaves as mere chattels? Senator Sumner said in his celebrated speech at the Metropolitan theatre, in 1855, 'By the law
of slavery, man, created in the image of God, is divested of his
human character, and declared to be a mere chattel, and said he
quoted from the law of two slave States, South Carolina and Louis-
iana."

"Nellie," said Mr. Thompson, "please hand me my scrap book
from my library. I have taken care to gather, as far as I could, all
laws on the subject of slavery, and codify them for my own information. It will therefore be in my power to see if the distinguished
Senator has done justice to our noble little sister State." After
turning the leaves for a few minutes, Mr. T. read aloud, "Slaves
shall be delivered, sold, taken, reputed and adjudged in law to be
chattels personal in the hands of their owners and possessors, and their
executors, administrators and assigns, to all intents, constructions and
purposes whatsoever." "If Mr. Sumner," said Mr. T., "was a plain
farmer, who knew nothing beyond his milk and cheese and butter,
and had read nothing but the Tribune, and had never heard any one
preach but Henry Ward Beecher or Theodore Parker, I should be
disposed to attribute to him all honesty of purpose, and he would
claim my most earnest pity. But for a United States Senator to say
that 'chattels personal' means 'mere chattels,' is to say that his ignorance disqualifies him for his position, or that his duplicity entitles
him to the reprobation of all truth-loving and honest people. The
law says 'chattels personal' to distinguish them from chattels real or
landed estates and fixtures, but a mere chattel is nothing more than
a chattel. Senator Sumner is an animal, and would not feel reproached
if I were to tell him so; but it I were to say, he is a mere animal, it
would be the same as to say, he is nothing but an animal. Senator
Sumner is a thing, but is he a mere thing, a thing only?"

"I see the point in your argument very plainly, uncle," said Nellie.
"Mr. Sumner has made an interpolation by substituting *mere* for
*personal*, and has thus materially altered the sense of the law. The
way he makes the law read, is to put slaves in the catalogue with

watches, furniture and the like, while the word 'personal' is placed before them to distinguish them from real estate. They were said in the Bible to be a man's money; this is the light in which your legislators view them, when they call them chattels. I suppose it simply means property or possession. This much, I believe, you have shown from the Bible, you are authorized to call them. Then they are chattels, and as they are not real estate, they must be personal. But the word chattel does not in the least interfere with their humanity. I wonder if such perversions are common with our abolition orators of the North? if they are, the 'blind are leading the blind,' and I do not see what is to keep us all out of the ditch of error, for the common people have no means of detecting these errors, however glaring they may be. We all gulp them down as the ox drinketh the water, and think them gospel truths. I remember reading Mr. Sumner's speech just before leaving home, and the impression made by it upon my mind was, that the South had lost all sense of justice and humanity. I never dreamed that the honorable Senator would mislead his readers. I must confess, Mr. Pratt, that I am not only unsettled in my opposition to slavery as a moral wrong, but my confidence in the candor and honesty of the statements of our Northern speakers on the subject of slavery is greatly shaken if not entirely destroyed. I discover now, what I never heard admitted at the North, that the subject of slavery has two sides. It admits of defence; and that upon moral and scriptural grounds. I cannot see any sophistry in uncle's arguments, and the texts he quotes are too much in point to be denied. As I heard you say once in a sermon, 'Let God be true, but every man a liar.' I am willing to commit the formation of my opinions on all subjects to the infallible word of wisdom and goodness. God cannot err."

A servant entered and handed Nellie a note, which after a silent reading, she gave to her mother, who referred its contents to her uncle and aunt. It was a polite note from Mr. Mortimer, asking Miss Nellie and her young cousin to take a ride the next afternoon, to see, what he considered a beautiful spring near his plantation. It was agreed that the invitation should be accepted, and Nellie sought her young cousin Alice that they might jointly answer the note. Tea being announced, the family retired to the dining room. While at supper, Mr. T. was informed that one of his servants was very sick at the cabins, whither he hastened without delay.

"Nellie," said Mr. Pratt, after they were again seated in the parlor, "I regret very much you so far committed yourself to the principles and practices of slavocracy You are giving them aid and comfort, and if we friends of human liberty have no more stability than that, we can never be of service to the down-trodden slaves. Your uncle has not convinced me, *nor do I ever intend to be convinced.*"

"Mr. Pratt," said Nellie, "I did not commit myself to the slavocracy, but to the Bible. I have been listening with the deepest interest for you to refute the scripture arguments brought forward by my uncle, by a reference to the same high authority, but you have disappointed me, and I have attributed it, not to a want of intelligence on your part, or an absence of familiarity with the Bible, nor could I presume you wanting in desire to demolish every proslavery argument; but I have attributed your failure to the weakness of your cause. You have not brought up Bible arguments, because there were none. As for being convinced, I hope always to be willing to listen without prejudice to scriptural truth. This you have taught me, as my pastor, from childhood; and I desire to have the candor and moral firmness to confess an error when discovered."

"But," said Mr. Pratt, "do you not know that the letter of the scripture is one thing, and the spirit is another. Paul says the letter killeth, but the spirit giveth life. Your uncle's arguments are specious, and I am surprised, and I had almost said ashamed of you, that you have not detected his sophistry."

"I wonder," said Nellie, "you did not point it out if it were so patent, especially as you seemed so hard pushed for an argument to sustain what you have always taught me to believe was God's truth. But you say the 'letter and spirit' of the Bible are different. Do you mean that the Lord speaks one thing and means just the opposite. That when He says 'Thou *shalt* buy bondmen,' He means thou shalt *not* buy bondmen? When He says, 'They shalt be your bondmen *forever*,' He means you shall emancipate them? No, sir, the letter and spirit do not, cannot thus contradict each other. That there are figures of speech in the Bible, I have been taught by my Sabbath School teacher, and I presume none will deny this, and I have also been taught, and correctly too, I presume, that these are to be interpreted just as the figurative writings of other authors. But if the Bible is not to be interpreted by its language, then I am utterly hopeless as to a standard of righteousness to which all may come. Should your opinion obtain popular currency, and you should prove yourself the man for the place, we had better have you appointed to give the spiritual meaning of the scriptures, and take away the word, for what use could we then have for the word? But this would be to darken counsel, or rather to extinguish the light entirely. Do you think it is right to say, 'You never intend to be convinced?'"

"Yes," said Mr. Pratt, "it is right to close the avenues to mental conviction against all such monstrosities. Do you think I would read Voltaire or Paine with my heart or mind open to conviction? Preposterous. Do you think I would listen to a Mormon preacher without fortifying every access to my convictions? Never! no never!! Be on your guard, Nellie, you are young and easily carried away by specious arguments and plausible pretences. Your uncle has met abolitionists before. He is well read and can make the worse, the better side appear. There is an air of straight forwardness about him, well calculated to deceive the young. He is a wily tactician."

"But, Mr. Pratt," said Nellie, "you are not fortifying yourself against infidelity, but against truth. Not steeling yourself against the fallacies of a Mormon preacher, but against utterances of a prophet of God. Not against an error, but against heaven's revelation. You are not required to believe a 'moral monstrosity,' but simply what God has spoken in plain language. The infidel would tell you it is a monstrous fabrication, that a just and benevolent God ordained a plan for human redemption, which made it necessary that his own son should suffer and bleed and die. He says you demand too much of his credulity. But you answer him by saying 'Thus it is written,' 'If they will not believe Moses and the prophets, they would not believe one though he rose from the dead.' The arguments of my uncle are not specious but scriptural, and to my mind conclusive; and though I am young, and on that account perhaps the more easily influenced, yet I have not been willingly convinced, and even now, while I cannot answer uncle's arguments, and it seems as plain as that 2 and 2 are four, yet I confess that my feelings of humanity do not so easily yield as my judgment, but this may be because I have not heard the humanity side of the question. I did not at first believe there was a scriptural side of the question, but as I have been convinced of that, I am still further open to conviction by the *power of Truth.*"

The conversation was interrupted by the entrance of Mrs. Norton and Mrs. Thompson, who, not knowing the nature, or even existence of the conversation, proposed that Nellie entertain them with some new pieces of music, with which her uncle had presented her on her arrival. The remainder of the evening was spent by the family, in the parlor, in social converse, interspersed with now and then a little music from Nellie or Alice.

Mr. Thompson, by the aid of his physician, was vainly endeavoring to arrest the effects of a congestion, which had seized hold on Reuben, one of his most pious and valued servants. The long hours of the weary night were spent around the bedside of this colored man; but the morning sun arose above his lifeless body.

The servants were notified to be present at the funeral obsequies at 3 P. M. The sermon was to be preached by "Uncle Jesse," the colored preacher, who, on that account, spent the day at home.

## CHAPTER V.

*Negro Funeral—Pleasant Ride—Plantation Piety—"All Men Born Free and Equal" Exposed—Rights of Slaves—A Picture of Free Negro Prosperity—Nellie's Opinion of Slaveholders.*

Nellie and Alice were early from their rooms, each anticipating a pleasant ride that afternoon, for Mr. Mortimer was known to both as a man of cultivation, and unusually fine social qualities. Nellie, seating herself at the piano, played and sang one of her most sentimental pieces, the meantime building air castles, when, where and how, we shall not say. She had a heart to appreciate the noble, the good, the generous, and her imagination, when unfettered by other attractions, was always filled with images of loveliness and beauty. She but seldom looked at the dark side of a picture; if it had a bright one, she delighted to gaze upon it; if not, she turned away as a true philosopher to hunt one that did.

At the breakfast table Mr. Thompson announced the death of Reuben, which cast a shadow over the bright faces of the young cousins, who had only heard of his illness before. The arrangements for the funeral were also spoken of, and when Nellie ascertained that "Uncle Jesse" was to officiate, she regretted the arrangement for the afternoon, for she was exceedingly anxious to attend a negro funeral; but it was too late, unless Mr. Mortimer was willing to stay, and she could not obtain her consent to approach him on the subject. Her mother, however, informed her she must forego the pleasure of attending the funeral, and in due time be in readiness with her young cousin for the ride.

Mr. Thompson was busy during the day, preparing for the decent interment of his servant; and Mr. Pratt took this occasion to gratify his Yankee curiosity, and feed his abolition sentiments, by walking about the cabins and prying into the condition of the slaves, observing the care taken of the aged and the helpless young, but was surprised to find so little to condemn and so much to approve.

When the hour for the funeral arrived, the white family, with Mr. Pratt, went to the house of worship to witness the ceremony and hear the sermon. "Uncle Jesse" was already in the pulpit. When all were seated, he arose and read a part of the 14th chapter of Job, and then lined out the hymn:

> "Hark from the tombs a doleful sound,
> Mine ears attend the cry,
> Ye living men come view the ground
> Where you must shortly lie."

It was sung in full and solemn strains by the entire congregation, whose feelings seemed to be in unison with the sentiments of the hymn and the solemnity of the occasion. The minister then knelt, and engaged in fervent prayer that this sudden visitation of Providence might be a warning to servants and owner. He expressed thanks that the one taken from them had put his trust in the Son of God, and was ready and willing to go.

He announced his text: "The righteous hath hope in his death." After giving some explanations of the nature and value of the christian hope, he drew a striking contrast between it and the sinner's hope which should perish. "The sinner's hope," said he, "will do for health, but the christian's is good in sickness too; the sinner's seems strong enough when he has no load to carry, but it is too weak when the heavy burden's put upon him. It is bright when the sun shines, but goes out in darkness; it is mighty pleasant in the sins of life, but not one spark of it is left for his death bed; and when he comes to judgment, he will call upon the great big mountains to fall on him and kill him so that the great Master can't find him to punish him. Where's his hope, then? He hain't got none, it's gone, gone forever. Poor sinner! he didn't love Jesus here, nor serve him, now Jesus won't take no notice of him. He cry for help, but Jesus, looking up yonder smiling on the good ones. He cry to the mountains, but the mountains no hear him; he call on the hills, but the hills no answer him. Poor sinner, he got no friend, no Savior at the judgment. But not so with the faithful servant; he done his day's work faithfully; he lived right so as to please his Master; he done what he told him; he mind his Master up yonder. He been looking all the time for his Master to come; he want to see

Him; be anxious for Him to come. He look all day for Him. He love his Master; he hope in His goodness and mercy, and as he sees the sun going down his heart is happy; ah! he says, "I'll see my Master soon. He'll be in a good humor; He'll smile and say, 'well done good and faithful servant.' He feels like the good preacher of old, 'Come, Lord Jesus, come quickly.' Blessed is he who the Master finds so doing. And when the mighty angel Gabriel shall blow his trumpet so loud that it will wake the dead in their graves, they will need no more hopes then, for they will see the Good Master standing near like He was to Lazarus' grave, and He will give 'em new wings, like the angels, to fly away with Him to that big house He is gone up into heaven now to make for them. Even now while we here are weeping and mourning, brother Reuben's spirit's gone up there to be happy forever. He had hope when he was well. You all know how he used to 'zort you all to bleave in Jesus; you 'member his good prayers and happy songs, and how he said he was ready when the Master called for him. So when he got sick, the Savior sent His good spirit to give him strength, and he had hope still. Last night, when death was coming, and the doctor and Mas George told him they couldn't do nothing to save him, he said, 'I am so glad I see the pretty angels coming for me, to take me up to my long home to be happy forever.' He said, 'Uncle Jessie, tell 'em all to be faithful servants to our good Master here, and to our heavenly Master above, for He says we must be good servants here to be happy there. Tell them all to meet me in heaven, for when they wake up in the morning I shall be there.' O Lord, make brother Reuben's dying sermon the loudest preaching these poor servants ever heard, may it stick to 'em and weight 'em down tell they come to Thee for help.

"And now, my fellow-servants, before I get through, let me say to you, who have not the hope of the righteous: The Lord sees you, His eyes are like two great balls of fire, set up yonder in the heavens, only they are there all day and all night too, looking down even into your hearts; and for every wicked thought and word he will bring you into judgment. Repent, repent, or you will all perish forever."

The preacher was much moved, and so were all who heard him. Mr. T. looked round at Mr. Pratt, who was just wiping the tears from his eyes. As the master arose, there was a general press forward to the coffin to take the last look at the breathless form of "brother Reuben." The wife came forward in silent grief, as the large tear drops fell from her face like pearly dew drops from the shaken grass, till she reached the corpse, when a wild shriek burst from her lips, and she fell prostrate upon her deceased husband. A moan of deep grief and heartfelt sympathy was audible in the congregation. After a moment she was gently removed, and the men designated for that purpose came forward, and, closing the coffin, marched slowly out of the house, followed by all, white and colored. As soon as they all cleared the door, the old ostler broke forth into a solemn funeral dirge, the refrain of which was echoed by nearly all in the procession, and, as they moved in slow and measured steps, the melody of death song filled the air, till they reached the grave, and placed the body in its last resting place. When the grave was filled up, a short prayer and the benediction by "uncle Jesse" was the signal for dismission.

While these solemn exercises were taking place, Nellie, Alice and Mr. Mortimer were enjoying the mild autumnal air, and regaling themselves with the fading beauties of the lovely forest. Passing near the residence of Mr. M., Nellie inquired, "have you any churches near you where there is a stated ministry?" "None," said Mr. M., "nearer than ten miles, and that enjoys only a monthly ministry." "Then," said Nellie, "your servants have but few religious opportunities, and make but little moral improvement, for I suppose that it is too far for them to attend unless you furnish them with facilities for riding." "We never permit our servants, except on unusual occasions, to go so far to church," said Mr. M. "We find it to our interest and for their good, to bring the minister to them rather than send them to him. You will observe a painted house standing out to our left—that is our church." "That with a short steeple?" said Nellie. "And have you a bell on it?" "Yes," said Mr. M., "I bought in Savannah a steamboat bell, which can be heard very well by all my servants, and we have it wrung just before the hour of preaching. We have a good deal of uniformity in our services. We have an educated and devotedly pious man for our minister, and he is greatly attached to the work of his ministry. He has been called to one or two city churches, and once I believe to a professorship in one of our universities, but he feels this is the work assigned him by Providence, and therefore he stays."

"How often," said Nellie, "do you have preaching in your church?"

"Preaching twice a month," said Mr. M., "and prayer meetings the other two Sabbaths and one night in each week. The weekly

H

prayer meetings, however, are held at the negro houses. They find it less labor after the fatigues of the day, and they procure a better congregation, and therefore, at their request, I have permitted them to use their own pleasure as to the location of these meetings."

"Have you many religious servants?" said Nellie.

"Yes," said Mr. M., "more than half of my adult servants are members of the church, and a large majority very conscientious and pious. They are more uniform and consistent, more regular in their attendance upon Divine worship, than any class of professed christians I have ever seen; and there is not one among them who refuses to pray when asked, and I believe all who have families are accustomed to hold prayer with them at least once a day. They are the most religious class of people in this or any other land. They have fewer temptations to the vices, vanities and cares of life. They are the most contented and happy people of our fallen race. I sometimes wish I had been born a slave, and reared in the lap of unaspiring contentment as they have been. I do not own one who is not to-day happier than I am."

"Can any of them read?" said Nellie.

"Several of them read well," said Mr. Mortimer, "and have their bibles and hymn books; and some have a knowledge of Scripture that would greatly surprise you. Before I became a church member, I used to argue the subject of religion, taking the negative, with a very faithful old servant of mine. He would answer from the Bible every argument that I brought up, till at last I denied the Divine inspiration of the Bible, telling him that it was written by a few wicked men just to see how foolish men were in believing a great story that pretended to be from heaven.

"Master," said he, "I'se seen a heap of bad men in the world, and I never hear them say good things like the Bible got in it. Bad men against the Bible, and the good things it tells 'bout they no write it. You think so, master? Ah! I know you don't. There's somethin' here," laying his hand upon his heart, "that says it's true, it's from yonder," pointing to heaven, "and your heart tell you so too. The wicked one make you say the Bible not true; he want you to burn in the lake of fire; he want to keep you out of heaven. Better take care, master, you too good a man for Satan to get, but he want you. You ought to pray, master, that the good Spirit teach you like a child how to be "wise unto salvation" and good like Master Jesus. I pray for you every day; I don't want the wicked one to get you; I want you to be christian, and lead we black folks in the right way. I tell you, master, if you be good man, your people be heap better and happier, and you be happier too. Master, do try to be good; please, sir, won't you, dear massa?"

Here tears came into the eyes of M., while he added, "under God I owe my salvation to the earnest and repeated exhortations and prayers of that good servant. I have often heard him pray for me when he was not aware that I or any one else was near him."

"Do they maintain anything like family discipline?" said Nellie.

"A few of them do," answered Mr. M., "and most of them command obedience from children to their parents. But, like all other families of the earth, there is much criminal negligence on this subject. Yet there is not that necessity for discipline among negroes that there is among a free people; at least a neglect of it is not so harmful. Their children are less exposed to temptation; they do not come in contact with the snares of a wicked and designing world as we do; the restraint which slavery places upon them is an admirable guard against the dissipations which ruin so many young men in our country. The pious among them generally take some pains in the religious training of their children, but many of them, like the whites of every land, are guilty of sinful neglect on this subject. Many white children are ruined for the want of proper religious instructions and restraints, and it is hardly to be expected that the servant should be above his lord in this respect."

"I suppose," said Nellie, "their standard of moral honesty is very low; their ability to discriminate between mine and thine must be very weak."

"They are not all honest, but there is less dishonesty among them than among any class of dependents in the world. Our house servants have opportunities to take anything we have, even our money, but either their sense of moral wrong, or their pride of character, keeps them from yielding to the temptations which are thus daily placed before them. Such of us as are bachelors, as myself, place even our keys at their disposal, so that they have free access to everything. I have no doubt, from my knowledge of their character, that generally they are influenced from a sense of moral honesty in abstaining from taking the things which belong to others. Nine cases out of ten of the robberies committed in our cities are perpetrated by white persons. There are more slaves in our cities, perhaps double the number, than of poor persons. Why do they not steal? They have better opportunities than the whites. They have access to every house; they know where the valuables are kept;

they have unrestrained intercourse with each other that they might form any collusion they chose, and yet they but seldom steal. The reasons seem to me obvious. Superadded to the one already mentioned, they have everything which their condition in life demands. They are fed bountifully, clothed well, nursed when indisposed, and afforded as suitable diet when sick as other persons enjoy, and if they need anything they have no hesitation at all in asking for it, and generally it affords a master pleasure to grant the requests, even though sometimes they may be very whimsical. Then again, most of our servants entertain such an affection for their masters that they consider themselves as much interested in what pertains to their interests as if it were their own. I have not a servant who would not labor as hard as I to save any piece of my property from destruction, or who would not now place himself in danger, if necessary, to save me from it. When I am sick they manifest the greatest concern for my recovery, and come in to see me every evening when they return from labor, and some of the more pious will come and propose to hold prayer for me. Under these circumstances, they pray most fervently and affectionately. On one occasion, when I was very ill, and so delirious I knew nothing, an aged servant came in at midnight and told those who were watching with me, that he could not sleep till he knelt by my bedside and prayed for me. His request was granted, and after a prayer in such broken English that it was scarcely understood by those who listened, for he was an African, he retired satisfied. His prayer, however, was heard in heaven, and the answer of mercy was enjoyed by me."

They arrived at the spring, and the conversation was turned upon the surrounding objects. The spring was so much less beautiful than many which Nellie had seen in New England, that she was not very profuse in its praise. As they rode home an agreement was made that on some day not far in the future they would ride up to Bonaventure and see that unique and ancient burying ground.

Nellie was convinced that slaveholding did not make a master the less a man in all the nobler elements of character. She had found a young bachelor who was an intelligent social christian, observing with scrupulous regard all the amenities of life, with a bearing dignified and even noble, a heart, too, true and generous, a sensibility cultivated and refined, free from that rude familiarity which she had been accustomed to see. In a word, she had found a man whom she felt was her superior, and for whom, to say no more, she entertained a profound respect.

Arriving at Mr. Thompson's as the sun went down, the party proceeded up the gravelly walk, ornamented with a variety of beautiful shrubbery tastefully arranged, while here and there still lingered on the parent stem an autumnal rose whose fragrance was not less fresh, and whose odor was not less sweet than when the first bland May morn was ushered in by the melody of the forest songsters.

Promising to call again soon to enjoy some new pieces of music of which Nellie had been speaking, Mr. Mortimer bid them good evening at the door, and retired.

The merits of Uncle Jesse's sermon and the scenes at the funeral were freely discussed at the tea table. Mr. Pratt said he had heard many sermons from ministers of finished education, which would compare unfavorably for strength of argument, scriptural illustrations and gospel purity with this, and he was convinced under such a system of religious instruction the colored people would not suffer for the bread of life. He added, "if all slaveholders were like 'mine hosts,' the institution would be much less objectionable to my mind. I would to God every slave of the South had such a master."

"I have found another such," said Nellie, "in the person of Mr. Mortimer; and am prepared to believe there are many more."

"I assure you," said Mr. Thompson, "my neighbors' servants, as a general thing, fare as well as mine, and such is public sentiment, that if a man treats his servants with inhumanity he is ruled out of society, and if that does not effect a reformation we apply the "weightier matter of the law" to him. Servants have their rights as well as masters, and we are scrupulously particular not to infringe upon them. The interests and rights of masters and servants do not conflict, but harmonize; they are different, it is true, and yet in some sense they are identical. It is like the relation of the subject and the sovereign. It is for the welfare of the subject that he should be subordinate and virtuous, honest and loyal; he thereby promotes the strength and perpetuity of the government which protects him in the enjoyment of his rights. and it gives him favor with his sovereign, whose good will is not to be lightly esteemed. On the other hand, it is the interest of the sovereign to regard the rights of his subjects, and, as far as possible, promote their welfare, for thereby he contributes to the strength and perpetuity of his throne, by obtaining a place in the hearts of his subjects. He makes it their interest to support him, by fostering their own individual welfare."

"I have often heard men at the North," said Mr. Pratt, "speak of the rights of slaves, but never expected to hear it from a Southern slaveholder. I did not know you recognized the existence of any such fact. Pray tell me what you consider to be their rights."

"There are many clever things at the South," said Mr. T., "of which you at the North know nothing, and for the supposed absence of which much odium is heaped upon us. But to the subject of your questions. The slaves have many rights. The right of life and limb, the right to be fed and clothed, to be nursed when sick, and cared for in old age when they become helplessly infirm. They are rightfully entitled to protection from ill treatment. They have the right to the uninterrupted possession of whatever they may accumulate by labor in their own time, or by honest trade, and this is universally awarded to them, although the amounts thus accumulated are considerable. They are entitled to protection from the pernicious sentiments of abolitionists which discontent them with their present condition by untruthful representations, but which do not afford them any relief. But again, servants have a right to the "tree of life," through faith in our common Savior. They have a right to our sympathy, esteem and confidence, and this right they enjoy at the South, but no where else in christendom. It is true that the rights of the negro are recognized nowhere on earth but in the South, and by no persons but slaveholders. Not that there is not a great deal of prating about "freedom, emancipation, inherent and inalienable rights," and a long catalogue of unmeaning jargon in its application to the slave; but they are despised and contemned and driven hungry and naked away from the doors of those whose professions of sympathy are loudest. Their Northern friends (?) will contribute money to free them from slavery, but not from hunger, cold and nakedness. How many refugees now at the North turn with longing eyes back to the comforts and privileges they enjoyed while in slavery. But their friends will neither help them back, nor relieve them there."

When seated in the parlor, after tea, Mr. Thompson referred to the conversation of the previous afternoon, and said: "I did not reply to all the objections you urged against slavery. I will now finish what I then began. Your proposition was, that slavery annuls the religious rights of the enslaved, and denies them the privileges of moral and intellectual culture."

"I will withdraw the first part of that proposition," said Mr. Pratt. "What I have witnessed of their religious and moral culture this day is more convincing than any argument you could produce. I am convinced that on this particular point the South has been misunderstood. I hold to the proposition that it denies them the right of intellectual culture, and I apprehend you will admit the fact."

"I think," said Mr. T., "I might well hold you to the proof that such right exists. If it does, from what source is it derived?"

"From their common brotherhood to the human family," said Mr. P. "God has endowed all men with intellectual powers, and holds them responsible for their improvement. Then it follows that there must be freedom to do that, for the doing or neglecting of which they will be held accountable."

"I hold," said Mr. Thompson, "they have no rights on this subject which are not in entire accordance with the obligations imposed by slavery, since in this particular God made them exceptions to the common brotherhood, entailing on them slavery with all its legitimate consequences. What rights to intellectual culture has their Creator bestowed on them? Go to the land of their fathers and ascertain. They have no written language, no schools, no teachers, no means for the increase of knowledge. God has withheld these privileges from them up to the present time. They are, as you know, an ignorant, degraded, indolent people. They have lain in ignorance for thousands of years without either the ability or inclination for improvement. More than two-thirds of the population of Africa are in the most servile bondage to the other one-third. The masters and slaves alike in the most stupid ignorance. This state of universal ignorance in Africa cannot be attributed to the moral and religious darkness that has settled as a pall of blackness upon the hearts of that people. Greece and Rome and Egypt in ancient days, and the Chinese at the present time, with their learning, their poetry, history, oratory, arts and sciences, and yet all having no knowledge of the living God, prove most conclusively that intellectual improvement may be wholly disconnected from moral and religious culture. As this is the only nation of people who have not advanced intellectually, there is much reason to believe they are providentially an exception to the general rule."

"You do not pretend," said Mr. P., "to deny the glorious principle asserted in the Declaration of Independence: that 'all men are born free and equal.' This would be a denial of a fundamental principle of republican government. This truth has thrilled the hearts of millions, and called forth the loudest plaudits from enthusiastic republicans. This part of our noble declaration is so eminently true, that he who denies it should deny the unity of our race. I hope, therefore, that my honorable host will not be guilty of such rashness."

"I suppose, then," said Mr. T., "you hold this declaration to be true without any restrictions or qualifications. The negro is as free as the American citizen, and is therefore his equal; he is consequently entitled to the elective franchise, and even more, to hold any office to which a white man is eligible. A negro, therefore, may one day be President of these United States—his beautiful thick-lipped spouse doing the honors of the White House, and graciously condescending to receive an introduction to, and entertain your wife and daughters. Under these circumstances, the wives and daughters of your Congressmen would have to receive the attention of the President and his sons, if he had any, and treat them with all deference as equals or superiors. But again, if a negro is thus equal, and therefore eligible to this high office, he has the right to choose his cabinet, and would, as we have invariably done, select them of his own color. Now, my dear sir, would this not be a beautiful illustration of the doctrine of equality. America ruled by Africa—white men ruled by negroes—the enslaved of the Lord dictating to those whom He made free. Verily your dogma would turn the world "upside down," annul the Divine order and reverse the decrees of nature. Nor can you deny that this is the inevitable result of the doctrine, that all men are born free and equal. We have always held the theory abstractly, but put it into practice and yet avoid these results if you can."

"What extremists you Southern people are," said Mr. Pratt. "I did not mean political freedom and equality, but social, religious and mental."

"Then," said Mr. T., "you believe in social equality with the negro, do you? You would be pleased to have them visit your wife and daughters upon a social equality: intermarry with them, have them for your sons and daughters, amalgamate the two races, to one of which God has given a white skin and straight hair, and to the other of which he has given a black skin and woolly hair. Thus, what God has joined together you would put asunder, and what he has put so far asunder you would join together. But pardon me, sir, if I say you abolitionists do believe in the political freedom of the negro, and for its accomplishment all your abolition societies have been organized, and all your speeches, sermons and petitions to

Congress made. Why this perpetual cry against slavery, if it is not that you want them freed in the political sense. Then, if you believe in universal freedom and equality, it must include political as well as social freedom. However, sir, I accept your limitation, and am glad that you do not believe in the political freedom of the negro, that you are content to leave him in political bondage, because he has no such right as freedom. He has rights, but the elective franchise is not one of them, as you have very properly concluded. Then what are his rights? Dr. Channing says the slave ' is subject to the community, and the community has the right, and is bound to continue all such restraints, as its own safety and the well-being of the slave demand.' Then what becomes of the equal rights of the slave according to this celebrated abolitionist? He is not to be owned by an individual nor controlled by one master, but by many, poor fellow, by the 'community.' The community are not to free him, not to restore to him his lost but inalienable rights. Oh, no, it is to ' restrain' him. The negroes, generally, are not fond of such prominence, nor has experience taught them that they fare better in a community who holds no property in them, and whose sole duty it is to restrain them, than they do in the hands of a man whose money they are, and who therefore is the vigilant guardian of their best interests. But again Dr. Channing says, 'If he (the slave) cannot be induced to work by rational and natural motives, he should be obliged to labor on the same principle on which the vagrant in other communities is confined and compelled to earn his bread.' Poor fellow, what a foot ball he would become out of the hands of his Southern master and sympathiser. Has the ' vagrant who is confined and compelled to labor to earn his 'bread,' any right to intellectual culture? Who confers it, and how is it available? These rights of the slave ' grow small by degrees and beautifully less' as they get further north. Now, sir, to admit the doctrine of equal rights without any restrictions, is to admit that every man has an equal right to the Presidency of these United States, be he wise or ignorant, virtuous or vicious, white or black. But these conclusions you very wisely and prudently repudiate, and in doing so, you virtually deny the premise from which the conclusion is drawn. 'The well-being of the slave' demands certain restraints. What these may be, are best known to those to whom providence has committed him. The Southerners alone, of all the world, understand negro character and capacity.

God never designed them for an intellectual race. China, isolated from the world and degraded in idolatry, has a history and a literature. She has her philosophers, her poets, her teachers, her graduates, her temples. But Africa, doomed to slavery, has neither. Ignorance, stupidity, imbecility, are characteristics of her people. Incapable of self-government and self-support, a gracious providence has sent them here to find governors and protectors, who will feed and clothe them, and lead their hearts and minds to the knowledge of the living God; while they pay less for the benefit than any other set of learners on earth.

The last thought you gleaned from Dr. Wayland is that "slavery restrains them from the employment of their own time for their own benefit." In reply to this, it is only necessary to say, that all experience and observation prove, that the welfare of the negro is best promoted when he is under the restraints of slavery. No doubt your knowledge of the condition of the free negroes at the North confirms this assertion. Most of our slaves (and it is so with negroes everywhere) work only under the pressure of necessity, then they do it cheerfully; they are only kept from vice, when too busy to go into temptation; they are only kept from sinking back into barbarism by contact with civilization and christianity among their masters. They are better fed, better clothed and more contented when in slavery. To prove the truth of what I have said, we have only to refer to the short history of the emancipated slaves in the West Indies. They were left in the possession of a most fertile soil, with all the appliances of husbandry, and the country in a high state of prosperity. What is it now? Dr. King says, "the marks of decay abound. Neglected fields, crumbling houses, fragmentary fences, noiseless machinery—these are common sights, and soon become familiar to observation. I sometimes rode for miles in succession over fertile ground which used to be cultivated, and which is now lying waste. So rapidly has cultivation retrograded, and the wild luxuriance of nature replaced the conveniences of art, that parties still inhabiting these desolated districts, have sometimes, in the strong language of a speaker in Kingston 'to seek about the bush to find the entrance into their houses.' The towns present a spectacle not less gloomy. A great part of Kingston was destroyed some years ago, by an extensive conflagration; yet multitudes of the houses which escaped that visitation are standing empty, though the population is little, if at all diminished. The explanation is obvious. Persons who have nothing, and can no longer keep their domestic establishments, take refuge in the abodes of others, where some means of subsistence are still left, and in the absence of any discernable trade or occupation, the lives of crowded thousands appear to be preserved from day to day by a species of miracle. The most busy thoroughfares of former times have now almost the quietude of a Sabbath."

The following is a report signed by several Missionaries and made in 1849:

" Missionary efforts in Jamaica are beset at the present time with many and great discouragements. Societies at home have withdrawn or diminished the amount of assistance afforded by them to chapels and schools throughout this island. The prostrate condition of its agriculture and commerce disables its own population from doing as much as formerly for maintaining the worship of God and the tuition of the young, and induces numbers of negro laborers to retire from estates which have been thrown up, to seek the means of subsistence in the mountains, where they are removed in general from moral training and superintendence. The consequences of this state of matters are very disastrous. Not a few Missionaries and teachers, after struggling with difficulties which they could not overcome, have returned to Europe, and others are preparing to follow them. Chapels and schools are abandoned, or they have passed into the hands of very incompetent instructors. H. C. Cary says, 'population gradually diminishes, furnishing another evidence that the tendency of everything is adverse to the progress of civilization. In 1841 the island contained a little short of 400,000 persons. In 1844 the census returns gave about 380,000.' "

The history of emancipation in South Africa is accompanied by the same sad results. While there is no population on earth, the rates of whose increase is greater than our slaves, yet in those localities where they have been deprived of the fostering care of masters and the blessing of slavery, they deteriorate in character and decrease in numbers with fearful rapidity. There can be no reasonable doubt but that slaves are the most intelligent of the negro race; and the reasons are obvious. As a rule they have not intellects susceptible of much cultivation—very seldom, if ever, do you find a really striking character—they must necessarily learn by contact and observation, and these means of information must be available constantly. Their contact and association with the superior minds of the Anglo Saxon race, throws upon their darkened minds a flood of light, some of the rays of which they cannot but retain. But take them away from these influences and let them associate only with their own race, and all the history of the past—the history of Africans for all past time, prove there is no progress, either in minds or morals. Theories are sometimes very beautiful, and no doubt but to the mind of an enthusiastic abolitionist, the theory of emancipation presents nothing for the slave but a bright progressive future, the development of a great and religious race which shall bless the world in some future age. But "facts are stubborn things," and often destroy the most beautiful and plausable theory. From the facts to which we have referred, we may justly conclude, that what freed slaves have done in Jamaica and South Africa they will do everywhere under the same circumstances. I therefore conclude that God never designed they should enjoy the rights of freemen; indeed unless they should be remodeled mentally and morally it would be the greatest curse that could befall them. How many promising boys have been ruined by being freed from parental restraints at too early an age. Just so it would be, because it always has been, with the negro. God gave the parent authority over the child, because it was for the child's good, and so He gave the master authority over the slave for his good. No man has a right to freedom when its exercise is injurious to the community, or if he has, there is a right vested in the community to restrain that freedom within such limits as will insure benefits to enure to the individual or the public or both. Negro freedom here would engender vice, degradation, vagrancy, penury, starvation, theft, murder, mobocracy, and every form of evil which could possibly be imagined, and would ultimately terminate in the extermination of the blacks by the whites or by starvation. Nominal slavery cannot exist here, because it would be unprofitable to the owner, and therefore reduce the slave to want. Nothing is practicable but absolute slavery, modified by christianity and the laws of the land. This results in a mutual interest and affection between the master and the slave. The master's interest demands kind and humane treatment to his slave, who in his turn claims the gratitude and wins the love of the dependent."

"You do not think that a slave has really any affection for a man who holds him in bondage, do you?" said Mr. Pratt.

"I can answer that question for you," said Nellie. "I tried to get uncle's carriage driver to go back home with mother and myself on our return north, but he said he would not, unless his master and mistress would go too, and stated as a reason that he loved them too well to leave them. I have talked to several others in the same way, and invariably received the same answer. I am convinced that they do not feel slavery to be a bondage, but are satisfied and happy, and instead of feeling that their masters are their oppressors, they look upon them as benefactors. The tears that are shed over slavery and the prayers offered for its bonds to be broken, are not by the enslaved, but by us, their misguided and less informed friends at the north."

"I will give you this permission," said Mr. Thompson to Mr. Pratt, "you may go among my negroes, and represent facts and fiction to them, and if you find one who will go with you home, I will defray all the expense of going, and you shall support him at the north until you get him into a business where he can support himself, and when he has tried freedom for one year, if he desires to return to slavery, you shall see that his desire is granted at my expense. The latter item I would incur from sympathy and humanity, knowing he would be unhappy where he met with neither friends nor sympathisers."

"I wonder," said Mrs. Thompson, "if you gentlemen will never get off your stilts. You really don't recognize our presence, much less address us a social word, nor has either of us been able to get in a word edgewise to night. Can't you play the agreeable for a little while—just a little while? We would feel complimented, honored, even flattered by a little notice from gentlemen so cultivated and intellectual. Come gentlemen, do give us a short opportunity to express ourselves. You have certainly forgotten that the ladies esteem it quite a deprivation to sit a whole evening in silence—such a thing is intolerable. You lords of creation must be a little more condescending: won't you?"

"Excuse us ladies," said Mr. Pratt, "it is not often I meet a slaveholder, or my friend an abolitionist, and we only wished to interchange views on the subject. I was endeavoring to teach Mr. T., and he trying to prove to me that he knew more than I, who proposed to become teacher. I desired to convince him that slavery was an evil, but he has convinced ——— Nellie, at least, that it is religiously right. But to your theme : did you ever hear of the lady that was so fond of talking that she held a conversation with a snake, out in the orchard?"

"No indeed," said Mrs. T., "I regret that one of my sex has so far lost her dignity as thus to condescend; or perhaps I ought not to condemn her, for she may have been some unfortunate widow who had lost her husband, or some old maid who never had one, and in either event, one might be excused for talking to almost anything, rather than to be forever silent. An apple orchard was indeed a poor place, and a snake a very unpromising subject, but 'necessity knows no law.'"

"I suppose," said Nellie, "Mother Eve was the lady, Satan the snake, and the garden of Eden the apple orchard."

"What a wit you are," said Mr. P., "you had better set yourself up as a candidate for tutor in astrology, conundrums, enigmas, &c., and have us elect you as general expounder of abstruse science."

"Thank you sir, I covet no such distinction," said Nellie, "and when our wiseacres learn to state their problems a little more clearly, the office you propose to create may well be dispensed with."

The conversation became general and social; but Nellie's mind being absorbed with other thoughts, she excused herself and retired to the room. Her cousin Alice, a miss of thirteen years, had just mastered her lesson for the next day, and laid down her books as Nellie entered.

"Alice," said Nellie, "I wish you had spent one summer north before I came south."

"Why, cousin?" said Alice.

"Because," said Nellie, "I want to talk with you about the difference in society and manners there and here."

"As I am only a learner anyhow," said Alice, "I will be very glad to hear you talk about your society at home. It will be very interesting to me. Do tell me all about it, my dear cousin. I will listen to every word, and not get sleepy."

"I don't care to talk so much about northern society, as to tell you how much I am disappointed in southern society," said Nellie. "I thought southern slave-holders were an ignorant, rude, bigoted, uncultivated and cruel people, who delighted in oppressing and tyrannizing over their slaves, and treating them as brutes. I thought they took pleasure in punishing them and at witnessing their sufferings; that they were destitute of the common feelings of humanity, and never sympathised with the sufferings of their slaves. I conceived them to be a proud, haughty, illiterate people generally; too ignorant to know their own deficiencies. But I am happily disappointed. I find slave-holders intelligent, many highly cultivated and intellectual—men of superior general intelligence, refined, polite, genteel. I find them to be men of highly refined sensibilities and tender sympathies—patterns of unselfishness. I have often been surprised that uncle could obtain his consent to make it his permanent home and rear his children among semi-barbarians, as you all have been represented to be by our abolition speakers and writers. But to my surprise, I find southern character superior, absolutely superior to northern character. I make this confession with unfeigned mortification, and would not do it elsewhere, and yet one should not be ashamed or afraid of the truth. There is a greatness of soul, an independence of character, a dignity of mien, a purity of thought, a manliness of carriage, an unselfishness of heart, so happily blended with unostentation and softness of deportment, so manly and yet so modest, so intelligent, and yet so free from pedantry, I must say that southern character claims my most profound admiration. There is no petty tyranny here—no brutality—no such oppression as I have been taught to believe universally prevailed among slave-holders. The line which marks the distinction between master and servant is most apparent, and yet the master does not lord it over his servant as I supposed. He does not abuse his power, but it is exerted in a kind, generous, condescending manner. He is a kind and amiable prince, who loves his subjects and is interested in the happiness and welfare of each one, not only because they are his property, but he really takes pleasure in their happiness.

"I am reminded of Jacob, whose paternal care extended to the remotest and smallest member of the family. I tell you, cousin, such an interest in the welfare of laborers at the north, if it exists at all, is the exception, not the rule. When a man there is well and does his work faithfully, his wages are paid regularly, but when he gets sick, or grows old and helpless, he is turned off without a thought as to his necessities. He has no more claims on his master. And even while at labor, the intercourse between the employer and laborer is not half so free and unrestrained, as here between the negro and his master. There is a total absence generally of that kind feeling so universally observed here. I attribute this to the much hated and slandered institution of slavery. There is something about, it don't know what, it is a mystery to me, that exerts a most favorable influence over your southern society. I have been highly gratified to find an absence of that little picayunish disposition and that low sensualism so distressingly prevalent in northern society, and the rapid growth of which threatens the overthrow of all good. Father has often spoken of that dreadful tendency in our society at home, and thinks it portends much evil in the future. I do wish he would come south and live, I am so fascinated with southern society and manners."

Nellie happened to cast her eye towards the side table, and saw

"Treasured Moments, by Sawtell." She took it up, and it opened at the first letter on slavery. Finding he was a New Englander, she concluded to see what he had written. She read aloud to Alice:

"The object of this letter is simply to correct some erroneous impressions as to the real character of slavery in this country. The prevailing impression at the north is, that the cruel treatment of the slave, and his consequent sufferings, are such as to demand his immediate and unconditional emancipation. This is one of the most cogent reasons urged why we should take no time to consult the future good and interests, either of the master or of the slave. And to deepen the impression, the most frightful pictures of sufferings and cruelty have been drawn, and held up to the imagination till the heart has become sick, and the very name *slave* is associated in the mind with all the horrors of the "middle passage" and the racks and tortures of the inquisition. Now, with all due respect to the *opinions* of others, I do know that such impressions are not in accordance with facts. On this subject southern character is either not understood, or grossly, though I would hope, unintentionally misrepresented. Bold and chivalrous as is a southern man in contest with his equals, nothing is more despicable in his eyes than a petty tyrant, who exhibits his powers only in inflicting wrongs and injuries upon the helpless and unprotected. Naturally high-minded, noble and generous in feelings and sentiments, he is found magnanimous and kind in spirit towards his dependents."

As a general fact, I doubt whether there can be found a class of people in the world that suffer less, mentally or physically, than the colored population of the South. None who have fewer cares and troubles, who wear happier faces, are more jovial and merry, and who sing louder and sweeter than they. For the truth of this, I appeal to every man who has visited the South, and examined this subject for himself with an unprejudiced and impartial mind. Exceptions I know there are, but these no more prove the general truth on this subject, than do the convicts in the penitentiaries of New England prove that all the old Puritans of that land of steady habits are grinding in the prison house. Hence, when a Northern man enters the Southern States for the first time, and witnesses the familiarity and kindness between master and servant, he exclaims with wonder, 'where are the long whips, the scourges, the groans and tears of which I have heard so much?' And often have I seen the tear start in the stranger's eye at beholding the ecstacy of joy with which the dependents gather around their master on his return from a long absence, seizing his hand and seeming to vie with each other in manifesting their love and attachment to him."

"Enough," said Nellie, as she threw down the book, "how singularly coincident are the results of his and my observation. Henceforth I shall refuse to join in the abolition cry against the South. Indeed, I will frown upon it as a wicked and malicious slander. It is really provoking to think how I have always been deceived—how gullible we poor Northern dupes are. Our politicians, editors and preachers take us by the nose and lead us where they please. Henceforth I will think for myself, always taking the Bible for my guide."

"I tell you, cousin, the negroes at the North are a down-trodden race; they are ignorant, mean, degraded, vicious, abandoned. Every man's hand is against them; no one respects or esteems them, if they can avoid it. They profess great love for the poor slave, but they are a nation of negro haters; and you have only to be there and see for yourself to know that I speak the truth. I do think you Southerners have much more reason to pity the free negroes at the North, than we have to sympathize with your slaves. I would ten thousand times prefer to be a slave in Georgia, than a free negro in Massachusetts. They are more respected, better cared for, and almost infinitely happier here than there."

Nellie discovering her young cousin's eyes were growing rather heavy, suggested they had better retire, to which Alice most cheerfully assented, and was soon lost in refreshing sleep. But Nellie's mind was full of ideas, and her heart of impressions. She thought of the elevated Christian character, the manly dignity, the superior intelligence, and the amiable, affectionate disposition of her new friend, with whom she had spent the afternoon so pleasantly. "I wonder if he is a genuine, true man. Yes, he must be; I cannot be deceived in him: he is too transparent, too guileless, there is no assumacy about him, he is certainly a gentleman of unusual moral worth. He seems timid, and yet very graceful; he is dignified, and yet has the *suaviter in modo*, as though he had been the pupil of Chesterfield. He is not at all pharisaical, and yet it is evident he is a true Christian. There is no religious cant about him, and yet he speaks as a man familiar with holy subjects. He has none of the pedant about him, yet he is certainly a finely educated and well read man. His mind is well stored with useful knowledge, and yet he claims no superiority over any one. He is certainly a model character—wish I had such a man for a —— hush, foolish heart—but

J

how I would esteem and love him. Oh, I would be so happy! I intend to study his beautiful and exalted character—I think the study will be quite as fascinating to me as was that of Botany, especially if I come in as frequent contact with him as I did with flowers." Sweet girl! there were visions flitting along her future path, "the beauty of which, like jewels, too rich to be exported, were not conveyable by expression to mortal fancy."

The next morning the gentlemen rode over the farm. When on approaching the "cotton-pickers" Mr. Thompson suggested to Mr. P. "that now was his time to make the experiment of a slave's anxiety to throw off the shackles of bondage and accompany him to the land of freedom." Mr. T. therefore rode another way to where some hands were ploughing in wheat, while Mr. Pratt rode up to the foremost cotton picker, and alighting from his horse and walking up very near, the following colloquy took place:

"Howdy, uncle. What is your name?"

"Jerry, your sarbant, sa."

"Well, Jerry, your master has agreed to give you your freedom if you will go home with me. As I know you want to be free, I am glad of being the bearer of such happy intelligence. There is no mistake about it, you are free to go home with me, and we have no slaves at the North, all are free alike there. You will be as free as I or any one else. Now, as your master has consented, you must not refuse, but be ready in a few weeks."

"Who say so? Mas George say I must go wid you? Dis nigga hab de considerashun ob de objection."

"Why, don't you want to be free? You can then work for yourself and have all you make."

"Eh, hab all he make. How he'gwine to make any ting?"

"Work for it, to be sure. 'Ye shall earn your bread by the sweat of your brow,' is the Bible rule since the fall."

"You make nigga free, and den make him work too. Plenty work here widout gwine home wid you."

"Yes, but then you can be free and do as you please. You all ought to be free. God made you so, and you would be better off in many respects. You could then go to church when you wanted to, have your own property around you, and send your children to school, and give them an education. You don't know how much happier you would be if you were free. Now you must not refuse to go home with me, since I have been so kind as to get your master's consent."

"I hab great considerashun for respect ob your feelins massa, but de colored folks, sir, is peculiar. Dey needs de considerashun ob de everdence to show unto dem de ducements of freedom. Work is work. If I hab to work when I free, and I hab to work when I no free, you see I no hab the everdence ob de vantage. Mas George gib me good home and plenty to eat and put on, and Sunday close too. I go to church ebry Sunday, and prayer meetin' twixt times; and I be happy, too, tank God, for he mighty good and merciful to colored folks."

"Well, then, you prefer slavery, do you? Had you rather stay here, and be a poor slave all your life, and work for your master, than go home with me and be free?"

"I is'nt molishus nor unconsiderate on dis present occasion; de subjick strikes berry much at de anxiety ob de cullud folks ginelly; but I hab peculiar purswashun on dis case. I gwine to stay wid Mas George and Miss Penny."

"You don't want to be happy as a freeman, then?"

"Ah, Massa! You tink freedum gwine to make de cullud folks happy. Dis is not de konsiquence. It de *tribulation* what makes him happy. He want what is perspicus to de feelins. He wants de Lord to send and descend and condescend wid his sperit, and cause to turn and return and overturn, and make his heart to joice and rejoice and overjoice. He want de Lord to lift up de lily white vail, open de dormur windows ob heben, wave back de dark curtins, drop his frown behin' de mountin, and take a peep ober into de camps ob Israel. Den, sa, de tribulation ob de occasion will be berry much wid de anxiety ob de cullud folks, and dey will break down at de foot ob de cross ob calvary and be happy. Dis, sa, is de perspicus consequence ob de sensible observation."

The disgusted clergyman mounted his horse and rode away to meet his friend, soliloquising as he went on the power of habit and the evils of slavery. Meeting with Mr. Thompson, he announced the failure of his mission with Jerry, and received the assurance of the master, that the result would have been the same with any other of his negroes.

## CHAPTER VI.

*A new Scripture against Slavery—Its misapplication—Opinion of an English writer—God uses the institution of Slavery as an illustration of Truth.*

The next day was spent by Nellie in writing letters to her New England friends. But "a change had come over the spirit of her dream" on the subject of slavery, and doubtless her sentiments sounded strangely to her New England friends, as coming from a descendant of the Puritans. She whispered in strict confidence to a special friend, the name "Mortimer," and spoke of the pleasure she enjoyed the day previous in his society. Completing the last letter, she entered the parlor, and finding her aunt alone, sat down near her. After a short pause, she said, "Aunt, why has Mr. Mortimer remained a bachelor so long? Is he a misanthrope, or is he waiting for his dulcinea to complete her education?"

"Neither, I presume," said her aunt. "He will never marry simply to escape the odium of being a bachelor. He is a man of taste and judgment, and will only marry when he thinks he has found a true woman. He is not a shallow-brained exquisite, to whom life is a dream and marrying a frolic, and the future a path of perennial flowers. He desires intelligence, refinement, neatness, good sense, economy and a pure heart, all combined. He is only waiting to find such a one, and he will offer her a home, which he will render most attractive and happy, and a heart as pure, noble, true and generous as ever throbbed in man's bosom. But why do you ask about him, my sweet neice, has he touched a cord in your heart?"

"O, you know, aunt, it is natural for young ladies to want to know all about those with whom they associate. I agree with you, however, that he is a very sensible gentleman, very graceful in his manners, and fluent in conversation. I know of no man who has more power to charm and fascinate than he, and yet he seems all unconscious of his merit."

"I shall be pleased to have him for a nephew," said Mrs. T. "Nellie Mortimer; why it would be really a romantic name."

Nellie blushed and left the room.

After tea the family again being assembled in the parlor, Mr.

Pratt took up the Bible and remarked: "You have said during our conversations that not one word was said by Prophets, Apostles, or by the Great Redeemer against slavery, and challenged the world to disprove it. Now I am a very small part of the world, but I accept your banter. I will prove that the Prophet Isaiah enjoins the emancipation of slaves, as a prerequisite to an acceptable fast, to a successful approach to an offended Deity. I will read from chapter 58 : 6—"Is not this the fast that I have chosen, to loose the bands of wickedness, to undo the heavy burdens, and to let the oppressed go free, and that ye break every yoke." Now, sir, here are three expressions which apply to slavery: 1. "Undo the heavy burdens;" 2. "Let the oppressed go free;" 3. "Break every yoke." What burden is heavier than slavery? Who are oppressed if not the slave? Where is a yoke, if it is not found upon the necks of slaves? Until you undo those burdens, liberate these oppressed, and break these yokes, all efforts at an approach to God in confession and reverence are unacceptable. But you have not done so; therefore your fasts have been an abomination in His sight. Ye exact all your labors." Now as you have not broken these, and let the oppressed go free, you are still in rebellion against the high and holy authority of heaven which commands it. Now, sir, as an honest man, and a christian, confess your sin, forsake your way, and obey the Almighty, that you may obtain pardon for this great iniquity, for I perceive wrath is coming upon you."

"I thank you for the exhortation and kind interest for our deliverance from Divine wrath, which you manifest," said Mr. T. "If I find your exegesis of the Divine word correct, I will endeavor to profit by it, for I desire to be not only a hearer, but a doer of the word. You dogmatize very flippantly, I must confess, but invariably fail in moral demonstration. You assert in a very positive and solemn manner, but never prove what you assert, and I must again repeat, that you possess the most remarkable tact of any polemic whom I have met, for taking as granted the very point that must be proved. I fear it is an infirmity with you Northern theologians to take superficial views of solemn subjects. You assert that three expressions in the text quoted apply to slavery, and in proof thereof you reassert it. The *onus probandi* rests upon you; but I waive all rights in the premises, and I will attempt at least to show what this Scripture means. Let us go back a little.

The laws of Moses abounded in commandments embodying the spirit of love. Mercy, kindness, compassion and beneficence were duties enjoined by that model code. These were given, not alone as evidences of the Divine character of the Great Law Giver, but also as rules of life to be observed by all the people. For the disobedience to these and other Divine injunctions, the prophet was sent to rebuke and reform the people. The hand of God had inflicted severe chastisements upon them, and they were exhorted by Isaiah to repentance, fasting and prayer. They seem to say in reply to him, "we have repented, and we have fasted and mourned and worn sack cloth, and yet the punishment has not been withdrawn; we have afflicted our souls, and thou takest no knowledge of it." Then the holy man of God shows them their error. Repentance was not of the lips, nor was mourning in the wail of the voice. "Behold in the day of your fast, ye *find pleasure* and *exact all your labor*, behold ye fast for *strife* and *debate*, and to *smite* with the fist of wickedness; ye shall not fast as ye do this day, to make your voice to be heard on high. Is it such a fast as I have chosen?—a day for a man to afflict his soul? Is it to bow down his head as a bulrush, and to spread sackcloth and ashes under him? Wilt thou call this a fast and an acceptable day unto the Lord? Is not this the fast that I have chosen? to loose the bands of wickedness, to undo the heavy burdens, and to let the oppressed go free, and that ye break every yoke. Is it not to deal thy bread to the hungry, and that thou bring the poor that are cast out to thy house? When thou seest the naked that thou cover him; and that thou hide not thyself from thine own flesh?" In the preceding chapter, which is the context, the prophet had rebuked the people for idolatry, and promised mercy to the penitent. Here he answers the objection which they had made—that is not a fast which simply abstains from food, and puts sackcloth and ashes on the body. A true fast implies genuine repentance, and genuine repentance includes reformation. While the Israelites fasted, they continued the very sins for which God was chastising them. The laws of God were forgotten, and when His strong hand was upon them they asked for mercy, but showed none; they prayed to be delivered from oppression, but continued to oppress; they felt the evil, but did not forsake it; they sought a blessing for themselves, but were unwilling to confer it upon others; they sighed for the favor which belonged to the obedient, while they were unwilling to forsake their disobedience. The prophet taught them that when they abstained from food, they must have the spirit of the fast, and repent and reform. Now you have before you a true exposition of the prophet's meaning.

"But you assert that the 'bands of wickedness' are the bonds of slavery; that the 'heavy burdens' are those which we impose upon our slaves; that to 'break every yoke' is to set our negroes at liberty. . An accredited expositor, who was an anti-slavery man, says of these bands: "The bands which we have wickedly tied, and by which others are bound out from their right, or bound down under severe usage. Those which perhaps were at first bands of justice, tying men to pay a due debt, become when the debt is exacted with rigor, from those whom Providence has reduced and emptied, 'bands of wickedness,' and they must be loosed, or they will bring us into bonds of guilt much more terrible." The same author continues: "It is to undo the 'heavy burden' thus laid on the back of the poor servant, under which he is ready to sink, it is to let the 'oppressed go free' from the oppression which makes his life bitter to him. Let the prisoner for debt, that has nothing to pay, be discharged; let the vexation be quashed; let the servant that is forcibly detained beyond the time of his servitude be released, and thus break every yoke."

"It was a law of Moses, that the Hebrew servants should only serve seven years, but this law had been forgotten, and many of this class had been held in perpetual servitude, in violation of this Divine law. The prophet may have meant to warn the people against this sin.

"Slaves are under a yoke, none will deny it—so are wives and children, as well as oxen. As we are commanded to 'break every yoke,' shall we therefore divorce every wife, release every child from parental authority, liberate every slave, and forbid the yoking of oxen? Certainly the breaking of every yoke requires this and much more to be done. Slavery is a burden, though among a christian people the lightest that is borne; but so are the duties of the minister a burden, the obligations of life, and the responsibilities of rulers. Shall you cease to preach and labor? Shall I refuse to be a member of society? Shall our governors and rulers resign? Shall the laborer cease his vocation, because all have to bear burdens? But all this and much more must be done before we can 'undo the burdens.' But these things, you are aware, cannot be done without a total disorganization of society and governments, and a most palpable violation of the laws of God. Then what yokes must be broken, and what burdens undone? Manifestly those which are unlawful, and none others. 'Bear ye one another's burdens, and so *fulfil* the law of Christ.' Now, sir, until you shall show that slavery is an unlawful yoke, and an unauthorized burden, you cannot claim that these words of the prophet apply to us, as slaveholders. This you have failed to prove—you have not even attempted it. I, therefore, take it for granted that you cannot do so."

"You affirm that slaves are oppressed. By this you mean that they are 'burdened with unreasonable impositions.' Your unavoidable ignorance of the institution prompts you to make this charge. No man at all familiar with the workings of the institution will believe that, as a general rule, any unreasonable labor is required of our slaves. They do less than any other laboring class of any land."

"Uncle," said Nellie, "let me read to you the opinion of an Englishman on this subject, who resided in Virginia for six or seven years—Mr. G. P. R James, 'the well known and English novelist.' He wrote for the Knickerbocker a very interesting article on Life in Virginia, in which he says the negro life in Virginia 'differs very little, I believe, from the negro life all through the South. In return for food, clothing, house room, medical attendance, and support in old age, about one-third of the labor which is required of the white man in most countries is required of the black. He performs it badly, and would not perform it at all if he were not compelled. The rest of his time is spent in singing, dancing, laughing, chattering, and bringing up pigs and chickens. That negroes are the worst servants in the world, every man, I believe, but a thorough bred Southern man, will admit; but the Southerner has been reared among them from childhood, and in general has a tenderness of affection for them, of which Northern men can have no conception. 'Great care is taken by the law to guard them against oppression and wrong; and, after six years' residence in the State, I can safely say I never saw more than one instance of cruelty toward a negro, and that was perpetrated by a foreigner. That there still may be evils in the system which might be removed by the law, and that there may be individual instances of oppression, and even bad treatment, I do not deny; but these instances are not so frequent as those of cruelty to a wife and child in Northern lands, as displayed every day by the newspapers; and, in point of general happiness, it would not be amiss to alter an old adage and say, 'as merry as a negro slave.' I think, said Nellie, that six years' observation of such a man as Mr. James, whom we know to have been unfriendly to the institution of slavery when he came to the United States, is a sufficient refutation to the charge that slavery *is* an oppression. He is certainly a disinterested witness."

"Thank you, Nellie," said her uncle, "for the testimony of this witness. It answers two points at once. It shows there are neither 'heavy burdens' nor 'oppression' in Southern slavery. Therefore, in these two respects, the prophet does not rebuke slavery at the present day.

"The mercy, kindness, compassion and beneficence taught by the divine law had been disregarded. It may be the King ruled as a tyrant; if so, he was to become a mild, just and virtuous sovereign. The husband may have been oppressive to his wife, or the parent to the children; these evils were to cease, these offenders to reform. The master may have done great injustice and wrong to his slave; these were to be discontinued and the master to treat his slave with the justice and humanity which his condition and right demanded. In a word, the higher virtues of political and social life, so admirably and unerringly taught in the scriptures, were to be observed."

"Uncle, did I understand you to say," said Nellie, "that this Scripture referred to the unlawful detention of the poor Hebrews, who on account of their poverty had been sold into bondage to their brethren, and who were entitled to their freedom in the year of release? We know there was a sad declension in the moral condition of the Israelites in Isaiah's time, and this may have been one of their sins for which the prophet so severely threatens them."

"That this was one of the sins of that day there can be no doubt. I think the prophet may have had remote reference to this in 61: 1–2, 'To proclaim liberty to the captive, and the opening of the prison to them that are bound,' seems to refer indirectly to the Israelites who were in bondage to their brethren, and who, contrary to the positive injunction of Jehovah, had continued their bondage past the year of release, perhaps from generation to generation.

"So Mr. Pratt, I still maintain my position that there cannot be found in the lids of the Bible, a single injunction to slaveholders, to liberate those held by them in bondage. Your quotation is inadmissable because not pertinent to the question."

"There is not the shadow of a doubt on my mind," said Mr. Pratt, "but that slavery was the crying sin of the Jews in Isaiah's day. It was for this offence that they were delivered over into the hands of the Babylonians. They were subjugated by their oppressors and made slaves themselves, that they might know from sad experience the bitterness of bondage. It was here the proud master was to be humbled, the callous heart to learn sympathy, the obtuse mind to understand the sin of slavery. It was here they were to learn the lessons of humanity so long forgotten. In drinking the bitter cup of bondage, they were to learn how to sympathize with bondmen; in bearing this heavy burden, to feel for others similarly distressed; in wearing this yoke, to resolve afterward to break it wherever found. Justice was meted out to them that they might learn in their humiliation to practice those virtues with which they should long since have been familiar. All the rebukes which slavery received were unavailing. The sin was never cured till the captivity. A severe remedy indeed, but not too much so for the disease. A sad fate, but it was just, because it was well deserved. A punishment so severe, should teach you a lesson. The south ought to have written in letters of living light, placed higher than Haman's gallows: 'Babylonish Captivity,' with a hand pointing to a negro slave, under whose feet should be written, 'The cause.'

"God chose the hand of a heathen prince in a foreign land, and the desolations of the fair fields which once flowed with milk and honey, as his teachers. The voice of sighing was heard from the heart of every Hebrew, and the tears of bitterness flowed from every eye, while every spirit crushed to earth sent up a lamentable wail for liberty, *liberty*, LIBERTY. But the echo of their sighs and wails were the only response that came. Unmoved they had heard the sighs and tears of the oppressed, now behold, the scene is changed, and there is no eye to pity and no hand to help them. Beware! "Be sure your sin will find you out."

"Why did you not go on," said Mr. Thompson, "and make the thunders of Sinai and the sighs of Calvary unite in the rebuke of slaveholders? To have completed, you should have brought in the apostle of the gospel as well as the prophet and jurist of the synagogue. The voice of nature and the voice of inspiration should both have been heard. Nay, the stars that fought against Sissera might have been made vocal to arouse the stupid Hebrews. But no, the voice of the prophet was not sufficiently distinct, the word of Jehovah was too ambiguous, the light of revelation was too dim. You had to take them down to Babylon, among a cruel and barbarous people, where tenderness was never seen, to teach them humanity. You carried them among the heathen to learn them christianity; among the rude to learn them good manners; among the ignorant to learn them knowledge; where God was not known to give them a knowledge of Him. You take away their priests that they may render purer offerings; their prophets and teachers, that they may learn the faster; and finally set up Babylon and a slave to teach the South that the Bible says slavery is wrong. Really, sir, you deserve a medal for originating this new logic, that is, if you are the author. On the same principle it might be well for us, who desire our children to be virtuous, refined, pious and intellectual, to erect houses and remove them among the Hottentots, and leave them there till they are grown. Exclude them from the sun that they may have light, take away their books and teachers that they may increase in knowledge, remove from them every virtuous example, and surround them with vice, that they may learn to be christians. This is your logic, sir. But your beautiful, poetic and pathetic theory all falls to the ground before the face of irresistible facts; and hence, I am sorry to say that your exhortation is as a 'tinkling cymbal.' You assert that slavery was the crying sin for which the Jews were carried into captivity, that this vassalage was necessary as a remedial chastisement to effect a permanent cure. But suppose I prove from the Divine record that the remedy failed to eradicate or even palliate the disease. They were slaveholders before the captivity, they carried their slaves with them into captivity, (for cruel as were these heathen, they respected the private rights of their captives,) and they brought their slaves back, when they returned under the proclamation of Cyrus, to the land of Judea. Hear Ezra's account of this fact: chap. 2: 64–65. 'The whole congregation together was forty and two thousand and three hundred and three score, besides their servants and their maids, of whom there were seven thousand three hundred and thirty and seven.' This fact shows that about one-sixth of the population that returned were slaves still in bondage. Now, as according to your declaration, the Almighty had these wicked Jews writhing under his chastisements for this very sin, is it not marvelous that He did not conquer the spoiled child and effectually cure him of this bad habit before he released him from the punishment? But how does your assertion and Ezra's agree? There is certainly a conflict between you and him. He says they brought back their slaves; you say the Almighty effectually cured them of this sin in Babylon. Do you yield to this testimony and give up the point, or do you think that this holy seer was so bound up in pro-slavery sentiments that he left on record a falsehood for the sake of his loved institution? What do you say, Elder?"

"Why, uncle," said Nellie, "you don't suppose my pastor would deny anything so plainly stated by an inspired historian, do you?"

"I prefer he should answer for himself," said Mr. T.

"I don't think Ezra means just what he says," said Mr. Pratt, "for we know that the Jews were very much reduced in their circumstances when they returned. They themselves were only emancipated slaves, and how could they be slaveholders?"

"We have," replied Mr. T., "many African slaveholders among us. I was in South Western Georgia, some time since, and saw a very thrifty little farm tended by slaves, all the property of a free negro. But I am digressing to pursue your ignis fatuus. You do not think Ezra meant what he said. Why, do you think he was too ignorant to express what he meant, or designedly concealed the truth? Or do you admit, that according to Ezra, your Babylonish speech, like that once mighty city, has fallen, fallen? I am amazed at the subterfuges to which error will drive even good men. O! candor, honesty, magnanimity, truth! leave not our fallen race, our sin-cursed earth, unblest by thy beautiful presence and holy power.

"But you bolster up your denial of divine truth with the idea that these Jews were too poor to own slaves. Doubtless in this fact and not the divine disapprobation is to be found the reduction of the number of slaves. Hoping that you may never, either North or South, find yourself so reduced as to resort to subterfuges so unlike a man of your profession and learning, I wish to call your attention to another fact: It is this: Some of the most beautiful and pious similes in the Bible are drawn from the institution of slavery. Instead of denouncing it, these holy men of God light the lamp of truth at its divine altars, and thereby, with greatly increased power, bring home to the hearts of their hearers and readers, the sacred teachings of heaven. But they never illustrate truth by poligamy, divorce, adultery, or any other crying sin of the age. Hear the 'man after God's own heart.' Ps. 123 : 2 : 'Behold as the eyes of the servants look to the hand of their master, and as the eyes of the maiden unto the hand of the mistress, so our eyes wait upon the Lord our God until he have mercy on us.' Now, sir, no man but a slaveholder could have thus graphically drawn the waiting, dependant, expectant slave; and it seems to me nothing else could have afforded an illustration of the submissive, patient, docile, dependent condition of a christian before the gracious Bestower of all good. It is certain the Psalmist could obtain nothing more appropos, or he would have done so.

"Job, 7 : 2, describes his weary watchings during his painful sufferings, by the burden of the tired slave, and the restiveness of the hireling. 'As a servant earnestly desireth the shadow, and as a hireling looketh for the reward of his work, so am I made to possess months of vanity.' The Lord himself resorts to this hated institution for an illustration, that the truth may be more forcibly impressed upon the minds of the degenerate Israelites. I wish you to observe how he places it side by side with the relation of parent and child. Mal. 1 : 6, 'A son honoreth his father, and a servant his master; if then I be a father, where is mine honor, and if I be a master, where is my fear." Here he honors the relation of master by assuming the same to himself, but he never assumes a name connected with error or justly odious. You perhaps would suppose that a slave does not honor his master, but here you are informed by the Allwise Creator, that he does. This fact is no less true now than it was in the days of Malachi, the prophet, notwithstanding the incendiary spirit that has so long and zealously endeavored to sunder the bonds of natural union between master and slave.

"I trust you are satisfied that there is nothing, not one word in the Old Testament, to condemn, but much, very much to establish, enforce, and regulate slavery. You have been met at every point and defeated in every argument you have brought forward, until I presume you are 'convinced against your will.' So I leave your sober judgment and christian faith to combat with the unconquered and unconquerable root of abolitionism still latent in your bosom, and which nothing, I fear, but death will eradicate; no, not even if one were to arise from the dead would you yield the point, for if 'you will not believe Moses and the prophets, you would not believe one though he arose from the dead.

> 'You may as well go stand upon the beach,
> And bid the main flood bate its usual height;
> You may as well use question with the wolf,
> Why he hath made the ewe bleat for the lamb;
> You may as well bid the mountain pines
> To wag their high tops, and make no noise
> When they are fretted with the gusts of heaven,'

as ask a prejudiced negranthropist to abate one jot or tittle of his opposition to slavery. Elijah's prayers brought up the clouds and produced the rain; and at Joshua's command the sun stood still, but fortunately neither of them was brought in conflict with the madness and unscrupulosity of fanatical abolitionism."

"Come, uncle," said Nellie, "I thought you were going to leave the 'prating' and the 'eloquent nonsense' to we Northerners, while you would stick to the scripture argument. Thus far I am satisfied you have truth on your side, and indeed it is all on your side. That the Old Testament is a pro-slavery book is clearly established, and I think my pastor ought to admit it, if it is not presumption for me to suggest to learning, wisdom and age. At least, I am now perfectly satisfied. But do you think, uncle, that the Gospel dispensation will sustain your institution? I have often heard it said that Christ and the Apostles left slavery where they found it, because they would abstain from all interference with the social and political relations of life. That they were determined to be known only as promoters of the spiritual interests of the world; and, also, that as they found the institution very popular, they would not rebuke it, lest they might bring odium upon themselves, and thereby greatly lessen their influence for good."

"If Mr. Pratt is willing, we will enter upon the investigation of the subject as held by Christ and the Apostles, next week. It may be pleasant to recreate for a few days; and besides, Mr. Mortimer, you remember, is to take you up to Bonaventure to-morrow; and if our Elder has no objection, he and I will visit Savannah."

Mr. Pratt readily assented, and the party retired to their rooms for the night—Nellie to think on the pleasures of a long ride with her new friend, and the parson to wish he had never consented to a discussion of slavery with a slaveholder.

## CHAPTER VII.

*Trip to Savannah and Bonaventure—Social Influence of Slavery—Superiority of the South—English Philanthropy—Slavery and Democracy—The South Superior in Morals.*

AT early twilight everything was astir at Mr. Thompson's. The city which he and Dr. Pratt were to visit that day was several miles distant, and they purposed an early start.

As the sun arose the carriage was at the door, and Jack announced himself ready. The two gentlemen took their seats, and promising to return that evening, were driven rapidly away.

With considerable impatience, Nellie awaited the arrival of Mr. Mortimer, to accompany her to Bonaventure. The gentlemen had been gone a full hour before he arrived. But here we must leave Nellie and her escort for a time, and listen to the conversation of the two gentlemen.

"Laying the injustice and inhumanity of slavery aside," said Dr. Pratt, "it is to the moral, social and educational interest of the South to abolish it."

"Why," said Mr. T., "do you believe we are inferior to those nations where African slavery does not exist?"

"I certainly do. And I can demonstrate to you by facts, perfectly cognizant to yourself and every other intelligent man, that the North, and every other free civilized country, is superior to the South."

"Proceed, sir, with your demonstration."

"Well, to begin," said the Doctor, "you get most of your teachers from the North. You send your sons and daughters there to complete their education, when you wish it thorough. Hundreds of your preachers are Northern men. Your authors live beyond the Potomac, and your books are all printed by our northern presses. Now, sir, deny these facts if you can. If not, tell me if stronger proofs of our superiority are required?"

"I admit," said Mr. Thompson, "many of the facts you have stated. Many northern men and women are teaching at the South. But the reasons are not as you suppose. It is not because we have not persons among us fully qualified for the work. You have just admitted that we have educated many of our sons and daughters at the same schools at which yours are educated, therefore, they must be their equals. A sufficient number perhaps have thus been educated to supply the demand for teachers all over the South. Many of our best educated young ladies are the daughters of wealthy men, who would not consent for them to teach. Your northern young ladies are generally poor, and obliged to do something for a living. They must become servants to the rich at home, or teachers at the South—they prefer the latter. We have generally given them employment, and when they have become independent and returned home, many of them have treated us like Æsop's serpent, which, when warmed into life by his benefactor, bit him in return. In many instances they have shown a heartlessness and want of veracity unworthy of a highly civilized people. Now, if this is what you mean by superiority, why I grant it to you. I can inform you of a fact which you may not have learned : that Yankee teachers are at a discount among us. Many have resolved never to employ one again ; so many have proved to be nothing but treacherous abolition spies, that they have seriously affected the standing of the honest and true ones among them.

"But many send their sons and daughters North to complete their education. Many, like myself, are of northern birth and education, and you know how natural it is for a man or woman to think that their educators are superior to any others, and on this account many send North. But there are many Southerners 'to the manor born,' who do the same thing :

'Distance lends enchantment to the view.'

"It is for this reason that the American ladies obtain their fashions from Paris. Do they admit thereby that French ladies are superior to them ? They would be insulted at such an allusion. I have always considered it a great mistake, as well as a useless expenditure of money, to send boys and girls North to educate them. It has made, as is obvious now, a false impression at the North, as to our educational facilities, while it has proved a serious injury to the South, by withholding much of the patronage from our own institutions, which was necessary to give them the position they justly deserve. We have four male universities in Georgia, not inferior to your best in New England—the standard of scholarship is the same generally, and we have as thoroughly educated and efficient faculties as are to be found, as the fruits of their labors most abundantly attest. Female schools of a superior character abound all over the State, and in every other Southern State, and their privileges are within the reach of all who desire to enjoy them. I may safely say, that the education of the young has become a contagion, which has seized hold of the masses of our people, and will no doubt soon become universal. So that now, southern patronage to northern schools will grow small by degrees and beautifully less.

"You are greatly mistaken when you assert that our books are all written beyond the Potomac. We have many southern authors, not inferior to any in the world; the list is too long to mention, and I would make no invidious distinctions. But, sir, we have our poets, our novelists, our scientific authors, our theological writers. In a word, every class of writers that you will find among a sober-minded, practical literary people, anywhere in the world. In contrasting authors North and South, my observation is, that there is a strength, energy, and simplicity of style, an elevated, ingenuous method of expression, a purpose at once palpable and commendable, that I do not find in northern authors. It is true however, that we have but few authors whose *trade* it is to make books. Our people never write, unless they have something which they conceive is of importance to the public. At the North your people make a *trade* of any and everything. They make a trade of preaching, of freeloveism, of abolitionism, of making wooden nutmegs and hams. We freely confess our inferiority in these respects, for we have no such humbuggery among us. When you speak of our inferiority, you forget the Washingtons, Jeffersons, Monroes, Madisons, Calhouns, Clays, and a host of others too numerous to mention—all born and reared in the slave States. You forget that the greatest orators of which this continent has ever boasted were southern men. You forget that the giant intellects of this government, which have commanded the admiration of the civilized world, were southern men. You forget that 'the Mother of States and Statesmen,' is at the South. Inferior indeed! Where do you find, at the North, or any where else, such an array of statesmen, patriots, orators and military captains. The South, sir, is the greatest land upon earth, considering it is now but in its infancy. Considering its brief career, it has given birth to the greatest number of remarkable statesmen, orators, heroes and theologians of any nation upon earth. Why, sir, did you know that a fourth of the pulpits in Philadelphia are occupied by southern men, and that they greatly prefer them to northern men, and the Presidential chair has been occupied for forty-four, out of fifty-six years, by slaveholders.

"But you are of the opinion that our social elevation is retarded by slavery. This is a common opinion at the North, especially among those who have never mingled with southerners at their homes. As this class is totally ignorant of social life at the South, their opinions are not to be trusted. Far otherwise has it been with those who have sojourned among us long enough to understand southern life and character. The Rev. Mr. Sawtell, an eminent methodist divine, who spent several years in the South, thinks that socially, slavery has been of no disadvantage to us. Mr. Van Evrie, a New Yorker, thinks it has greatly promoted our social elevation. The Hon. Miss Murray, Maid of Honor to the Queen of England, after making the tour of the United States, gives it as her opinion that we are quite in advance of the anti-slavery portion of the union. Her testimony is valuable, as coming from one who began the tour with all the strong prejudices of an English abolitionist, against slavery and slaveholders. But in her letters home she wrote a most able vindication of slavery, which lost her the position of honor she had so long and gracefully occupied. But how can slavery retard the successful advances to that highest point of civil and social elevation towards which a great people should always aspire? Distress and pauperism, are the great obstacles; the fruitful progeny of these: 'vice and misery, wretchedness, suffering, ignorance, degradation, discontent, depravity, drunkenness, and the increase of crime,' form one mighty incubus, which hangs like a pall upon the public mind and forbids any commendable progress. But these evils are scarcely visible at the South—they do not accompany slavery, but flee before it, like the darkness does before the light. There is no such competition of labor here as to reduce any man to pauperism. There cannot be. But at the North and in England, you never have a financial reverse but what thousands of your poor are thrown out of employment, and reduced to extreme want. This engenders vice, misery, despondency, and degradation. The poor among us are never thus tempted, as a class. They are generally a contented, virtuous, happy, prosperous people, and are as perfect exemplars of virtuous principles as any in our land. Civilization advances in proportion to the virtue of the people. Where the standard of morality and intelligence is good among the private citizens of a country, it may be said to be in a high state of civilization. No better state of morals exists in any country than at the

South. Indeed, while I would not boast nor appear egotistical, I would give my adopted land the praise of being in advance of any country, where slavery does not exist. What section of this country gave birth to mormonism and freeloveism? not the South. What section elevates the law of conscience above the law of God? not the South. What country has dethroned Deity to make a place for *reason?* not a slaveholding people. Who deny many portions of Divine Revelation, or torture their plain and palpable meaning to prove the reverse of what the scriptures say? not slaveholders, but abolitionists. Where is the Bible declared to be not of God, because it is a pro-slavery book? not at the South. What people are prepared to give up the Word of Life, rather than part with their own private opinions on slavery? You at the North. You are now verging towards the most fatal forms of infidelity that ever cursed any people. Dangerous, because it comes in the guise of religion; it is in the church, in the pulpit, in your theology, in your religious convocations; in everything that is to go before the public mind, or impress the early convictions of the young. When carried out to its full development, it will not only make infidels of you all, but it will terminate in anarchy. Thus far we have been, in the main, delivered from these errors. We are in danger of contracting this contagion from you, and I sometimes tremble at the thought. A dark future awaits you at the North, unless Divine Providence interposes to arrest this increasing tide of infidel sentiment. 'Come and let us reason together.' Our Maker has established four cardinal relations in life—the strict observance of each is essential to the political and moral welfare of the people: 1. That between the ruler and the governed. 2. Between husband and wife. 3. Between parents and children. 4. Between master and servant. These all claim in the Bible the same divine origin, and no one but an infidel can or will deny it. But the North denies the latter relation. To do so effectually, they have so far shaken the others, that two of them are now meeting with disfavor, and the other is in danger. Already have several northern States rebelled against the national law on slavery, thus most effectually denying the first relation. Already, too, have free-love societies been established in northern cities, thus again denying the relation to be divine between husband and wife. With such a state of society as this will ultimately develop, the spirit of rebellion against parental authority must necessarily be instilled at a very early age. Then will come anarchy. All these are to be the mature fruits from the tree of abolitionism, for 'an evil tree cannot bring forth good fruit,' and those who cultivate the tree must eat of its products.

"Now, sir, wait till there is a manifestation of our want of civilization, before you charge it upon us. None of these evils have as yet made their appearance among us; if they had, the civilized world would have become vocal with the noise you would have made about it. As it is, you charge us with the want of civilization, without offering a word of testimony in proof of the fact.

"Now, if slavery is right, morally and religiously, as I have already proved to you, but which I intend to demonstrate more fully before this discussion closes, then it cannot give rise to the evils of which you speak. 'A good tree cannot bring forth evil fruit.' It is not opposed, as facts have shown, to the highest developments of national greatness. There is no branch of industry necessary to this end that it discourages, no moral culture that it hinders, no literary, intellectual or scientific attainments that it does not foster.

"The South abolish slavery! no, sir, never. We have too much regard for the welfare of our slaves. We know too well what is for *their* good, and we feel too deep an interest in them to throw them off, uncared for and unprotected; and devoutly reverencing God's institution, we will perpetuate it.

"Slavery is the *normal condition* of the negro, as much as freedom is of the Caucasian. He has always and everywhere been a slave; he always will be. Free him from his master, and he is a slave to the baser appetites of his nature. He becomes an indolent vagabond, a prowling thief, a midnight rogue, a brawling drunkard or an indifferent, filthy sloth, and dies of hunger. He is more virtuous, more prosperous and prolific, and much happier in a state of bondage. He lapses into physical, mental and moral degradation in a state of freedom, as the history of emancipation abundantly proves."

"Do you not believe," said the Doctor, "that there are thousands of slaves in the South that would be glad to be free?"

"No doubt of it," said Mr. T., "just as there are thousands of children who have loving and indulgent parents, yet would rejoice to be free from parental restraints. But it is best for the children, as you know, that these desires cannot be realized. It is no less true that the negro would be injured by his freedom. Simply, then, as a philanthropist, I am in favor of slavery."

"You have strange views of philanthropy," said the Doctor. "The moral and religious sense of the world is against you, and yet you stand out 'solitary and alone.' Why, sir, did you know that the interest on the amount invested by England for the emancipation and moral elevation of the negroes of the West Indies, amounts to five millions of dollars annually? Here, sir, is a philanthropy which speaks for itself."

"Yes, sir," said Mr. T., "I knew the fact. I also know that when Parliament voted forty thousand pounds to educate England's poor, it voted *eighty thousand pounds* to repair the queen's stables; thus making the comfort of her horses double the importance of the moral well-being of her poor! This, too, is *speaking* philanthropy from the same source. And further, I know that while England taxes her people five millions to elevate the negro, she does not allow her own people but one hundred thousand, or about one fiftieth of the amount, for the elevation of her own oppressed serfs. The truth is, negro slavery is democratic—it is opposed to monarchism—it is a death blow to it, and England was wise enough to find it out. Serfdom disappears at its approach; the two cannot live together in the same government. The whites will be free, where the negroes are slaves. England intended to keep her poor whites in slavery, and to do this effectually and peaceably it was necessary to emancipate the slaves in her colonies." Hear what Mr. Van Evrie, a Northern man, says on this subject: "To hold in check the tendency of democratic ideas, to sustain and prolong its sway over the masses, European monarchisms, and especially the British portion of it, originated the 'idea' of 'free negroism' and a crusade in favor of *inferior races*. Its design was two-fold: as an *antagonism for holding in check* the *progress* of *American democracy;* and, in the second place, as a *false issue* to its own *oppressed masses*. It began with Johnson, Wilberforce, Pitt, and others of the most bigoted school of British tories. As a general thing, both in Europe and America, those most *bigoted and most hostile to the freedom and equality of their own race* have been its special advocates. The time, perhaps, has not yet arrived to estimate this negro movement at its true value; but it will come, and, when it does, British philanthropy and 'humanity,' 'freedom,' 'emancipation,' 'abolition,' or whatever it may be termed, will be known, as it is, in fact, the *widest spread imposture* and the *vilest fraud* ever practised on human credulity." Now, sir, I would not charge a love of monarchism upon all the Northern abolitionists. They have strong imitative powers, and with all are exceedingly vain. Love of applause is a controlling element of character with them. They are frequently thrown with the English people, commercially and socially. They have thereby caught the spirit and desire to ape the motherland. Besides, you Northern people have been taunted by the English in a manner, it would seem, well calculated to disgust and insult you. But a fawning sycophant is willing to pay dearly for his privileges. They assert that slavery has demoralized the Northern States. To prove to them it is a mistake, you are goaded on in your opposition to slavery, till you have outstripped them in your denunciations of it. They charge to it all the violations of good order, even the "Mormon murders," the "Philadelphia riots, and the exterminating wars against the Indians." Your leading abolitionists, doubtless, say amen to all this, and then your orators and writers say "the half has not been told." So, Jehu like, you say to them, "Come and behold my zeal for human freedom;" and so you far outstrip them in your efforts to destroy this Pandora's box of evils.

"The statesmen of England are far-seeing; those of the North are not. The latter are willing to be led by the greater minds across the water. Lords and nobles will do anything to sustain the crown, but the crown can only be sustained by the perpetuity of monarchism, and this cannot long be done where negro slavery exists. Monarchies are opposed to Republics, and would like to see the last one crumble into dust, or be drowned in blood. But this can never be done in America till slavery is abolished. It is, therefore, to the interest of the monarchies of Europe to foster abolitionism here. No doubt the sagacious statesmen of England are chuckling at the increase of abolition sentiments on this continent, and see in it the precursor of a strong government, and think they hear in the emancipation clamor of the North the death knell of republicanism. I fear the sequel will vindicate their wisdom. But the blind abolitionists of the North have been dazzled and led on until the "things that make for their peace are hidden from them." They do not see the tricks of English diplomatists, nor will they until they are involved in ruin."

"What a desponding man you are," said the Doctor, "to see danger where none exists, to apprehend evil where it cannot by any possibility arise!"

"The wise man said 'The prudent man foreseeth the evil and hideth himself, but the simple pass on and are punished,'" replied Mr. T. "But again, sir, permit me to call your attention to the inconsistencies of English philanthropists. They denounce slavery and slaveholders in unmeasured terms. They protest against the institution as a system of robbery and fraud. Yet they are eager for the purchase of the products of slave labor. They grow rich upon them—they are the staple commodities of their commerce. Indeed, if they were to refuse our cotton, many of these zealous denouncers of slavery would have to go to bed supperless. Their pliant consciences are at rest when slave labor brings money into their pockets. They forget, then, the 'tears and sweat and blood' of the poor slave. And may I say, sir, that the consciences of Northern abolitionists are not less pliant, and their philanthropy is not less selfish. They write, and speak, and legislate, and pray, and preach against slavery; but, when they can make a dollar on cotton, their objections to the hated institution evaporate into thin air. Well has Inspiration said: 'The love of money is the root of all evil.' None but a Yankee brain could have invented the phrase, 'Almighty Dollar;' for none have ever *felt* the *mighty influence* of the dollar so sensibly as they. With them it is stronger than patriotism, philanthropy or local attachments. If what I have said is not true, if English and Northern abolitionists really desire the freedom of our slaves, why do they not reject the products of their labor? By purchasing them from us they only encourage us in multiplying our slave force. *They* rivet the chains of slavery upon our bondmen—they perpetuate the institution—they foster slave labor. If slavery is wrong, they are *particeps criminis.* Nor are they blind to this fact. It has undergone extensive discussions, both at the North and in England. It is really amusing to see the subterfuges to which the moralists(?) who opposed slavery have resorted, to justify the purchase of its products. The following may serve as a specimen: 'The master owns the land, gives his skill and intelligence to direct the labor, and feeds and clothes the slaves. The slaves, therefore, are entitled to only a part of the proceeds of their labor, while the master is also justly entitled to a part of the crop. When brought into market, the purchaser cannot know what part belongs rightfully to the master, and what to the slaves, as the whole is offered in bulk. He may, therefore, purchase the whole innocently, and throw the sinfulness of the transaction upon the master, who sells what belongs to others.' Now, how revolting to an honest mind, and how preposterous in a legal view, is such a proposition! Suppose two men to farm in co-partnership, one is entitled to one-tenth, the other to nine-tenths of what is made. How much each is entitled to is not known to the public, but simply that each has a share, the quantity of which is known only to the parties. Now, I am a produce merchant, and the man entitled to one-ninth brings in all the corn in his own name, and I, knowing the fact, purchase it. Have I done so innocently?

If I have, then no one is guilty who purchases stolen goods. But if slavery is wrong in itself, then the master's claim to its products is at the expense of the rights of the original producer, or slave, then to the purchaser, with a knowledge of these facts, they are stolen goods. In the eye of the law, the master is guilty of a fraud in 'confusing' the goods. But to purchase them from him, paying him for all, is to give him the advantage of his own fraudulent act; this the law never does knowingly. Now, if slavery is wrong in itself, as abolitionists say it is, then to obtain its products from the master, and yet justify themselves in so doing, requires the Jesuitical argument, 'the end justifies the means,' i. e., so we get the money it does not matter how—it is none of our business whether this planter came by his cotton or sugar honestly or not; we will not go back to see, that is his business. Such a course shows the fallacy, (to use the very softest word possible,) of English and Northern philanthropy, and it shows the elasticity of the consciences of these characters, who would set themselves up as public instructors of good morals."

But Nellie and Mr. Mortimer are passing us just now, and the curious reader may desire to hear the subject matter of conversation between them.

"How are you pleased with our climate and people, so far as your observation has extended to the latter?" asked Mr. M.

"Delighted with both. But why do you ask such a question? I am sure you could not think a lady of taste would be otherwise than pleased. This must be an approximation to the beautiful and delightful home of our first parents, before it was polluted by the appearance of the tempter. Nature, wild and untamed by the hand of art, is always attractive to me. Compared with my own frigid home, you have perennial spring and flowers. The birds sing the season round, the air is soft and mild as May. I have formed but few new acquaintances since my arrival, but have been much pleased with those. Society at the South is very different from what I expected to find it. I concur in the opinion expressed by Miss Murray, when she says of a Southern city: "I met there several pretty Southern ladies; their voices and way of speaking struck me as more refined and graceful than those of the other States I have visited. I find society here most agreeable."

"I am glad you are so highly pleased with the South and Southerners. So many visit us and return with prejudices against us, either because they do not stay long enough to form correct ideas, or from early education they are blinded to our virtues. The South is not appreciated generally by Northerners or by foreigners, and I suspect that it is on account of slavery. The whole world is in arms against us; but, after all, we are right. By the way, how does the controversy between your uncle and Dr. Pratt progress?"

"I have been very much interested in it," said Nellie. "Last night they closed the old Testament argument, and on their return are to enter upon the new."

"How did it terminate? Who had the better of the argument, you being judge?"

"Well, sir, I must confess to great disappointment. I never, for one moment, questioned the ability of our people at home to prove the sinfulness of slavery, to show that it was a palpable violation of the teachings of the Bible. I have so often heard it denounced, by our best and ablest men, not only as wrong, and sinful, but as villainous: I have heard every epithet applied to it which human ingenuity and eloquence could invent; till I had no idea that an intelligent and pious man, such as I know uncle to be, would ever attempt a defense of it. Slave-holders have been accused of such manifest injustice, oppression and cruelty to their slaves, that my feelings of humanity have often shuddered at the thought. I believed all was true, and true of all masters, for universal cruelty has been asserted, and I had no means of disproving it, even if I had possessed the disposition, but even that was wanting. I really believed that Southerners were as bad as untutored, idolatrous barbarians. Nor was I alone in this opinion; the masses of the people have no means of information as to the character of you Southerners, except what they read in our popular newspapers, nine-tenths of which are abolition sheets, and their editors as ignorant as those whom they would enlighten, or else they are wickedly deceiving the people. Occasionally we in the villages have a lecturer, but they are under the employ of societies which send them out to raise funds for the 'amelioration of the colored people.' They usually draw horrid pictures of Southern oppression and brutality, all of which is received as gospel truth. I assure you, if our Northern people could see slavery, as presented in its practical workings, and as taught in the Bible, I verily believe there would be a radical revolution in public sentiment."

"I think it doubtful," said Mr. M. "The masses are always controlled by the greater minds. At the North, these greater minds are designing politicians, and whatever will effect political capital for them, will be the last from which they will be willing to part. They

M

can never be convinced. Then you have a class of religionists, with whom *humanity* is the supreme law of right; the word of the Divine Being is of inferior authority. They would abandon the Bible if they thought it a pro-slavery book. These two classes include the leading politicians and many of the most prominent among the clergy. These exert an irresistible influence upon the people, and they can lead them anywhere, even to ruin: towards which they are now rapidly tending."

"I had very honestly thought," said Nellie, "that negro slaves were the most ignorant, debased, oppressed and miserable people in the world; that the serfs of the veriest despot upon earth enjoyed a paradise of happiness compared with them: but I am happily disappointed in finding them the most cheerful, virtuous, pious and contented dependents I have ever seen. I can say of every plantation I have seen, as Miss Murray did of one in this portion of Georgia: "A happy attached negro population surrounds this abode; I never saw servants in an old English family more comfortable, or more devoted; it is quite a relief to see anything so patriarchal, after the apparently uncomfortable relations of masters and servants in the Northern States. I should much prefer being a 'slave' here, to a grumbling, saucy 'help' there." Miss M. asks a question which I presume none of our Northern or English Abolitionists can answer in the affirmative: 'Is there any part of Africa, the West Indies, or South America, where three millions of negroes are to be found as comfortable, intelligent and religious, or as happy as in the Southern States?' She says, also, 'The system of slavery has been blamed for the ignorance and vices of the Africans: are they less ignorant or more virtuous where slavery does not exist? It has pleased Providence to make them barbarian, and as barbarian they must be governed, however Christian may be the feelings and principles of their masters.' These are sensible views, *if they did come from a woman*, Mr. Mortimer."

"Certainly, madam," said Mr. Mortimer, smiling, "the ladies are the only connecting link that binds us to the angels, and they are constant remembrancers of purity and perfection. I have often wished I was a lady, but recently I have concluded to be content, if I can only obtain one for my better self. But to return to our subject. I wonder that the refined sympathies of Northern and English philanthropists are not more excited by the oppressed of other lands. Their objections to slavery seem to grow out of the abstract idea of slavery, rather than from the physical and moral condition; or else it feeds upon envy of the wealth and prosperity of the South. They seem not to be moved by the sufferings of those who are nominally free. There is tenfold more sufferings in some portions of the world among the Caucasian, than in the South among the African race. Indeed, there are many in every land, whose physical, moral and intellectual condition is unspeakably inferior to our slaves. Yet these poor sufferers of other lands excite no sympathy in their behalf. I will give you one instance of labor and suffering, ignorance and degradation. It exists in the Brampton coal pits in England, 'where if their own citizens were blessed with the liberty and ease of our slaves, it would be a most glorious act of emancipation.'"

"Boys from eight to twelve years old are forced to pass through narrow pits, where each has a space of two feet headway; they go half-bent, because they cannot straighten; the mud through which they pass is one or two inches deep; they draw their barrows with one hundred weight of coal, sixty yards, sixty times a day. That is four miles a day through mud and water, half-bent or on their knees, and half that distance with a rolling load of one hundred pounds."

Were slavery to impose such labor, a cry of holy horror would go up from every nation.

"Robert North, one of the miners, says: 'I went into the pit at seven years of age to fill skips. I drew about twelve months. When I drew by the *girdle* and *chain*, my skin was broken, and the blood ran down. I durst not say anything. If we said anything, the butty, and the reeve who works under him, would take a stick and beat us.'

"Here was a boy harnessed as a beast, and worked and treated as a brute. No parallel to this inhumanity can be found on slave plantations in the South. But hundreds such occur in the Brampton coal mines.

"The wages paid to these degraded, ignorant serfs, is from $2 50 to $7 50 per month, according to age and ability, and out of this they must support themselves. They work twelve hours each day.

"The destitution and suffering in England is fearful. In a report made to Parliament by its commissioners, it is stated that forty thousand persons in Liverpool, and fifteen thousand in Manchester, live in cellars, while twenty thousand in England pass the night in barns, tents, or the open air. 'There have been found such occurrences as seven, eight, or ten persons in one cottage, I cannot say for one day, but for whole days, without one morsel of food. They have

remained on their beds of straw for two successive days, under the
impression that in a recumbent posture the pangs of hunger were
less felt.' No such destitution as this is known in the South, either
among the whites or blacks.

"The morals of this wretched class just alluded to, if indeed they
can be said to have any, are of the lowest grade. 'A *lower condition* of
morals,' says an eye-witness, 'in the fullest sense of the term, could
not, I think, be found. They have no morals. Their appearance,
manners and morals, so far as the word morals can be applied to
them, are in accordance with their half-civilized conditions. Their
ignorance is not less astounding.' Robert Crucilow, aged 16 years,
when catechised, answered: 'I don't know anything of Moses.
Never heard of France. I don't know what America is. Never
heard of Scotland or Ireland. Can't tell how many weeks in a year.'
Ann Eggly, aged 18, said: 'I never go to church or chapel. *I
never heard of Christ at all.*' Others said: 'The Lord sent Adam
and Eve on earth to save sinners. I don't know who made the
world. I never heard about God. I don't know Jesus Christ. I
never saw him, but I have seen Foster, who prays about him.' The
employer said to the catechiser, 'You seem surprised at Thomas
Mitchel's not hearing of God. I judge there are few colliers here-
about who have.' Slavery could not be worse than this, were it all
that its worst enemies have represented it to be. But all this hard
labor, vice, poverty, and ignorance, is in glorious Old England, our
father-land, whose very air is perfumed with the incense of liberty.
Of whom Cowper says:

> "Slaves cannot breathe in England, if their lungs
> Receive our air, that moment they are free.
> They touch our country, and their shackles fall
> That's noble, and bespeaks a nation proud .
> And jealous of the blessing."

"Yes, free, indeed. Free to live in ignorance of God, free to bear
a heavier yoke of bondage than ever galled the neck of slave in
Southerland. Free to starve for bread, free to go naked, free to go
houseless, homeless, friendless. If this be freedom, give me
slavery. Would it not be interesting to see one of the poor straw-
ridden skeletons of Liverpool or Manchester, or of Lowel in your
own New England, for there are hundreds such there, totter to their
door, and feebly thrusting out their pale wan faces, cry out,

> "O Liberty,
> Parent of happiness."

And then hear in hollow tones from a spectral object across the street, echo back the sentiment,

> "'Tis *liberty alone* that gives the flower
> Of fleeting life its lustre and perfume,
> And we are weeds without it."

Then let some slave from the South, pampered on the fat of the land, as they generally are, respond in the fullness of his heart,

> "So let them ease their hearts with prate
> Of equal rights, *which man ne'er knew*,
> I love a freedom too"—
> A freedom from the cares of state,
> A freedom which is known by few—
> *Contentment, plenty, peace.*

"Where did you obtain the facts to which you have just referred, about the poor miners?" said Nellie.

"From the report of the Commissioners appointed by Parliament. I have referred to only a few of the facts contained in that report. Some things are said about their moral condition, and also the poor alluded to, that so shocks our moral sense, that I have not mentioned them. The truth is, Miss Norton, negro slavery is infinitely to be preferred before the pauper freedom and serf-vagrancy and degradation of England and the North. Negro freedom would be no better. Indeed, it cannot exist; it never has in the past, it never will in the future, in that enlightened and virtuous sense, with which it should alone be connected. Break the chains of involuntary servitude, and they will reconstruct them by entering into voluntary slavery, or what is worse, become nuisances to society, and perhaps starve at last. God has united slavery and negroes, and no man can put them asunder. Nominally he may, but really he cannot. It is their natural condition; their whole organism, mental, moral and physical, proves their providential adaptation to it. They are vastly our inferiors, and of this they themselves have a most feeling consciousness. Even in Africa, a white man is looked up to as some superior personage, as we are told by Rev. Mr. Bowen, who was for many years a missionary among them. Their faculties are developed, in a state of slavery, more successfully and to a higher degree than can be effected in any other condition. This has been demonstrated by the emancipation experiment made in Hayti. Our slaves are vastly superior, morally and intellectually, to the Africans of that island. Not because they are naturally superior, for they are not, but simply for the reason that they are where providence placed them. They are more honest, more virtuous, better contented, and freer from the temptations which will surely lead this imbecile and plastic people into error. I can say, without the fear of successful contradiction, that there is less crime in the South, to the population, than anywhere else, even among your own citizens, who consider us but one grade above the barbarian. This being true, England would contribute largely to the cause of morality, virtue, religion, and more especially to human happiness, were it again to enslave its West India negroes."

"How do you prove that there is less crime at the South, to the population, than anywhere else? I do not acquiesce in your opinion. Our people may be *deceived* about slavery, and therefore oppose that which is right, but we are a law-abiding, virtuous and christian people."

"I establish my assertion by statistical facts, published by yourselves, and therefore ought to be correct, for a people are not apt to make themselves appear worse than they really are:

"The population of Massachusetts in 1850 was nine hundred and ninety-four thousand five hundred and fourteen. Out of that number there were seven thousand two hundred and fifty convictions for crime. In Virginia, in the same year, there was a population of one million four hundred and twenty-one thousand six hundred and sixty-one, and out of this number there were only one hundred and seven convictions for crime. In Boston, one male out of fourteen, and one female out of twenty-eight, was arraigned for crime. The records of our criminal courts show no such alarming state of demoralization any where in the South."

"O! is this Bonaventure? How beautiful, how picturesque. These spreading oaks, with their long arms reaching up towards heaven as if they would embrace their Maker. That beautiful moss, so exquisite, that hangs like long drawn veils, as if to half conceal their natural loveliness, but which really adds so many charms to this unique mausoleum of the dead. Eden was made for the living, it therefore had its flowers, its fruits, its songsters; but Bonaventure was made for the dead, it therefore has neither. Still as night, somber as the tomb, sweetly sad, with a melancholy visible every where, so well suited for the last resting place of the noble dead.

"'Tis a goodly scene—
Yon river, like a silvery snake lays out
His coil i' th' sunshine lovingly, it breathes
Of freshness in this lap of flourless meadows."

But my readers do not wish to hear all the enraptured maiden said of Bonaventure. So we will return to the residence of Mr. Thompson, and hear more of slavery. Some new views are doubtless to be presented by him, which may prove interesting and profitable to the inquirer after truth.

## CHAPTER VIII.

*Who were enslaved by the Hebrews—History of the descendants of Canaan—Jewish slaves and Southern slaves from the same ancestry—The negro incapable of mental development—Nellie's soliloquy.*

"As you have attempted to establish slavery from the Bible," said Dr. Pratt, "and as the descendants of HAM alone were to be enslaved; tell me how you proceed to derive Southern slavery from Bible slavery. Do you hold in bondage the people doomed by God to slavery? and if so, did the Jews the same? I think you will find this a knotty question, and though you may succeed in the answer to your own satisfaction, your arguments will, I opine, be too feeble to convince any one else. But I must not condemn before I hear you. So proceed."

"The first question to be settled," said Mr. Thompson, "is, 'Who were enslaved by the Hebrews? It I can succeed in proving that they were the descendants of Ham, then it follows that the Hebrews and we, under the Divine injunction, hold in bondage the same people, and that slavery now is what it was under the Jewish Theocracy, and is the same which Christ and his Apostles so emphatically sanctioned in after years; as I will show when the time arrives.

"Whom did the Jews bring under bondage? 'Of the heathen that *are among* you, of them shall ye buy bondmen and bondmaids.' Then they were the heathen who inhabited the land when the Jews went up to possess it. This you will not deny."

"I grant it," said Dr. P.

"Then, who were these heathens? In the 9th Chapter of Joshua we are informed they were the Hittite and the Amorite, the Canaanite, the Perizzite, the Hivite and the Jebusite." These tribes were descended from Heth, Jebus, Henor or Amor, Gergashi, Hevie or Hivi and Canaan. The above were six of the eleven sons of Canaan.

After the confusion of tongues at Babel, they emigrated to this goodly land, where they were living in the days of Abraham, for he purchased a burying ground of Heth. They were there in the days of Isaac and Jacob, for Esau grieved his parents by marrying one of the daughters of the same tribe, hence Jacob was sent back to take a wife from among his father's kindred. When Joshua led the Israelites into this land of milk and honey, these six tribes confederated together to drive him out, but they were defeated, routed and terribly slaughtered. Some fled back to Africa, some were exterminated and the rest were enslaved. The other sons of Canaan lived in the adjucent country, and many of them were gradually brought, like the Gibeonites to be "hewers of wood and drawers of water," for the Hebrews. Now sir, I have shown you, that the slaves among the Jews were descended from Ham. So I will proceed.—Those who fled the country, may be traced by the light of history. Procoporus says : "They first retreated into Egypt—but advanced into Africa, where they built many cities, and spread themselves over those vast regions, which reach to the straits, preserving their old language, with but little alteration." In the time of Athanasius, these people still said, they were descended from Canaan, and when asked their origin they would answer, "Canani."

"Who was this historian, upon whom you seem to rely? I cannot call him to mind. Is he a credible witness?" said Dr. P.

"Procoporus, or as he is sometimes called, Procopius, was one of the most celebrated historians of the Eastern Empire. He was born in Cesarea, in Palestine, and was afterwards professor of Rhetoric in Constantinople. Athanasius, you recognise as a celebrated christian bishop of the fourth century, and an Egyptian by birth. He had every opportunity of knowing the facts whereof he affirmed. 'In the mouth of two or three witnesses every word shall be established.' Now I have proven : 1. That the Jews enslaved the Canaanites, i. e. those who were descended from Canaan. 2. That many of those who escaped the sword fled back to Africa, and populated that vast and almost unknown continent. 3. That eighteen hundred years after the conquest by Joshua, they were spreading over the dark land of Ham, and tracing their lineage, by tradition, back to 'Canani.' The Jebusites, you will remember, could not be dislodged from their strong hold by Joshua. It remained for David to storm their citadel and reduce them to vassalage, taking their city for his capital. You will remember, also, that the inhabitants of Gibeon, a city of the Canaanites, when they heard of the destruction of

Jericho and Ai, by Joshua, made a treaty of peace with him, deceiving him as to what nation they belonged. He afterwards made them, as has before been mentioned, 'hewers of wood and drawers of water,' that is, he reduced them to slavery."

"Are you sure," said the Doctor, "that a more learned investigation of this subject will sustain you in the views presented?"

"I think," said Mr. T., "more light might be obtained to prove the correctness of my position, if we had the facilities at hand for further investigation. Dr. Gill, one of the most profoundly learned commentators, and a man who arrived at his conclusions from the deepest research, throws some additional light on this subject. He says, that some of the most ancient versions of the Bible read, 'the father of Canaan,' others 'Canaan,' and says, 'as both, the father and son were-guilty, the curse rested upon both;' that Canaan means 'to depress, humble, and make mean, and abject.' 'God shall enlarge Japheth, and Canaan shall be his servant,' means, says Dr. Gill, ' that the posterity of Canaan shall be servants to the posterity of Shem. This was fulfilled in the time of Joshua, when the Israelites, who sprang from Shem, conquered the land of Canaan, slew thirty of their kings, and took their cities and possessed them, and made the Gibeonites, one of the cities of Canaan, hewers of wood and drawers of water, or the most mean and abject servants. The posterity of Canaan servants to the posterity of Japheth; as they were when Tyre, which was built by the Sidonians and Sidon, which had its name from the eldest son of Canaan, fell into the hands of Alexander the Grecian who sprang from Japheth; and when Carthage, a colony of the Phœnicians of Canaan's race, was taken and demolished by the the Romans of the line of Japheth, which made Hannibal a child of Canaan say, *ignoccre se fortunam Carthaginis*, that he owned the fate of Carthage, and in which some have thought that he refers to this prophecy.'"

"I, at least, am satisfied uncle," said Nellie, "that you have proved all you proposed. Whether the Canaanites held in service by the Jews, had black skins and woolly heads, white eyes and ivory teeth, I do not know, or whether, by some interposition of Divine Providence, this mark has been put upon them since, I cannot tell, nor is it necessary to know; suffice it to say, they were of the same blood, and doubtless bore the same physiological marks. It does really seem to me that our Maker has placed a physical difference between us, as wide as the conditions between master and slave. *He* has stamped *inferiority* upon the negro. This mark, like that in the forehead of Cain, is one of which he cannot rid himself, whether in Massachusetts, Africa or Georgia. It has been placed there by the hand of God, and none but He can remove it."

"You frequently hear of the black *skin* of the negro," said Mr. Thompson, "as though by some accident of climate or occupation, or mode of life, his skin had become so; but he is *black to the bone*. Open his mouth, look down his throat, dissect him, and you will find he is no more a white man internally than he is externally. Examine his head phrenologically, and you will find he belongs to the *prognathous* species of mankind—that is, that the jaws are before, or anterior to the brain. This is not the case with the Caucasian or Mongolian races; but it is a feature of the monkey and of the orangoutang. Now, Doctor, don't become restless, as though you thought I was going to prove the negro not to be of the *genus homo*—no such thing. He is a man—a human being. Nor do I intend to deny the unity of the race. But to show that every development of body and brain, skin and wool, show them to be designed by their creator for a different sphere in life, and an inferior position to the white man. Now, Doctor, I assure you it is worth the time it will occupy, for a scientific man to investigate this subject. It will prove to any mind that God never designed the African to be equal with the white man. It also proves that no development of the negro character can make him a full man, capable of all the responsible duties of self-government. Wilberforce, and other English statesmen of his day, entertained high hopes of the future development of this race, as their speeches in Parliament, their zeal for emancipation, and the power they exerted, seem to indicate. But their hopes were not realized, indeed they were sadly disappointed. For as soon as the wholesome restraints of slavery were removed, he became an indolent good-for-nothing vagabond. He retrograded rapidly towards that point from which he started when he was brought from the dark and superstitious land of his fathers.

"You may suppose they would advance in knowledge if they could read and had facilities at their command, but such is not the fact. I suppose there are at least five thousand negroes in Georgia who can read, but out of that number, I presume there are not twenty who ever read anything but the Bible and hymn book—and yet these are the most intelligent and enterprising of their race. They never read for pleasure or for information, but from a sense of duty. They have no thirst for knowledge, no desire for information.

One negro alone in Georgia has ever shown a knowledge of anything beyond the medium of his class. The only negro, so far as I know, who has ever written anything original in the South. It is a singular and significant fact that he wrote a pamphlet against Black Republicanism, and in favor of the system which held him in bondage, for he was a slave. Ordinarily, when they read they do not comprehend. Their minds seem dark, obtuse. To illustrate, there was a pious mistress who took great pains in learning a servant boy to read; taught him herself, with great care, and furnished him with every private facility for improvement as he grew up. One day, after he was grown, he was setting reading to his mistress the third chapter of John. He came to the words, "Verily, verily, I say unto you, ye must be born again." He had been taught to call on his mistress for instruction whenever he felt the need of it. So turning to her, he said 'Missy, was Verily the brother of Jesus, or who was he?' 'Why do you ask such a question?' said she. 'Because he is talking to Verily. He says, Verily, verily, I say unto you, and as he was talking so much to him, I wanted to know who he was.'

"Many of our negro preachers, indeed most of them, can read, and yet they pronounce words just like the illiterate ones do. Now and then you will find an exception to this, but it is seldom.

"These facts prove what the negro is. You may settle it in your mind forever, that man can make no more of the negro than his Maker designed he should be."

"Then," said the Doctor, tauntingly, "you suppose that his Maker designed that he should always be a poor ignorant slave, do you?"

"I think uncle has already proved that," said Nellie. "He has asserted nothing but what he has substantiated by satisfactory testimony, to me at least. But I thought you were going into the discussion of slavery, as taught in the New Testament. After all, perhaps my good uncle is reluctant to come directly to the question in the clearer light of the gospel dispensation. Perhaps he prefers Moses and the prophets as witnesses, rather than Christ and his Apostles. Now, uncle, don't mistify the subject, don't run off from it after shadows, trying to convince us that they are collateral points of the great issue, as I heard a young lawyer once say. But seriously, I am very anxious to have you return to the divine standard, the law and the testimony."

"And so am I," said the Doctor, as if he really thought Mr. Thompson desired to avoid the issue.

"And so am I," said Mr. Thompson.

"But," interposed Mrs. Thompson, "I hope you do not intend to sit up all night. Be temperate in all things, is in the Bible, as well as slavery. I think you had better sleep on the subject, and rest till to-morrow night, and then we all will listen to you with deeper interest."

"I always submit to whatever the ladies say," said Dr. P. "But I wish a word with my little truant pet about her visit to Bonaventure, before we retire."

"I suppose, Nellie, the real pleasure was as great as anticipated, and you had a delightful time with your excellent young friend. Did you find him all your heart desired—all you could wish for?"

"He is a perfect Adonis in person, as you perceive," replied Nellie. "He is not so wise as Solomon, I presume, but certainly much more interesting to *me*. Bonaventure is an exquisitely beautiful place, but if I had been with you or uncle I should have appreciated and enjoyed the scene much more, for I should then have been able to give it my *whole* attention—my undivided observation. But the greater attraction was at my side, instead of in the prospect. Would you wish any further information on the subject?"

"I do not wish to be considered impertinent, and therefore fear to push my inquiries further."

"I am glad you are so chary of your reputation. It might be well for pastors not to ask their young lady members too many questions about their young gentlemen associates. They might thereby 'lead them into temptation,' from which they should always endeavor to deliver them. So good night." Nellie arose and ascended the flight of stairs leading to her room, repeating mentally from Spencer:

> "Love is life's end, an end, but never ending;
> All joys, all sweets, all happiness awarding;
> Love is life's wealth (ne'er spent, but ever spending)
> More rich by giving, taking by discarding;
> Love 's life's reward, rewarded in rewarding;
> Then from thy wretched heart fond care remove.
> Ah! should'st thou live but once love's sweets to prove,
> Thou wilt not love to live, unless thou live to love."

"Ah," said she, as she entered her room, and found Alice was soundly sleeping, "I would not have had that old bald-headed abolitionist—my dear good pastor, I mean—to have seen deep down in my heart for a world. I am afraid my tell-tale face betrayed me. What a pity I was'nt made of brass—no, it is'nt either, for then I would'nt enjoy loving as I do. Why it is a real *pleasure*, I do declare. Who would have believed that I, a Massachusetts girl of eighteen summers, holding the South in such unmitigated contempt, and looking upon its people as but half civilized, should have fallen so violently in l——; pshaw, what am I talking about. But he is really the first and only young gentleman I ever saw, to whom I could think of surrendering my heart. And to think he is the only young man whose acquaintance I have formed in Georgia—wonder if there are any more Mortimers here—but surely, I am a very silly girl. Well, wonder who could help it? I can't. Mrs. Tighe is right ;

"O have you never known the silent charm
That undisturbed retirement yields the soul,
Where no intruder might your peace alarm,
And tenderness have wept without control
While melting fondness o'er the bosom stole;
Did fancy never in some lonely grove
Abridge the hours which must in absence roll!
Those pensive pleasures, did you never prove?
O! you have never loved! You know not what is love."

But perhaps my reader is a staid old bachelor, or a sceptical old maid, whose heart was never touched with the sentimental, who conceives all such feelings as sickly and childish, and who would rather hear,

"From Greenland's icy mountain,"

than to spend one moment in sympathy with this sweet girl who is enjoying the happy impulses of her first love. Or perhaps some noble specimen of a true man, who wishes the highest success to this first essay of my unpracticed pen, may prefer Bible facts to love's sweet dreams of fancied bliss. Then from deference to what may be the wishes of my readers, I will leave Miss Nellie's happy thoughts to herself. She would doubtless take it as an unkindness in me to spread them before a curious public. So, wishing sweet dreams, and a happy realization of these bright anticipations at an early day, to our young heroine, we bid her good night, and enter the room of Dr. Pratt and look in on him for a moment. He is reading Miss Murray's travels. Her correspondent, which Dr. P. is reading, says :

"The phenomenon of African slavery, as it is sometimes called, is in truth no phenomenon at all. Where is the country or the period of history wherein slavery did not exist in some shape or other? Slavery has always existed, and will continue so long as there is a disparity in the intellect or energy of men. I do not enter into the question of the Unity of Races, which is supposed to be derived from the authority of the Bible: it will be sufficient to assert that this race, known as the African, is inferior to the Caucasian. As a people, the blacks are sensual and stupid, lazy, improvident and vicious; unless under guidance, they have no idea of cherishing those virtues which elevate our common nature; they have an alacrity for sinking, nothing more. In their own country they are either savages or slaves," (both savages and slaves.) There is at this time, and there has been for long periods, a large number of free colored people in the slaveholding and non-slaveholding States of the Union; but even constant attrition against Yankee sharpness and shrewdness has failed to elicit one scintillation of talent or genius from this race. When they pass from bondage, it is only to swell the volume of insignificance or vice which has characterized their past history. But besides this, I would remark that we should reflect upon the fact of slavery more than upon the manner of its regulation. The Virginia negro, who is held by law as a slave, is really little more a slave (not half so much) than the man who works in the mines and manufactories of England. The first is held in subjection by a well-devised system of police; the other by a *necessity* stronger than any police. It is no answer to say that the Englishman can, if he chooses, leave his employer—that power only exists in theory, as the penalty for severing his bonds is *starvation*. His real master is capital, which, being in its nature greedy, grasping and selfish, doles out to human labor the smallest possible amount which will sustain life, and keep the working machine in order. There are three millions of slaves in the United States, and they constitute the only black people who are progressing in civilization and christianity, who are orderly, quiet, contented and industrious. They are well fed, well clad, and in physical comforts will compare advantageously with the same number of operatives in any part of Europe. The only favorable results yet marked out for the African race are due to the American system of slavery."

"There is some truth in this," said the Doctor as he closed the book and sat musingly. "So far as the happiness of the negro is to be considered, I have never seen free negroes at the North so happy, so well fed, so neatly clad as Mr. Thompson's are. They are more virtuous and religious, too, than those North; indeed, they have better religious privileges, and a deeper sympathy is felt for them here than there. We have not done justice to our free colored people. We look down upon them, we frown on them, we will not associate with them. The truth is, they are such a mean and despicable race that we cannot treat them otherwise without contamination. I have been surprised at the liberties which Mr. Thompson and his slaves take with each other, and yet they are perfectly subordinate, and really seem to love him. Well, there is something strange, mysterious, about all this; but I will keep my thoughts to myself. It will never do for me to change my sentiments—*never!* But really Thompson gets the advantage of me at every turn; but he shall never know that I feel so. 1 may be wrong in this concealment, but I cannot help it. I never will yield to a slaveholder.

## CHAPTER IX.

*Nellie's Hint to her Father—The " Golden Rule" and Slavery— Dr. Wayland's Admission—His Subterfuges Exposed—Christ could not enforce Abolitionism, and therefore would not try—Left it to Modern Abolitionists.*

The following day was spent by Nellie in writing letters to her numerous correspondents at home. Among others she wrote to her father, of whom she jocundly inquired if he would not like a nice little winter retreat neatly kept by his little Nell, where he could escape the icy bonds of the New England winters, and concluded by referring him for further information on the subject, if he desired it, to Mrs. Julia Norton.

But the evening arrived, and, after tea and prayer, the family were again assembled in the parlor. Mr. Mortimer was present also, for the purpose of listening to the discussion, and perhaps with a slight ulterior design of which none perfectly know but himself, others might suspect; but one young heart felt she knew, for " as in water face answereth to face, so the heart of man to man."

Mr. Mortimer was a Union candidate, though he had not avowed the fact publicly; but Nellie's shrewdness was not slow in detecting his intentions, and she was decidedly at heart in favor of his success.

"This evening," said Mr. Thompson, "we are to enter into the discussion of slavery as taught in the New Testament. Where shall we begin?"

"I have some idea," said Dr. Pratt, "of pleading an estoppel, as the lawyers would say."

"How?" said Nellie. "I hope you are not opposed to proceeding with the discussion. You said last evening you were anxious to proceed. I hope no change has come over the spirit of your dream, unless it be that you announce yourself with us, convinced that you have been on the wrong side all the time. If this is what you mean we will give you the right hand of fellowship, and then proceed with the investigation. For that we must have, for my benefit, if for nothing else."

"Well, you need not be in a hurry to offer your hand just yet. I might not be willing to take it. I meant I would give your uncle a *poser* at the start, from which he will not recover in time to proceed with the argument during life. I propose to give him a Bible argument against slavery, which he will never be able to answer."

"Do, Mr Pratt, if you can," said Nellie, "for I think so far you have utterly failed; but then you have come to the dispensation of *light*, and we may be more able to see the darkness by contrast."

"I am anxious to hear your *poser* from the Scriptures," said Mr. Mortimer. "If there be one verse or sentiment in the Divine Word against slavery, it is time we slaveholders knew it, for we have been accustomed to believe it was taught, not denounced, by heaven."

"So I have ascertained," said the Doctor, "but interest, you know, greatly blinds the mental as well as the moral vision sometimes, and this may be the reason you have never seen it. All the rest of the world have long since discovered it in the Bible. 'A reward perverteth the judgment,' says Solomon. Perhaps you would see clearer if you had no slaves. But to my argument. It is found in Matt. 7: 12, among the holy sentiments contained in the Sermon on the Mount. It is, therefore, from Christ himself, and demands the most devout and immediate obedience. Here it is: 'Therefore all things whatsoever ye would that men should do to you, do ye even so to them; for this is the law and the prophets.' You, gentlemen, are masters—you would not desire to be held in bondage by your slaves; therefore, if you hold your slaves in bondage, you violate this precept. You are bound by this law to do unto others as you would have them do unto you. If this does not extirpate slavery's terrible hold upon your hearts and consciences, I shall think that the things which make for your peace and welfare are hidden from you. There is no excuse for a misinterpretation of this precept, every one knows what he wishes others to do for him, and this must be the rule of his conduct to them, at all times and under all circumstances."

"We are all very familiar with your test," said Mr. Thompson. "It is one by which we endeavor to be governed, even as masters. We call it 'the golden rule,' on account of its unselfishness and freedom from the counterfeit morality of the mercenary age in which we live. But, Doctor, is your construction of this passage of Scripture the correct one? If so, and I owe you a thousand dollars, and you, in thinking over the sacrifices it will cost me to pay it, conclude that, were our positions reversed, you would prefer me to release you from the payment, then you are bound to give me the debt. Let us see further what will be the results of your interpretation. In his moral science, Dr. Dagg says: 'The Sheriff, who is about to hang a murderer, may argue, were I in the murderer's place, I would not desire to be hung; therefore I must not hang him. The jailor who is about to turn the key of the prison door may argue, were I in the place of the prisoner, I would desire the prison door to be left open.' Therefore the murderer and the felon must be turned loose upon an innocent community, after they are justly condemned by the court, and that, too, in obedience to the best and most unselfish rule ever given by heaven to erring man. The result would be, that obedience to the Divine law, given to restrain evil and foster good, would bind the hands of retributive justice, and turn loose upon the world those wicked spirits against which there would be no protection. That cannot be a correct application of the Scripture precept, which would make these officers neglect duties so important to society. And equally wrong is its application to slavery. The murderer, the imprisoned felon, and the discontented slave, may all desire that liberty should be proclaimed throughout the land; but the Scripture precept does not require that therefore they should be turned loose on society. *It requires that we divest ourselves of selfishness in deciding how we should act towards others. It limits our wishes on the one hand, and our actions on the other, to what is right and reasonable,* ACCORDING TO SUBSISTING CIRCUMSTANCES. In view of the mischiefs which would result, I ought not to desire that the murderer, the felon and the slave should be turned loose on society, even if I myself were the person, and therefore it is not my duty to turn such persons loose, if society has entrusted them to my charge." Now take one more case, akin to those I have quoted from Dr. Dagg. Suppose the keeper of a penitentiary were to look in on the degraded and suffering inmates till the deepest and tenderest sympathy of his nature was moved in their behalf. He says to himself, "I would greatly dislike to be in their places; this must be a very miserable life. If I were they I should desire that the keeper would, either by accident or purposely, leave the gate open that I might make my escape. In that event, Doctor, you hold that, according to this Scripture precept, the keeper is bound to do as he would be done by, and therefore turn them all out. From selfish motives he would desire the keeper to betray his trust, to violate the law, and turn loose upon society a band of murderers, robbers and felons, and because he would desire another to do wrong he must do wrong himself. If this construction were correct, no humane sheriff would ever arrest a lawless offender, no jury would ever convict a guilty criminal, no judge could ever pass sentence of execution against the convicted murderer; therefore all penal law would be suspended, and the wicked would run riot, while the innocent would have no protection against them. Can that be a legitimate construction of the word of God, which would lead to so many wicked consequences? Surely you will not persist in maintaining your position. But if Jesus intended this Scripture to apply to slavery, it is very singular indeed he did not allude to it in the many instances in which he came in contact with the institution. But instead of that, he enjoined upon the slave obedience to the master, and on the master justice and kindness, (not emancipation,) towards the slave. Its application to slavery may be correct this far. I am bound to treat my slave *as such* with that justice and humanity which christianity enjoins. But that it demands of the master to liberate his slaves was never once contemplated by Christ or His Apostles, or they would certainly have said so."

"Uncle," said Nellie, "I wish you would repeat again the meaning of the 'golden rule,' as given by Dr. Dagg; it strikes me as being very excellent and undeniably correct. I desire to remember it for all time."

"I will do so with pleasure, for I think it the clearest and most correct interpretation I have ever seen. 'It limits our wishes on the one hand, and our actions on the other, to what is right and reasonable according to subsisting relations.' Dr. Pratt would place no limit to the desire; he would make nothing to depend on 'subsisting relations.' Indeed, he would revolutionize society, revoke the Divine laws for public safety and protection; he would break down all barriers between good and evil, right and wrong, virtue and vice, and give the freest scope to the wildest licentiousness; indeed, he would break every yoke, political, social, marital, parental; in a word, totally disorganize society, enthrone *socialism*, the modern pet idea of Northern vice and libertinism. I do not mean that you would desire to do all this, Doctor; but such would be the legitimate consequences of your interpretation of the golden rule, when applied to all these relations. Such a state of things would subvert, instead of foster, the Divine purpose."

"Then it follows," said Nellie, "that if slavery is taught in the Bible this rule does not interfere with it. Slaves being lawfully in bondage, the law does not require a reversal of its own decree. They being scripturally bound, cannot be scripturally set free, for this would make the Bible contradict itself, which cannot be true of its infinitely wise and perfect Author."

"And I suppose," said Mr. Mortimer, "the scriptural proofs on this subject will accumulate as the discussion advances, so that the Doctor will have a clearer view of 'subsisting relations.'"

"But," said the Doctor, "you have not removed the injunction from the rule, 'Do unto others as you would have them do unto you.' There it stands out in frowning aspect upon you selfish slaveholders. There it is, look at it, listen to its rebuking voice, as you drive your slaves against their wills to the field of toil."

"Listen to it!" said Mr. Thompson, "as you drive your reluctant child to the school room. Listen to it as the judge pronounces sentence of condemnation against a guilty criminal, who reluctantly yields to the judicial behest. Listen to it as the jailor drives the prisoner into the dungeon against his will and bolts the heavy doors. Listen to it as the member of society reluctantly bears the burdens which his relations thereto necessarily impose upon him. Aye, listen to it as *you* urge a man whose heart is evil, and only evil, and that continually, to cease to do evil and learn to do well. You urge him against his will, and would, for his good and that of society, *force* him if you could. Every member of society must yield certain privileges and preferences for the general good, and, if he refuses to do so, society must have coercive power to enforce it. This is the conservative element of social well being. Under this, the slave *must* labor. His own welfare and happiness, as well as that of society, demand it."

"You do not illustrate," said the Doctor, "the cases you mention are not analogous. The cases to which you allude are inevitably right; therefore their enforcement is according to the spirit of religion."

"And so is slavery right, and its enforcement is according to the Scripture. Now, if slavery is taught in the Scriptures, you must admit that this rule is not designed to interfere with it any further than this: the master shall treat his slave *as such*, with the same justice and lepiency that he might lawfully desire extended to him if he himself were a slave. It no more contemplates breaking up one lawful relation than it does another. Slavery is as safe in its hands as marriage. It no more requires me to emancipate my slave than to separate from my wife. It does not revoke 'subsisting relations;' it only regulates our deportment under them. Governments, marriage, parental and filial obligations, master and slave, are all 'subsisting relations,' instituted and regulated by the same Divine authority; and the 'golden rule' no more sunders the obligations of one than it does of another of these relations. So that, instead of breaking the chains of slavery, it is designed to remove its rigors, correct its evils, and place it upon a christian basis. I am to be a kind, good, just and benevolent master, but a master still. I am not to impose burdens unnecessarily heavy. I am not to be a tyrant, an oppressor. And these duties it enforces in every relation of life. The ruler, the husband and wife, the parent, the child, the master, the servant, all, all alike are affected by this delightful precept."

"I am delighted, Uncle, with your views," said Nellie. "Now you are coming to a recognition of a truth for which I have been long and anxiously listening—that slaveholders take the Bible as their rule in the treatment of their slaves, as well as authority for holding them. This is right. But do all slaveholders the same?"

"No more so, my child, than all parents are governed by the Divine rule in the treatment of their children," said Mr. T. "It is really sad to think how little we regard the authority of God in our actions. There are but few in any relation of life who discharge the duties connected with those relations with a conscientious regard to the Divine rule laid down for their government."

"You have admitted a fact," said the Doctor, "which I always believed to exist. That is, that Southern masters are not influenced in the treatment of their slaves by those high principles of moral obligation inculcated by the Divine Being. I am glad you were candid enough to make the confession."

"I profess to be sufficiently honest and candid to admit truth, at whatever cost it may be," said Mr. Thompson. "But you misunderstood me. I have made no admission as to slavery that does not also hold good as to families. I do not believe masters are more remiss in this respect than parents, husbands or wives. As a general thing, masters are but seldom guilty of injustice or rigor to their slaves. So far as my acquaintance extends, I *know* of no exception to humane and just treatment. That such exceptions do exist, is not to be denied. There are brutes in the shape of men in every relation of life, whether as ruler, husband, wife, parent, child, master, slave; they are abandoned, low bred, cruel, coarse, brutal. But these are the exceptions to our race wherever found. One bad master no more proves that masters generally are bad than one cruel husband argues the cruelty of all husbands."

"Mr. Mortimer, you are intimately acquainted with the general treatment of slaves in our portion of the State. What do you say of it?"

"I know of no case where the master lives on his plantation with his slaves but what they are treated with justice and kindness. There are some cases where the master lives at a distance, in which the slaves are not treated with that tenderness which their state of dependence requires, and which the Bible commands. There has, however, for the past few years, been a great improvement in this respect. If the abolitionists would stop their presses, and close their mouths, it would enable us to do much more for the slave population than is generally being done. Their unwise, unscriptural and fanatical efforts to ameliorate the condition of our slaves have proved a serious injury to them. It is such an interference as it would be for a man to come to my house and propose to regulate the discipline of my family, or for England to propose to this government to regulate its machinery and remove evils which our national men had not seen, and which they knew did not exist. The result of this abolition interference has been to tighten the chains, and shut out much light from the slave, and to awaken a general spirit of indignation and resentment among Southerners. A spirit of crimination and of dictation on the part of the North have effectually closed the doors at the South against them. We feel capable of attending to our own business and of deciding what is right, and will therefore regulate our own institutions, in the fear of God, not of man, as we may think right."

"I would like to know," said the Doctor, "why you Southerners make such a great parade over the word *servant* in the Bible as though it necessarily meant *slave*. You have certainly forgotten that there are *hired* servants, and that the word applies to more relations in life than one. The king calls his subjects servants, the Savior called His disciples servants, the God of the Old Testament called His people servants, and the Apostles themselves said, ' We are the servants of Christ.' Now you would not so far risk your reputation as a scholar, Mr. Thompson, as to say that servant means *slave* in all these relations, or indeed in any of them. And if you cannot maintain this fact, then of what use is it to attempt any proof of slavery from quotations where the meaning is ambiguous?"

" For instance," said Nellie, " I was reading this morning in the 8th chapter of Matthew, where a centurion came to the Savior, saying: ' Lord, my servant lieth at home sick of the palsy grievously tormented,' and the Savior said 'I will come and heal him.' Now, was this a slave or a hired servant? How am I to know which he was?"

" Are you acquainted with the Greek language, Nellie? If you are not, your honored pastor is. So, Doctor, we will let the original decide this question for us, for in the Greek we can ascertain whether he were a slave or a hired servant. As it will take us some time to go through with the philological examination of slavery, perhaps we had better defer it till to-morrow evening, and give that occasion entirely to the subject."

"There is one fact, to my mind of great importance, to which I would this evening call attention. It is this: *In the catalogue of sins denounced by the Savior and His Apostles, slavery is not once mentioned.* This fact is worthy of record; this of itself forms conclusive evidence of the fact that slavery was not looked upon by them as an offense against righteousness. Paul, in his first chapter to the Romans, records, under the inspiration of the Holy Spirit, the sins of the people—it is a fearfully long and dark array of wrongs. He says : ' Being filled with all unrighteousness, fornication, wickedness, covetousness, maliciousness, full of envy, murder, debate, deceit, malignity, whisperers; backbiters, haters of God, despiteful, proud, boasters, inventers of evil things, disobedient to parents, without understanding, covenant breakers, without natural affection, implacable, unmerciful.' Again, in Gal. 5: 19-21, he says : ' Now the works of the flesh are manifest, which are these—adultery, fornication, uncleanness, lasciviousness, idolatry, witchcraft, hatred, variance, emulation, wrath, strife, sedition, heresies, envyings, murders, drunkenness, revellings, and such like.' I might go on to fill whole pages with the dark and grievous, or lesser sins of the people, and yet you would not find slavery once mentioned among them. If it were a sin, is it not remarkable that Christ and his Apostles left the people ignorant of the fact?"

"Not at all," said Dr. P. "There were two reasons for not condemning the institution: 1. It was not the purpose of the gospel to interfere with the social relations of life. 2. It would have retarded the gospel to come out in opposition to an institution so deeply rooted in the public mind, and, with all, so very popular. So from motives of policy they forbore."

"These are the reasons given at the North, uncle," said Nellie, "but they do not seem to me now to accord with either the spirit of the gospel or the practice of Christ and the Apostles. But then I am no judge."

"You judge very correctly on this subject," said her Uncle. "You think the gospel was not designed to interfere with social life, Doctor. Slavery is a relation of social life; therefore it would have nothing to do with it. But does not the gospel interfere with social relations? Did not Jesus rebuke polygamy and divorce? These were social relations, but they were sinful. Did not John rebuke Herod for marrying his brother's wife, and lose his head for it? This was a social relation, but this was a sin. Indeed, the Divine precepts descended to every relation of life, and gave rules for their regulation, and pointed out the several obligations growing out of them. He tells the husband how to love his wife, the wife what are her duties to the husband, the parents how to train their children, and the children how to obey and honor their parents; the servant how to obey and please his master, and the master how to treat his servant. And yet you, Doctor, a minister of the gospel, a student of the teachings of heaven, say the gospel was not designed to interfere with the social relations of life! I do not wonder, sir, at your being an abolitionist."

"Your second reason why slavery was not condemned by Christ and his Apostles is the popular hobby at the North; but is, to speak in the mildest terms, a slander against the Lord and His Apostles. *Policy.* This word, which you apply to the Savior and His servants, has been pertinently defined thus: 'To serve God so as not to offend Satan.' This seems to be precisely your definition. Slavery was a sin. Satan was its great author, and man his servants to execute his wicked purposes; but it would not do for the gospel promoters to rebuke this darling pet sin of the great adversary, lest his satanic majesty should be aroused into furious opposition to righteousness, and, being stronger than the man of sorrows, he might hinder the progress of his kingdom. Truth must fraternize with error, and if it come across a very popular sin, which had taken strong hold of the hearts of the people, it must shut its eyes and close its lips, and not arouse the lion, lest destruction follow. The gospel must begin with little sins, such as polygamy, divorce, adultery, idolatry. It must rebuke at first only those sins which the people were not strongly attached to, such as covetousness, pharisaism, Judaism. Preposterous!"

"It was right, you think, for them to denounce slavery, for you do so; but then they feared to arouse the passions of the people; they must not give offense; it would injure the cause of righteousness. As Paul says, you falsely accuse them of doing evil that good might come. They could not, they dare not, offer the sacrifices of righteousness and put their trust in the Lord! They could condemn other sins, but not this one. Jesus could take a whip and beat the thieves and salesmen out of the temple; but it would be unpopular to condemn slavery. He could tell the whole race of pharisees 'Ye are the children of the devil,' but must not say slavery is wrong. He told them they were hypocrites and robbers of widows and orphans, but was afraid to condemn slavery. The Apostle would preach the truth, though it incensed a whole multitude and brought down the direst persecution on his own head; but you think he was afraid to give the slightest intimation that slavery was wrong. But you are not afraid to say so; therefore you have more courage than Christ or His Apostles."

"You are not afraid it will hinder the progress of the gospel. You say it will advance it; that slavery is an incubus upon the civilization of the age, and a disgrace to christianity. O how much christianity and civilization have lost by the delay of the advent of abolitionism to so late a period! Now, if you and Dr. Barnes and Dr. Wayland had only been in the place of Peter, James and John, to have given the Savior and the Apostles the benefit of your superior foresight, your clear discriminating powers, and, more than all, of your fearless, undaunted spirit, what an impetus you might have given to human liberty and to the glorious gospel. How shall we ever be reconciled to this great loss? 'But what can't be cured must be endured.' So I will try to be patient."

"Why, Uncle, you surprise me," said Nellie.

"Excuse me, Nellie, and you, too, Doctor, for really when I see men of sense, men professing christianity, resort to such subterfuges to carry a point, which has no argument or truth, it destroys my respect—not for you, Doctor—you are my guest and a gentleman, but you are in bad company, and 'evil communications corrupt good manners.' But to advert to your hypothesis. 'That the gospel was not designed to interfere with the social relations of life.' Has it changed its design since the time of our Lord? You abolitionists think it *demands* of you to change those relations now. Was it true then—has it changed now? Was non-interference right then, and is it wrong now? Was silence on the part of Christ and the Apostles both right and prudent then, and is just the opposite course right for those who would accomplish the same end now? Where do you learn this new lesson? But if silence and non-interference were right then, and you say they were, then they are right still, and you are estopped. The silence of Jesus rebukes the noisy abolitionist. But Christ was not silent, nor were his missionaries, and yet they do not utter one syllable of condemnation, or even of censure against the institution. Dr. Wayland himself admits 'That the New Testament contains no *precept* prohibitory of slavery.'"

"He makes that admission," said the Doctor with strong emotion. "But what else does he say? Do not garble him. I will quote him, and *do him justice*. 'You may give your child,' he says, 'if he were approaching discretion, permission to do any act, while you inculcate upon him principles which prohibit it, for the sake of teaching him to be governed by principles rather than by any direct enactment. In such cases you would expect him to obey the principle, and not avail himself of the permission.' Now, sir, you have a most beautiful and forcible illustration, in this sentiment of Dr. Wayland's, of why there is no *precept* in the gospel prohibitory of slavery."

"Forcible, indeed, it is," said Mr. Thompson, "but very discreditable to the Father of Mercies. According to this illustration, He gives his children permission to continue in what you consider a sin of appalling magnitude, and yet does not give them the slightest intimation of the fact; they have His consent to 'practice this frightful enormity,' to live and die in this 'sum of all villainies,' without even saying, 'I would rather you would leave it off.' And why does He not say so—why not give a *precept?* Simply to teach them *not to follow his permission*. The *permission*, I suppose from the illustration, being in direct antagonism to the *principles* which He enunciates. He must teach them *disobedience* to the Divine permission, in order to learn them rectitude of life. How very complimentary you are to the wisdom and consistency of God and to the word of inspiration. Abraham was commended by God because he *commanded* His children; but if He had given them permission to do the sins which He forbade, he would, according to Dr. Wayland, have been, for all that, as pure and good as the Father of Mercies. And these, Dr. P., are the 'miserable straits and impious sophisms to which even divines are reduced, when, on the supposition that slavery is a sin, they undertake to vindicate or defend the Word which they profess to preach."

"But you are aware, Mr. Thompson," said the Doctor, "that it was no part of the scheme of the gospel revelation to lay down anything approaching to a *complete* system of *moral* precepts. To enumerate everything *enjoined* and *forbidden* by our religion, the New Testament would have formed a library in itself, more voluminous than the laws of the realm of Great Britain."

"The revelation is incomplete, I suppose," said Mr. Thompson. "And you of the North must add the important matters which were left out for want of room. The great Reformer thought the 'Word of God a sufficient rule of faith and practice.' All Protestants since have given their hearty assent to this view, and have adopted this theory. But now you must 'add to this incomplete Bible in order to root out one of its greatest sins, which the Divine spirit could not put in for want of space.' Does it not seem there might have been room added to say 'Slavery is wrong, repent of and forsake it.' It would not have enlarged the inspired volume much. And then the precepts regulating it, and teaching the duties of masters and slaves, could with great propriety have been entirely omitted. Indeed, if these precepts had been left out, there would have been room for a whole chapter, giving in detail the evils of slavery. How much it is to be regretted that Dr. Wayland or yourself had not been there to make the suggestion; for I know either of you would do so, if you had the making of a Bible now."

"But who is to fill up this deficiency in the moral precepts of the gospel scheme? Northern and Southern men, Americans or Europeans? Jews or Gentiles, Catholics or Protestants? Or shall it be left to be inferred by each fallible creature?"

"Is it not a sad misfortune that so many lesser sins are rebuked repeatedly, and this *great sin* should have been entirely omitted?"

"But," said the Doctor, "What good, as Dr. Wayland says, would a simple precept or prohibition have done? They are, of all things, the easiest to be avoided. Lord Eldon used to say that 'no man in England could construct an act of Parliament through which he could not drive a coach and four.' We find this to have been the case with the Jews in the time of our Savior. The Pharisees, who prided themselves in their strict obedience to the *letter*, violated the *spirit* of every precept of the Mosaic code."

"Perhaps," said Mr. Thompson, "Lord Eldon was a shrewder rogue than most English thieves, for it is certain that under acts of Parliament many were caught who attempted to drive through with much less incumbrance than a coach and four, and were brought to summary punishment. But, Doctor, is not a *principle* as easily evaded as a *precept*, and *vice versa?* What is the difference? But how are principles to be inculcated except preceptively? Again: if the Author of the Bible would lay down principles instead of precepts for the discontinuance of slavery, because it was seen by him to be the most effective method, why not adopt the same plan with polygamy, idolatry, covetousness, and every other sin? Why make this the single exception? Why forbid any sin, if precepts are so easily evaded as to be useless? The evangelical prophet thought that the Divine plan was, 'precept upon precept, precept upon precept, here a little and there a little.'"

"Do you raise your children by Dr. Wayland's rule? Do you teach your congregation without precepts? If so, when you return home, be kind enough to suggest to the Abolition fraternity to adopt the same method towards Southern slave-holders, and thereby prove your consistency, for 'faith without works is dead, being alone.' Try your theory with the South. Who knows but it will work well, and bring out a new era in the slavery question. If it were not worth while for the Savior to give a precept to the people, because they would not obey it, it would seem to be presumptuous in man to do so. But it was his custom, as you know, to give precepts, whether the people 'would hear or forbear.'

"Now, Doctor, does it not seem strange that you and Dr. Wayland should say there was room in the gospel for the *principle* but not enough for the *precept?* It really does seem you are hard pushed for a way of escape. You cover yourselves with inconsistencies. How such gauzy sophistries can blind the minds of an intelligent people, I cannot see. Yet the scripture must be fulfilled. 'Eyes have they, but they see not: ears, but they hear not.' Now, Doctor, here is your position: Slavery is a sin 'always and everywhere,' but then it was not worth while for the Lord to tell the people so, for they would neither believe nor obey Him. But then he would lay down a *principle*, embodying the precept, and though ambiguous, it *must* be obeyed. Though He who raised the dead and cast out devils was not able to enforce a precept against slavery, yet Phillips, Beecher, Wayland, Channing, Parker and others, were especially commissioned to do so. But He might have lightened their task by giving them a precept, (had He not been deterred by the knowledge of the fact that it would do no good,) a plain enactment, pointed and forcible, unambiguous and palpable "——

"Oh, uncle," said Nellie, "why don't you argue the question?"

"Because, my daughter, the proposition is too preposterous, too presumptuous. A man to say that his Maker did not condemn a sin, a vile sin, just because it would do no good; because He could not give a precept which would not be evaded. And yet man is better and mightier than his Maker, and therefore undertakes the correction and reformation of this sin. Such a subterfuge does not deserve a serious consideration.

God forbade other sins, which are yet perpetrated, why not this? He gave precepts by the thousand, which are till yet disregarded, why not have given a precept against slavery, if it were a sin? He forbade adultery, but he knew the sin would not be discontinued. He forbade covetousness, but He knew the people would still covet, and so I might go on with a whole volume, if I would. But slavery He did not denounce. He gave no precept against it, because, says Dr. W., an English statute can be driven through with a coach and four, and because the Jews violated the spirit of the Mosaic code. Wonderful logic. Surely Dr. Wayland must be inspired, to have so clear an insight into the Divine reasons for omitting the condemnation of so great a sin."

"Well, gentlemen," said Mr. Mortimer, "you will please excuse me for the evening; I will come over to-morrow evening and hear you through with the philological question. Good evening."

One of the chief attractions being gone, Nellie soon excused herself, and retired.

Life's future was bright and cloudless to her. No storms were to beat upon her path; no sorrows, she imagined, would ever befall her. She had made up her mind to live at the South, and own slaves, if invited to do so. True, the matter was not fully arranged between Mr. M. and herself, but in her mind the question was settled, and she entertained no doubt but his determination was fixed. He had said some things which she felt sure were *intended* to be understood, and her susceptible heart readily acquiesced in his intention. But she would have felt freer, if he had *said* all he meant, and all she knew he felt. " Why," thought she, " is a true gentleman so timid, so backward; he seems embarrassed, if even the thought comes into his mind. Ah! he is a man of very delicate and refined sensibilities and could not bear a disappointment, and I am sure I am too much of a lady to be forward in hints and approaches. He would, as he should, be, disgusted, instead of encouraged. 'In your patience possess ye your soul' is the good rule, so I will quietly wait; 'it will all work out right.' 'All's for the best,' said a good old Christian, and I believe it." Thus she gently fell asleep.

## CHAPTER X.

*Definition of Greek words settled—" Doulos" means " slave," proven by the best authorities—" South-side view"—Illness of Mrs. Thompson—Dr. Pratt's troubles.*

Mrs. Thompson, being quite unwell, did not make her appearance in the parlor. Mrs. Norton preferred to remain with her sister, though the latter persuaded her to go in and listen at the discussion, as her maid would remain in the room and afford any necessary assistance. But Mrs. N. said she did not understand Greek, and was tired of the discussion any way; she wished they would drop it, she did not see what good it was doing, and they might enjoy themselves much better socially, and then she was afraid her hot-headed brother might hurt the feelings of her good pastor.

But the reader is anxious to hear the discussion, so we will leave the two ladies to their own enjoyments, or sufferings, and enter the parlor.

" I will now proceed to answer your question, Nellie," said her uncle.

" Before you proceed," said the Doctor, " I wish to say, this is a question you cannot settle, even in the original, with any degree of certainty. The Greek word upon which you will rely to establish slavery is *Doulos*. Dr. Barnes says of this word : 'It is so extensive in its signification as to be applicable to any species of servitude, whether voluntary or involuntary. The word denotes servant of any kind, and it should never be assumed that those to whom it is applied are slaves.' So you see, it denotes a servant of any kind, whether voluntary or involuntary. Now, sir, you can proceed."

"Do you, Dr. Pratt, as a *scholar*, not as a Northern man, but simply as a *scholar*, endorse this view of Dr. Barnes?"

"Certainly I do, sir," said the Doctor.

"Very well, then," said Mr. Thompson, "I will prove that both you and Dr. Barnes are very deficient scholars, or very much blinded by prejudice, just as you may choose to be considered.

"Mr. Mortimer will you please take the Greek Testament there on the table by you, and turn to Luke vii: 2. I refer to Luke instead of Matthew, because, in the latter, *pais* is used, which signifies a child. In Luke, the description is fuller."

Mr. Mortimer announced that *Doulos* was the word used in Luke.

"Now, then," said Mr. T., "we will see if the definition is as ambiguous, as vague as the Doctors say. Robinson's Greek and English Lexicon of the New Testament says: '*Doulos*, a bondman, slave, servant by birth.' In the family, the *doulos* was one *bound to serve*—a slave—and was the property of his master; a *living possession*, as Aristotle calls him. The *doulos*, therefore, was *never* a hired servant, the latter being called *misthios*, *Misthotos*.

"Here, Doctor, you have the definition in full, also the fact that another word, viz: *misthios*, *misthotos*, express the idea of a hired servant. *Doulos* always means a bondman. Now, Mr. Mortimer, turn to Luke xv: 19, where the prodigal said, 'make me as one of thy hired servants,' and see if *doulos* is used."

He turned to the chapter and verse, and announced that the word used was *misthion*.

"Mr. Robinson says that *misthios* means 'hired, salaried, one hired, a hired servant. It is from *misthos*, hire, wages, recompense.' Now let us examine further into the meaning of *doulos*:

Liddell and Scott say, '*Doulos*, a slave, a bondman, strictly; one born so. Doulos, like the latin *servus*, slavish, enslaved, subject.'

"Grove, in his Lexicon, says: '*Doulos*, a slave,' &c.

"Alford, in his Greek Testament, says: '*Doulos* means a slave.'

"Hodge, on Ephesians, says: '*Doulos*, from *deo*, to bind, means a bondman or slave, as distinguished from a hired servant, who was called *misthios*, and *misthotos*.' Dr. Hodge adds: 'It is evident, both from the meaning of the terms here used, and from the known historical fact, that slavery prevailed throughout the Roman Empire during the apostolic age, that *this* (viz: Ephesians vi: 5–9,) and *other passages in the New Testament refer to that institution*.'

• "Bloomfield says· 'The word *doulos*, contracted for *deolos*, was properly an adjective, signifying *bound;* but used substantively, denotes a bond servant, usually for life.'

"Trench's definition of *doulos* is this: 'One in a permanent relation of servitude to another.'"

"But," remarked the Doctor, "you will remember, there are other words besides *doulos, misthios,* and *misthotos,* that are translated servant and servants, in our version. 'Moses as a *servant* was faithful in all his house,' Heb. iii: 5. The word translated servant in this place is *Therapon*. In John ii: 5, 'his mother saith unto the *servants*.' The word translated servants here is *Diakonois*. Now, then, how, if our wise translators gave them all the same rendering, are we to ascertain definitely that either one means slave, and the rest do not? I think you are in a dilemma from which your scholarship will not deliver you."

"I suppose," said Mr. Thompson, "you will admit that Richard Chenevix Trench, B. D., Professor of Divinity, King's College, London, author of the 'Study of Words,' 'The Lessons in Proverbs,' &c., &c., is good authority on the difference in the meaning of these words? If you will not, we will turn you over to Dr. Barnes as an incorrigible neophyte.

"*Therapon*. Of this word, Mr. Trench says: 'From the fact that the septuagint translates the same Hebrew word now by *doulos*, now by *therapon*, it will not follow that there is no difference between the words; nor yet that there may not be occasions when the one would be far more appropriately employed than the other; but only that there are other occasions which do not require the bringing out into prominence, of that which constitutes the difference between them. *And such real difference there is.* The *doulos* is one in a permanent state of servitude to another, and that altogether apart from any ministration to that other at the present time rendered; but the *therapon* is the performer of present services, without respect to the fact whether as a freeman or a slave he renders them, and thus there goes constantly with the word, the sense of one whose services are tenderer, nobler, freer, than those of the *doulos*.' Moses therefore was a *therapon*, doing honorable service for his Divine *Master*. Liddell and Scott say: 'It implies free and honorable service.'

"*Diakonos.* Says Trench : 'The difference between *diakonos* on one side and *doulos* and *therapon* on the other, is that diakonos represents the servant in his activity *for the work*, not in his relation either of servitude as that of the *doulos*, or more voluntary as in the case of *therapon to a person*. The attendants at a feast, and these with no respect to their condition as one of freedom or servitude, are as such *diakonos*. What has just been said of the importance of maintaining the distinction between *doulos* and *diakonos*, may be illustrated from the parable of the marriage supper, (Matt xxii : 2–14) : " With us the king's 'servants' bring in the invited guests, (vs. 3, 4, 8–10,) and his 'servants' are bidden to cast out him that had not on a wedding garment (v. 13); but in Greek, those, the bringers-in of the guests are *douloi*; these, the fulfillers of the king's sentence are *diakonoi*—this distinction being a most real one, and belonging to the essentials of the parables."

"In this long quotation from Mr. Trench, you have clearly drawn the distinction between the words so often confounded in our version. My interpretations of the scriptures, to which I may hereafter refer, will be founded on these distinctions. Wherever I find doulos, or douloi, I shall be sure to call it slave and slaves, and to know I am right, Dr. Barnes to the contrary notwithstanding."

"Let me see if I comprehend these distinctions," said Nellie, " for I suppose my understanding of the scriptures to which reference may be made, will depend upon my retention of them. *Therapon* is the performer of present services, without reference to the fact whether as a freeman or as a slave. *Diakonos* represents the servant in his *activity for the work*, not in his *relation* either of voluntary or involuntary servitude. Neither of these words can be relied on to prove slavery, though in our Bible they are rendered servant.

" *Doulos* means : 'One in a permanent *relation* of servitude to another ;' a bondman, a slave. This last, then, you rely upon to prove slavery. It 'always and everywhere' means slavery. Now I am ready for you to proceed."

" Dr. Pratt," said Mr. Thompson, " I have proved by a number of the best witnesses I could produce, and those, too, whose scholarship the learned world has acknowledged, that *doulos* means *slave* and nothing else. As a lawyer would say, 'I close for the present.' If you have any further testimony, produce it, ' or forever after hold your peace.' Dr. Barnes is your only witness so far ; and as interest, prejudice, and a want of information destroy the credibility of his testimony, I await the introduction of others. If you have no other witnesses, I shall claim a confession."

"I never confess," said the Doctor, "without an imperative necessity. I always go before the jury, to carry out your own figure. You can proceed."

"Then, in the first place, I shall proceed to *discredit* your only witness. You look surprised. I do it, not for the sake of the argument, but for the honor I would pay to Greek literature. As Greek scholars, Dr. Barnes would have us believe that *doulos* may mean a 'hired servant,' just as well as a slave, not that he would urge the usage of Greek writers as proof of his assertion, but upon his own unsupported word. We look for evidence to sustain the Doctor, but find none, not a single witness, save Dr. Pratt. Dr. B. says: 'It is often used in these senses in the New Testament, just as it is elsewhere'; but he gives no single instance in which it is thus used, nor can he. 'If the term *doulos* signifies a 'hired servant' or 'an apprentice,' it is certainly strange, that out of the long list of learned lexicographers, *not a single one* ever found it out. Stephens, in his Thesaurus Ling. Grace. Art. *doulos*, was equally ignorant of any such use of the term. Now, is it not to be regretted, that as Dr. Barnes is the only man who has ever made this discovery, he did not give us some insight into the sources from which he derived his information, but he has not condescended to adduce a single example in which his definition is applicable. 'The Greek word, *doulos*,' says Dr Smith, in his Dictionary of Antiquities, 'like the Latin *serus*, corresponds to the usual meaning of our word slave.' Aristotle, whom we may suppose to have understood Greek as well as any one else, (save Dr. Barnes,) defines a slave (*doulos*) to be a living working tool, a possession, to be not a servant of any kind, but a *slave*. Dr. MacKnight renders the word *doulos* slave. . But I will not weary you with these proofs. 'In the mouth of two or three witnesses every word shall be established.' The scholarship of the world has passed judgment against you and Dr. B., and you must suffer the penalty."

"You remind me very much," said the Doctor, "of one of our good preachers at the North, who, when he establishes a point, is so proud he stops to crow over it. Your crowing is rather more noisy than one would expect of a staid, prim, scholarly Christian like yourself. Better do as the blacksmith, who, when he has driven the nail, only stops long enough to clinch it, and ——"

"That is just what he has done," said Nellie, with a glance of triumph towards Mr. Mortimer. "His proofs are certainly conclusive. But, uncle, you need not think we would grow weary of additional testimony, for while you have certainly afforded enough, yet, if you have more, you can 'make assurance doubly sure.'"

"Well, then," said her uncle, "one or two more witnesses. Donnegan says: '*Doulos* a slave, a servant, as opposed to *despotes*, a master.' But he never applies it to hired servants.

"Conybeare and Howson; '*Doulos* a bondsman' They say of Paul's letter to Philemon: 'This letter is not only a beautiful illustration of the character of St. Paul, but also a practical commentary upon the precepts concerning the mutual relations of slaves and masters, given in his contemporary epistles'

"Dr. Kendrick, of Rochester, New York, in a few articles written for the New York Examiner, a few years ago, gives the meaning of *doulos* to be *slave*. He argued the question with his Abolition brethren with a 'scholarly ability that quite put them to the blush. I am sorry I did not preserve his articles, that you might see how he puts the question forever at rest. I remember his articles created quite a fluttering among the Abolition theologians at the time, and they put on a doleful face, and sighed through their papers, and expressed many regrets that brother Kendrick should have spoken at all, if such were his views; but they did not, so far as I now remember, attempt to controvert his positions.

"Dr. Hackett, of New England, in his revision of Philemon, states in a foot-note that *doulos* means slave. In the body of the letter he says servant, to please, perhaps, the Abolitionists; but he was afraid to risk his reputation as a scholar, and therefore adds the marginal note.

"Mr. Sumner makes a great ado about slavery and the Bible, and declares that slavery cannot be proved from the New Testament, but that the very opposite can. But Senator Sumner has no reputation as a scholar, so far as I know; certainly none as a theologian, and if he has any for veracity, it has not made its way thus 'far from his home. Like many of his class, he asserts a fact, and when asked for the proof, re-asserts it with vehemence. But this is quite enough to satisfy the Northern mind; they never ask for proof from an Abolitionist—they want none; the wildest and most reckless assertions are received as true beyond all question.

"But, sir, I have done with the philological part of my argument, and am prepared to show, that according to the definition given by the learned world to *doulos*, slavery existed in the apostolic age; that it was known and understood by Christ and his apostles; that they recognized it as one of the social relations of life, and endorsed it; that they commanded slaves to be obedient to their masters; that they commended the faith of slaveholders and received them into their churches.

Mr. Mortimer, will you turn to Ephesians vi: 9 and see if the word translated servants is not *douloi*."

"It is, sir," said Mr. Mortimer, "but I would suggest that Dr. Pratt have the Greek Testament, so as to place all imposition out of the question, so I will hand it to him."

"Mas George, Miss Penny mighty sick, sir; she want to see you," said Phebe, entering, and interrupting the conversation.

Mr. Thompson hastened to his wife's room and found her very ill with incipient pneumonia. He immediately sent Jack for the doctor. Returning for a moment to the parlor he excused himself for the evening, and stated that from present indications the discussion would have to be suspended till a change was effected in his wife's health, which might be several days, for she was violently attacked.

Mr. Mortimer took his hat, and bidding them good evening, retired. Nellie ran into the room of her aunt, whom she loved most dearly, to see if she could afford any assistance. Dr. Pratt, after sitting for a full half hour in a brown study, went to his room, where he found a warm fire brightly blazing. Looking to his left, on a centre table, he discovered a small book, but finding it was entitled "South Side view of Slavery," he was tempted to put it down again, but finding no other book in the room but the Bible, and not feeling in a very devotional frame of mind, he opened the book at chapter seventh, and seeing in large letters "Revolting features of Slavery," he read:

"Passing up the steps of a court house in a Southern town, with some gentlemen, I saw a man sitting on the steps with a colored infant wrapped in a coverlet, its face visible and the child asleep.

"It is difficult for some who have young children not to bestow a passing look or salutation upon a child; but besides this, the sight before me seemed out of place and strange. 'Is this child sick,' said I to the man, as I was going up the steps.

'No, master, she is going to be sold.'

'Sold! where is her mother?'

'At home, master.'

'How old is the child?'

'She is about a year, master.'

'You are not selling the child, of course. How comes she here?'

'I don't know, master, only the sheriff told me to sit down here and wait till twelve o'clock, sir.'

"It is hardly necessary to say that my heart died within me. Now I had found slavery in its most awful feature—the separation of a child from its mother. 'The mother is at home, master.' What are her feelings; what were they when she missed the infant? Was it taken openly or by stealth? Who has done this? What shape— what face had he? The mother is not dead; 'the mother is at home, master.' What did they do to you, Rachel, weeping and refusing to be comforted. Undetermined whether I would witness the sale, whether I could trust myself in such a scene, I walked into a friend's law office and looked at his books. I heard the sheriff's voice, 'the public outcry,' as the vendue is called, but did not go out—partly because I would not betray the feelings which I knew would be awakenened. One of my friends met me a few minutes after, who had witnessed the transaction.

'You did not see the sale,' he said.

'No; was the child sold?'

'Yes, for one hundred and forty dollars.'

"I could take this case so far as I have related it, and go into any pulpit or upon any platform at the North, and awaken the deepest emotions known to the human heart, harrow up the feelings of every father and mother, and make them pass a resolution, surcharged with all the righteous indignation which language can express. ('Yes, and you ought to do it,' thought Dr. P. quite audibly.)

"On relating what I had seen to some Southern ladies, they became pale with emotion; they were silent; they were filled with evident distress . . . . During my stay in the place, three or four estimable gentlemen said to me, 'I understand that you saw that infant sold, the other day. We are very sorry that you happened to see it. Nothing of the kind ever took place before, to our knowledge, and we all feared that it would make an unhappy impression upon you.' The manner in which this was said affected me almost as much as the thing which had given occasion to it. Southern hearts and consciences, I felt re-assured, were no more insensible than mine. The system had not steeled the feelings of these gentlemen. . . I received three or four statements of the case, and this is the substance of them: 'The mother of this infant belonged to a man who had become embarrassed in his circumstances, in consequence of which the mother was sold to another family in the same place, before the birth of the child; but the first owner laid claim to the child, and there was some legal doubt with regard to his claim. He was disposed to maintain his claim, and it became a question how the child should be taken from him. A legal gentleman, whose name is familiar to the country, told me that he was consulted, and advised that, through an old execution the child should be levied upon and be sold at auction, and thus be removed from him. The plan succeeded. The child was attached, advertised and offered for sale. *The mother's master bought it at more than double the ratable price,* and the child went to its mother. Nor was this all. In the company of bidders there was a man employed by a generous lady to attend the sale, and see that the infant was restored to its mother. The lady had heard that the sale was to take place, but did not fully know the circumstances, and her purpose was to prevent the child from passing from the parent. Accordingly, her agent and the agent of the master were bidding against each other for some time, each with the same benevolent determination to restore the child to its mother. Rachel was comforted. Rather, she had no need of being comforted, for the sheriff was, in this case, to be her avenger and protector. Here was slavery *restoring* a child to its mother; here was a system which can deal in unborn infants, redressing its own wrong. Moreover, the law which forbids the sale of children under five years, was violated in order to keep the child with its mother. The man who had the claim on the unborn child was from *Connecticut.*"

"Who is this 'South Side view of Slavery' written by," said the Doctor, mentally; "let me see. Nehemiah Adams, D. D., published in Boston, by T. R. Marvin. What! a Massachusetts man writing this way! Well, we will never put down slavery at this rate; this is bolstering it up. This is not the side of the question I want. This Southern nabob has given me too much of that already. I wish I was better prepared to meet him. But the truth is, he has the scholars of the age on his side; there is no doubt of that, and I shall touch that question as lightly as possible; prudence suggests *silence,* so far as I dare maintain it. But if the scholars were his only strength I could do better; but much as we condemn slavery, I fear I shall not be able to bring one single precept from the New Testament against it, for some how or other I cannot quote one that he does not make it mean something else. Even Dr. Wayland has made that unfortunate admission, that there is no precept in the New Testament against it. He never should have made any such admission, even if it be true. There was no necessity for it. The Scriptural condemnation must be by implication, and that will never reach the hearts of these incorrigible Southerners, especially when we cannot deny that Christ and the Apostles lived in a land of slavery and saw the institution in all its bearings. I know Senator Sumner says the Bible is against it; I could quote him, but then Thompson is such a stickler for *proof*, that I know he would riddle him at once, and that would only show the weakness of my cause. I don't know what I shall do. Yes I do, I will play the man; I will stand up to the last; I'll fight slavery, though I have to do it without a weapon. I'll not do as Adams did. They shall not gull me in that manner, never, no never. There is too much sternness in this heart, too much iron in this will, for such puerile vacillation. But really I am a little troubled about it. Christ did not rebuke it, the Apostles did not, neither did they pray for its discontinuance, but I do. Then it follows that I and the abolition world are, as christians, doing that for which there is no apostolic *precept* or *example*. Are we better than they? "How shall I curse whom God hath not cursed? or how shall I defy whom the Lord hath not defied?" But pshaw! What a train of reflection I am indulging. I do believe I am about to go crazy. Ah, its a temptation. 'Get thee behind me.' I am in the land of slavery, and it is very natural I should not be so strongly against it, where all I hear is in its favor, as if I were where the reverse is true. Well, I will think of wife, and write her a letter to-night."

So we will leave the Doctor to commune with his loved one far away, hoping he may become a more devout lover of divine and apostolic precepts and examples, at some future day.

## CHAPTER XI.

*Mrs. Thompson's illness—All remedies fail—Negroes pray for her—The sick room—Affecting scene—Effect of prayer.*

After Mr. Thompson had dispatched a servant for his family physician, he applied such remedies as he hoped would afford Mrs. Thompson temporary relief. On the arrival of the Doctor he pronounced the disease pneumonia, and informed Mr. T. that the attack was one of unusual violence, and would require prompt treatment and the most vigilant care in nursing. He was well known to the family as a skillful physician, and as a man who never gave needless alarm. Mr. T. felt the most painful anxiety for his wife, upon whom he had always looked as one of God's best gifts to him. Nellie proposed to watch by her aunt's bedside with her uncle during the night. It was with unfeigned reluctance that she retired when informed by her uncle that he might need her more at another time.

For several days Mrs. Thompson grew worse. Every effort of the physician was ineffectual; till at length her life was despaired of. Mrs. Norton had been all attention and tenderness. She loved her sister; and then she felt so deep a sympathy for her brother and his interesting family of children. Nellie, too, who had found a congenial spirit in her accomplished aunt, felt a distress at her condition almost beyond endurance. She had looked forward to so many happy, joyous days in the society of her whose spirit now seemed vibrating between two worlds, and sighing to "depart and be at peace." Even Dr. Pratt was moved to earnest prayers for her recovery. But all seemed unavailing. The hand of the destroyer was, it seemed, upon her, and his terrible hold none could break.

"Uncle Jesse," said Phebe, when at twilight the good old servant came up to inquire how his mistress was; "Uncle Jesse, Miss Penny mighty low; the doctor says she's gwine to die. You been prayin' for her, Uncle Jesse?"

"Don't you know I been prayin' for dear Miss Penny. I pray most all night last night. I couldn't sleep. I been on my knees twenty times, I speck. Poor Miss Penny, God bless her and spare her to us a long time yet, I pray, if it be thy blessed will."

"Uncle Jesse, can't you and Uncle Dick and Gabriel and the rest of you, go and hold a prayer meeting for Miss Penny? I 'member

Mas George read in the Testament that Jesus cure sick people when he here on earth. He can cure Miss Penny but the doctor can't."

"Yes, I go now and see the brothers, and we will pray for her. The Bible say 'the prayer of faith shall save the sick.' O Lord, increase our faith. Sister Phebe, you pray too."

"I have been prayin' all the time," said Phebe, as she burst into tears and turned away, wiping her eyes with her apron.

Uncle Jesse went out to hunt up "the brothers." Very soon they all assembled in the house of pious Dick, the ostler. Uncle Jesse arose and stated the object of the meeting as follows:

"My brothers, God been good to us, to give us a kind mistis like Miss Penny always been to us. She always speak good to us; she treat us well all the time. She nuss us when we sick; she kind to our wives and chilens. Nobody got good mistis like we is. God send sickness on her. The doctor can't do her no good; he say she gwine to die. I call you here, my brothers, to pray for our dear good mistis, that Jesus, the Great Physician, come and cure her, like he did when he was here on earth, if it be his holy will. He say, the prayer of faith shall save the sick. He say wheresomever two or three are gathered together, there I am in the very midst. Now, brothers, Jesus is here to-night with us. I feel in my heart he is here. He will help us to pray, and he'll hear our prayers and break off the monia from Miss Penny. Only *believe*, brothers, when you pray, for Jesus says all things are possible to them that believe. O Jesus Master, help us to believe! Brother Dick, you pray first." All knelt, and Dick lifted up his heart in fervent supplications, while his lip gave utterance in broken accents, with sobs and tears, to the following prayer: "O dear Master God, for Jesus sake, help this poor servant to pray for his poor sick mistis. He would not ask for a. form, nor for a fashion, but for de lone sake of Master Jesus, dy dear Son. O, for his sake drop dy frown behind de mountain, and come over de hill of our transgreshums and hear de prayer of dese dy poor servants. O Daniel's God, help dy poor creature to pray aright 'fore de dis afternoon. Be dou de good Physican to stand by de bedside of my dear mistis and buke de fever and de monia, and give her to us once more, if it be dy holy will. Take her by de hand and raise her right up, and put dy strong arm under her to make her strong. She been kind to dy poor servants, she been good to all de people. O Master Jesus, cure Miss Penny. She got little chilens too; what will dey do widout her! O spare her for dey's sake. And Mas George; he too mighty good—what will he do? His heart be broken! O Master Jesus, don't take Miss Penny away from him, our dear master. O please, if it be dy will, break off her sickness and make her well. She teaches us dy blessed word; she read it to us ebry Sunday; she tell us about blessed Master Jesus. O for his sake give us Miss Penny, our dear, good mistis; don't take her away now, if it be dy holy will. O, broders, pray for our dear Miss Penny, dat de Lord may give her to us, for dy dear Son's sake. O Lord, please, dear Master God, don't send my dear mistis down to de cold grave dis time, if it be dy most holy will. We all begs for Christ's, sake. Amen."

The meeting was continued till about eleven o'clock, when it was resolved to go to the house and ask "Mas George" to let them see Miss Penny and pray with her. About twenty, male and female, went up to the door and halted, while Uncle Jesse softly approached the door of the sick chamber, and while looking in on the pale, wan face of his emaciated mistress, the big tears chased each other in rapid succession down his black cheeks.. He beckoned to his master, who came to the door. Taking him a little out, so as not to disturb the sick, he informed him that about twenty of the servants were at the outer door and in the yard, and wanted to see Miss Penny, and if he would let them, pray with her. Mr. Thompson beckoned to the doctor, who came to see what was wanting. When informed of the mission of Uncle Jesse, the doctor entered his protest, and said it must not be done—they must not come in to see her, much less to make a noise; it would excite Mrs. T., and she might sink immediately under the excitement. "Do you think she will live through the night, doctor?" asked Mr. Thompson, as his lip quivered and his voice became tremulous with emotion.

"I think it *possible* she may, but there is no certainty about it."

"Then," said Mr. Thompson, "if my negroes do not see her tonight, they may never look upon her living form again. Unless you are very positive in your opposition to it, doctor, I am disposed to grant the request of my servants, at least so far as to let them come in and see her. Can't I leave it to her, doctor?"

"It may hasten her death, Mr. Thompson, but you can do as you please. But don't ask her if she is *willing* to see them, but if she *desires* to; don't let her know they are here."

This conversation was carried on in a low whisper just outside of the sick chamber. Mr. T. approached the bedside of his sick wife, on one side of which Nellie was sitting, with a countenance that indicated deep mental pain and anxiety; her face was pale and her eyes

R

were wet with weeping. Her mother reclined on a soft couch near by, with her eyes fixed upon the face of her invalid sister. Phebe stood at the foot of the bed, with her hands resting on the back of a chair, ready to go at the behest of any one who commanded her for her mistress. Dr. Pratt had come in an hour before, and was sitting in an easy chair near the fire. Deep sadness was visible on every face, and a death-like stillness reigned through the room. Mrs. Thompson lay with her eyes closed, her hair brushed neatly back from her forehead, with a brow as colorless as marble and a slight flush upon her cheek. She had been fully conscious of her critical state all the time; but was resigned to the Divine Will, whatever that might be. She loved her husband devotedly, and her children with a fondness which none but a mother ever feels. For a few days after she was attacked, she did not feel that she could give them up and leave them. But she was now content. God, her Father and Friend, would take care of them. He would guide and comfort them, and bring them all at last to the scenes of bliss which her faith portrayed in the near prospect. But Mr. T's heart was wrung with bitterest anguish. A dark and lonely future was before him. His prospects for this life he felt were to be forever blighted; his precious little children soon to be bereft of a mother. With such a *mother* but few were ever blessed. Though a man of great faith and fortitude in trials, generally, now they seemed to fail him. God was *just*, he knew, he felt it, but was there *love*, was there *mercy* and *goodness* in a providence so sad? Could *love* tear asunder hearts so lovingly united? Could *love* bereave five young children of the best, most tender and faithful mother that ever blessed a family by her example and influence? Could *love* tear away from an affectionate and devoted husband the wife of his bosom, the only object that made life sweet, and without whom existence itself would scarcely be tolerable. Could *love* do all this? But then he would cry for help from Him who is his people's *Strength*, and his faith would increase, till, by Divine assistance, he could say "though He slay me, yet will I trust in Him."

The whole family, white and colored, were in great distress. The servants did not feel that they could forego the sad pleasure of once more looking upon the face of their beloved mistress; and Mr. Thompson, believing that this night would close the earthly pilgrimage of his wife, was unwilling to deny them this privilege. He therefore approached his wife softly and asked her if she desired to see the servants. She opened her eyes and looking around the room to see who was present, answered emphatically, "Yes." He then told her they were at the door, and he would let them come in, one at a time, and see her, but that she must not let it disturb or excite her. "No," said she, "let them all come at once." Mr. T. stepped back and told them to go in as easily as possible, one following the other.

"Uncle Jesse" led the way, and approaching the bed, held out his hand, and, taking hold of Mrs. T's hand, said "God bless you, my dear mistis, and make you well again." Juda came next, and holding out her hand, burst into tears at the sight of her emaciated mistress. All who were not too deeply affected to speak, had some kind word for "Miss Penny," as they took her hand. Dick, for a wonder, was behind. When he came up, she said, "Sing for me, our good old song—
'O sing to me of heaven.'"

Dick paused, cleared his throat, and looked at "Mas George," who did not shake his head. So he stepped to the door and softly called those who were just leaving. They all returned, when Dick led off, followed by all the rest—

"O sing to me of heaven
When I am called to die—
Sing songs of holy ecstasy,
To waft my soul on high.

When cold and sluggish drops
Roll off my marble brow,
Burst forth in strains of joyfulness,
Let heaven begin below.

When the last moment comes,
O watch my dying face,
And catch the bright seraphic gleam
Which o'er each feature plays.

Then to my ravished ears,
Let one sweet song be given;
Let music charm me last on earth,
And greet me first in heaven."

A sweet, heavenly smile played over the face of Mrs. T., while the negroes were singing. Nellie, poor dear girl, sobbed irresistibly, and even Dr. Pratt wept big tears of mingled joy and sympathy. Mr. T's whole frame shook; while many voices among the colored songsters were tremulous with deep emotion.

"Uncle Jesse," said Mrs. T., feebly, "I want you to pray for me."

Jesse looked round for his master's approbation, but his face was concealed and his frame almost convulsed, so Uncle Jesse feeling that "prayer never hurt no body," he said, "Brothers and sisters, let us all pray. Do please, Master Jesus, hear us this one time more for our dear mistis. You have said whatsomever we ask in faith you will give it to us. You say in your word, Ask and ye shall receive; and you told us the prayer of faith shall save the sick. We bleaves thy word. Darefore, O Jesus, bless my Miss Penny. Be the Good Physician, to heal her sickness and make her well again once more, if it be thy holy will. O Master God, look upon poor servant, for Jesus' sake, and listen to his prayers. Poor sick mistis ask this poor servant to pray for her once more—O give us back Miss Penny as alive from the dead. But speak the word, and she shall get well again, for you did say, Lazarus, come forth! and the dead did live and come up out of the grave. Do please, my Heavenly Master, give her back to us again, for Jesus' sake, if it be thy most holy will, and we will praise thee forevermore, for Jesus' sake. Amen."

The colored people all retired to their houses after the prayer. Uncle Jesse, however, lingered at the door till he could catch his master's eye, then beckoning to him, he walked to the outer door, and stopping, said, " I mighty sorry for you, but the Lord is good—his mercy endureth forevermore—it never fail him. I bleave Miss Penny gwine to get well." " But, Uncle Jesse," said his master, " the doctor says she cannot; that she will die to-night." " The doctor can't cure her, Mas George, but the Lord Jesus can. He fetch up Lazarus from the grave after he be dead four days, and he able to make Miss Penny well again, too. You look to Jesus and trust in him, and not in the doctor, and you see if Miss Penny don't get well agin."

Nellie and her mother had just given Mrs. Thompson a little wine, lest she might sink under the reaction from the excitement.

Having lain about two hours, with her eyes closed, save when she made a feeble effort to cough, she opened them, and motioning to her husband to come to her, she said in a soft whisper, " Husband, I am going to get well."

" I hope so; but why do you think it? do you feel so much better?"

" ' Whatsoever ye ask, believing, ye shall receive, that the Father may be glorified in the Son,' is just as much intended for our servants as for us," she replied, " and I believe uncle Jesse asked in faith, don't you?"

" Yes, my dear, I do," replied her husband, with deep emotion.

The Doctor had retired to a room, to obtain a little sleep, as the servants entered. He gave instructions, that if any, the slightest change for the worse, took place, to have him waked immediately. He was surprised, therefore, when a servant called him, to find it was to prepare for breakfast, instead of being an urgent summons to the sick room. On entering Mrs. T's room he gave her a careful examination, and looking at Mr. Thompson with a grateful smile upon his face, said, "Decidedly better."

"Thank God!" said Mr. Thompson, as the tears involuntarily filled up his eyes to the brim.

At the breakfast table, visible signs of the reappearance of the day of joy were seen in every face, and heard in every word. The night was far spent, and the rising rays were seen to gild the horizon. The cloud was being dispersed, and the light struggling through its hitherto dark bosom.

The reader may feel relieved to know that Mrs. Thompson began to improve, and continued steadily to grow better and strengthen daily, till she was, in two weeks time, able to join the family again in the parlor—whither we will soon conduct you to hear more of Bible slavery.

## CHAPTER XII.

*Slavery demonstrated in the New Testament—Obedience to Masters as taught of God—An endorsement of the rectitude of Slavery—Inspired picture of modern Abolitionists—Secession a positive command.*

MRS. THOMPSON made her first appearance at the tea table, which added greatly to the pleasure and happiness of all present. Mr. Mortimer had been invited to tea. His sparkling wit, the repartee of Nellie, the puns of Dr. Pratt, and the presence of Mrs. Thompson, gave a joyous zest to the tea party, that made all forget the sorrows of the past, only to be grateful for their removal. The cloud had entirely disappeared, and the sunlight of joyous pleasure again filled every heart.

A fervent prayer of thanksgiving was offered up by Dr. Pratt, when all adjourned to the parlor.

"To your Greek Testament again, Mr. Mortimer," said Mr. Thompson, who held a Bible in his hand.

"I have resigned that honor in favor of our clerical friend," said Mr. Mortimer, rising and handing the Greek Testament from the table to Dr. Pratt.

"Then," said Mr. T., "Doctor will you turn to Ephesians, vi : 5-8. 'Servants be obedient to them that are your masters according to the flesh, with fear and trembling, in singleness of your hearts, as unto Christ; not with eye service, as men-pleasers; but as the servants of Christ, doing the will of God from the heart ; with good will, doing service, as to the Lord, and not to men. Knowing that whatsoever good thing any man doeth, the same shall he receive of the Lord, whether he be bond or free.' Now the first question to settle, is, were these servants bondmen or free, were they slaves or hired servants. What is the Greek, Doctor?"

*Douloi*, sir."

"Then, according to the scholarship of the present and last centuries, they were slaves. Conybeare and Howson, in their "Life and Epistles of Paul," translate *douloi* in this place 'bondsmen," and in every other place, I believe, where Paul uses this word. They give it but one meaning—I believe, Doctor, you have not shown it to mean anything else."

"I will grant," said the Doctor, "in the language of Dr. Wayland, that 'the New Testament contains no *precept* prohibitory of slavery.' Ask me for no further admissions."

"This is quite enough, Doctor, I am sure," said Mr. Thompson. "I should certainly be hard to satisfy, were I to ask more. For where do you find a *sin* practised by the people, in the days of Christ and the Apostles, against which they did not utter a prohibitory precept ? Not one, either among the high or low, rich or poor, Jew or Gentile. There was no evasion or compromise with them. Christ and his Apostles condemned *all sin*, but they did not condemn slavery; therefore slavery is no sin. But I wish us to understand the meaning of the quotation just made, as Bible students, as seekers after truth.

"'Bondsmen obey your earthly masters, with anxiety and self-distrust, in singleness of your heart as unto Christ; not with eye-service, as men-pleasers, but as bondsmen of Christ doing the will of God from the soul. With good will fulfilling your service as to the Lord our Master, and not to men,' &c.

"In this quotation we have : 1st. Obedience to their masters, enjoined and required of slaves by the authority of heaven. But if slavery is wrong, then its obligations are usurpations, and must therefore be wrong. Now, whatever authority enforces obedience to error, by requiring submission to its behests, partakes of that wrong. It, therefore, follows, that if slavery is wrong, the precept above given to enforce obedience to it is wrong also. But if there be wrong in the precept, then God is the author of that wrong. But God can do no wrong. Therefore this precept which He gave is right; then it follows that the obligations of slavery are right—and how can this be unless the institution is right also? 2d. It is required that this obedience be 'in singleness of heart, as unto Christ.' Not only is the body to submit, but the heart also. The mind is to acquiesce in the moral and religious validity of slavery, and the conscience of the slave to be at rest in its entire approval of the institution which holds him in bondage. He must take his obligations and service to Christ as the model after which he is to pattern, in his service to his master. Olshausen says on this thought: 'This working of Christianity, directed to the inmost state of the soul, renders it the power which transforms the world. It makes each, in his place, what he is intended to be: the master a true master, the servant a true servant. But further, not merely is the *whole* will of the master to be done, even in secret, where no eye observes the performance, but it is to be done from the heart also; i. e., with willingness and joyfulness. The will of the earthly master is here conceived *exactly as the will of God*, because the relation of dependence comes from God, and thus also its individual manifestations. Finally, *here* too again it is self-evident, that this obedience to the earthly master does not extend to that which is forbidden by God; he that serves his master as if he served God, will never fall into the temptation to sacrifice God's will to his master's.' This able German commentator makes fidelity to earthly masters a means of promoting piety to God. 3d. Here is a most emphatic *endorsement* of slavery: 'Be obedient unto your masters. \* \* \* Doing the will of God from the heart, with good will doing service as unto the Lord.' Here is the *expressed* will of God, that slaves should be obedient to their masters. *Obey*, do not rebel, do not run away, do not idle away your time. *Obey*, do not stop to question whether your master has a right to your service; whether his commands are just and proper; whether heaven has given him the power to order you against your will, or without consulting your wishes. Not a sparrow falleth to the ground without your heavenly Father, much less could you have been brought into bondage without Him. He has done it because it was right, because it was best for you; therefore obey. Do them service with the same cheerfulness, with the same fidelity you would to the Lord, 'as unto the Lord.' 'Doing the will of God from the heart.' His will in what respect? What is He speaking about? Why of the obedience of slaves to their masters. How, then, is His will to be done? By obeying their masters—by obeying them 'from the heart'—a conscientious obedience, a cheerful, ready, willing obedience; this is the way in which they are divinely directed to do the will of God. Then disobedience to masters is disobedience to God; and rebellion against masters, is rebellion against God; to escape from their masters is to flee from a Divinely appointed authority. 'Hagar, return to Sarah, thy mistress, and submit thyself unto her.' Paul sent Onesimus back to his master. Now, then, if obedience to masters is doing the will of God, if disobedience to them is rebellion against God, is not this a full, explicit, and unqualified endorsement of slavery by the Supreme moral authority of the universe? None certainly can question this who believe the Bible. When God says: 'Children obey your parents in the Lord, for this is right,' does he not thereby sanction the right of a parent to control the child? Does he not endorse the relation as right? Who would deny this? And yet it rests on the same basis as the other; only that higher and holier obligations are imposed on the slave, and stronger and more oft-repeated reasons are given why he should obey. But the authority for both is the same. Do not 'be obedient,' and 'obey,' mean the same thing, whether given to the slave or to the child?"

"But, Mr. Thompson," said the Doctor, "the Scriptures say 'children obey your parents in the Lord, *for this is right*.' They do not say 'servants be obedient unto your masters, for this is right.' The one is endorsed as being *right*, the other is simply enforced without a reason. Now, sir, what do you say to that?"

"Then, I suppose, you understand it to be thus: 'Children, obey your parents, for this is *right*, and you servants be obedient to your masters, for this is *wrong*.' But you cannot make God enjoin a wrong act, without making him a party to the wrong; to make him a party to the wrong certainly destroys the perfections of Deity, which it seems you would do to destroy slavery. The same Apostle, in the preceding chapter, says : 'Wives submit yourselves unto your own husbands as unto the Lord,' but he does not add 'for this is right.' Then, I suppose, you think he means it is wrong, or that it is of such questionable propriety, that he will not give it his fullest endorsement. He also says: 'Husbands love your wives,' but he does not add even to this, 'for it is right.' He says to Christians, 'Be ye followers of God, as dear children.' But here, also, he fails to give the reason. It is always presumed, and universally admitted by all but infidels, that when Deity commands an act to be done, the performance of that act is right, without any express language to that effect. Obedience to the commandment just as it is given, is the highest obligation known to man; because it proceeds from the highest authority. If God was held to give a reason, then the Bible would abound as much in reasons as it does in precepts.

> 'Not Gabriel asks the reason why,
> Nor God the reason gives.'

"'Even so, Father, for it seemeth good in thy sight.'

"When it pleases him God gives a reason; as in our passage on slavery, the reason given is, that in obeying the master, the servant honors Christ. Matthew Henry says: 'When servants, in the discharge of the duty of their places, have an eye to Christ, this puts an honor upon their obedience, and acceptableness into it. Service done to their earthly masters with an eye to Him, becomes acceptable service to him also.'

"Now, sir, it is apparent that slavery is from Heaven, and that every obligation of religion is but an additional fetter to bind the slave to his bondage, and that he cannot sunder bonds which bind him to his earthly master, without breaking those which unite him morally to his Redeemer. Doctor, will you now turn to——"

"Stop, sir; you run too fast to look up all the truth. You take such as you like, and leave the rest unnoticed. Let us see what the Apostle says to masters, before you leave this book. 'And ye masters, do the *same things* unto them, forbearing threatening: knowing that your master also is in Heaven; neither is there respect of persons with him.' Now, sir, here is a divine injunction requiring obedience of you to your servants."

"Where do you find obedience in this passage?" said Mr. T.

"In the words, 'do the same things'; i. e., do the same things to them, which are required of them in the above Scripture, to do for you. Do you not see it?" replied the Doctor.

"Not at all," said Mr. T., "nor anything like it. Olshausen says on this verse: 'Paul makes a transition from slaves to masters, and exhorts the latter, not as one might suppose (Mr. O. we may be sure was an Abolitionist,) to make their slaves free, that is left to the free motion of the Divine Spirit; but only on their part to *exercise mildness towards* them, in the consciousness that they, too, like the

S

former, have a master in heaven, with whom personal considerations are of no avail.' The motive which was to constrain the slave in obeying his master, was, that he might please the Divine being; the same motive was to influence the master in the exercise of a mild temper and kind treatment towards the slave. By way of enforcing this precept, Paul mentions the fact, which should be remembered by every master and slave, that both have one common Master in Heaven, who will hold each responsible for every violation of the injunctions given to them.

"Now, sir, if you have nothing more to say on this subject, be kind enough to turn to Colossians iii: 22–24, which is the next Scripture on slavery. Please tell us the Greek word used there for servants."

"*Douloi*, sir, as a matter of course," said the Doctor.

"Bondsmen or slaves, then. 'Slaves, obey in all things your masters according to the flesh; not with eye-service as men-pleasers; but in singleness of your heart, fearing God; and whatsoever ye do, do it heartily as to the Lord, and not unto men, knowing that of the Lord ye shall receive the reward of the inheritance, for ye serve the Lord Christ.' Here we have much the same injunctions enforced as in the preceding verses; only these unite the obedience of the slave, with the Divine favor, more intimately and forcibly than in the other. Here the slave is taught, 1st. That in his obedience to his master, he 'serves the Lord Christ.' His fidelity to his master is an acceptable service to God. Why? Because God commands the obedience, and its performance to the master, is its performance to God also. Disobedience to the master would, then, be rebellion against God. 2d. That the reward of the slave for his fidelity to his master, will be given by the Lord himself, knowing that of the Lord ye shall receive the reward.' How strong an avowal of the Divine approval of slavery is here expressed. As if He were to say, 'go work for your master; I am the author, the originator of this institution. I have brought you into servitude, I perpetuate the yoke of bondage, it is all of me; I am responsible for it. You slaves obey your masters according to the flesh, and I, the Lord, will reward you.'"

"You do not mean to say, that the reward spoken of there is simply for obedience to the master, and not for general Christian fidelity?" said the Doctor.

"I mean it is the reward of grace. And grace produces general Christian fidelity, one of the obligations of which is obedience to the master. This obedience is one of such great importance in the Christian system, that the Apostle found it necessary to place it by itself, that it might be the more obvious, and attract the more attention. I might, were I such a stickler as you Abolitionists are, deny that any other duty is referred to, but as a conscientious man, having all the truth on my side, I can afford to be liberal, and certainly always truthful. This, though, I would be, were it to sacrifice my cause "

"I hoped," said the Doctor, "you would have proceeded to quote the first verse of the fourth chapter, and save me that trouble. I did not know but your liberality would induce you to advocate both sides of the question."

"It would afford me great pleasure to accommodate you in doing so, sir, if the question had two sides. But after several days close application, investigation and discussion, you have failed to show yourself to be in possession of a side of the question, though you have proved yourself a student, and an adroit tactician in polemics. Indeed, you have admitted you have no argument to offer in the New Testament, by saying with Dr. Wayland, that there is no precept against it."

"I do not mean by that admission, sir, as you very well understand, that there is *nothing* in the New Testament against slavery," said the Doctor, rather impatiently, "and lest I be further misunderstood, I take back that admission, which I ought never to have made, and beg leave to differ from Dr. Wayland in this respect. But I will not suffer myself diverted from quoting the verse to which I referred, Col. iv : 1. ' Masters give unto your servants that which is just and equal, knowing that ye also have a master in heaven.'

"Now, sir, I maintain that here is a precept against slavery. If this text is obeyed, slavery must be abolished. Then if my construction is right, not only the principles, but the precepts also, of the New Testament are opposed to slavery. ' Give to your servants that which is *just* and *equal.*' Do justly by your slaves, and they will have freedom ; do that which is *equal*, and you are obliged to place them upon an equality with yourself. Then this quotation destroys your foundation, and slavery is gone."

"Your exposition is wonderful, indeed," said Mr. T. "Whose commentary do you study at home ? Has Beecher ever published one ? They all lean to the side of Abolitionism. But seriously I am surprised that you should give, as an honest opinion, the views you have just presented. Let us again consult Olshausen, the German

Abolitionist, and see if he concurs with your view: 'Here the *dikaion*, which is translated just, refers to what the slaves are justified in requiring, *clothing, food*, &c., but of course *isotes*, which is translated equal, cannot mean equality with their masters; that would be abolishing slavery, which is *against Paul's intention*. The expression rather denotes the equal treatment of all, which excludes the preference of one at the expense of another.' The '*just*' refers to the master's obligation to furnish the slave with what he, in his condition as such, needs; and the word '*equal*' forbids that partiality which would discriminate in favor of one and to the injury of another. Now, sir, if there had been any abolitionism in your text, this learned German would have found it. But he says this was contrary to Paul's intention. His views correspond with the early Christians. Bunsen, in his picture of the Church as it existed in the days of Commodus and Severus—the third century, drawn from the writings of Hippolitus, says: 'Almost all the questions of the day came under discussion, and eminently among them, the important one of slavery. The resolution at which the Church arrived on this point, bears the impress of high moral faith and courage, as well as of Christian wisdom. A slave even of a heathen was not admitted unless he promised to deserve his master's good will by honest behavior, and to abandon every practice which was incompatible with his Christian vow and confession of faith in the proffered salvation. He was taught that it became a Christian to fulfill all righteousness.'

"Now obedience to masters was justly considered by the ancient Christians as a part of 'all righteousness,' because it was commanded by the Righteous Judge; therefore they required a special pledge or vow to that effect. But you Abolitionists would require no such promises; indeed, you would pledge him to a contrary course. You would inform him that religion enjoins no obligations of obedience to masters; that when the inspired word says 'be obedient unto them that are your masters, according to the flesh,' it means that the master ought to set him free, and in the event he does not, the slave is at liberty to run away, or do anything else that would break the yoke of servitude. Aye! you would put the torch in one hand and the sword in the other, as John Brown, the 'Martyr'(?) did, and tell them to burn and butcher their masters and their families. Does not this present a singular contrast between the spirit of Abolition Christians(?) and primitive disciples? But this is attributable to the moral advancement(?) of the age. It is hardly to be expected that those under the instruction of the fishermen of Galilee, and the pupil of Gamaliel, would be so thoroughly imbued with the spirit of the gospel as the descendants of the Puritans, now taught by Channing, Beecher, Parker, and Wayland. *Those* could enjoin the obligations of slavery; but *these* know better. *Those* thought the institution was from God; but these have found out it comes from Satan. *Those* said 'servants be obedient to your masters, according to the flesh'; these say, masters liberate your slaves, you have no right to the service enjoined by the Apostles. According to the gospel of Christ, slavery was right; according to the gospel of the Puritans, it is wrong. The Holy Spirit said servants obey your masters; the holy (?) Puritans say, 'its bonds shall be broken, and they shall not obey.'"

" A thought has just occurred to me," said the Doctor, " for which I acknowledge my indebtedness to Dr Wayland. I think you will find it a 'hard nut to crack.' Do you believe in the slave trade?—is it right? If not, then to enslave Africans is not right; and if it be wrong to *enslave* them, then it is wrong to perpetuate their servitude; or if not, then can an act, having its inception in error, be made right by perpetuating it? Can a wrong act become right by continuing in it? If slavery was wrong at first, does its perpetuity for one hundred and fifty years make it right?"

" I thought, said Mr. T., " your 'hard nut,' would not come from Paul, or Peter, or Christ, or from any ancient Christian, but from some of our modern self-appointed instructors in morals and Christianity. But as I have allowed you great latitude heretofore, it would seem a hardship to curtail your privileges now; so I will proceed to answer your questions, or, in your own classical language, to 'crack your hard nut.' You ask me if I believe in the slave trade? I am subject to the powers that be. My country has decreed against it, and I acquiesce cheerfully in the decision. Were it not for two reasons, superadded to the one above mentioned, I would be in favor of the slave trade. These are my two reasons for opposing it: 1st. We have negroes enough in the South. A greater number, with the present ratio of increase, would soon become burdensome. 2d. The inhumanity generally practiced in obtaining them on the coast of Africa, and bringing them over to this country. The slave trade has produced the most cruel and desolating wars, and these wars have devastated many fertile portions of interior Africa, and depopulated many large cities. I cannot favor anything which is accompanied by such disastrous results. I am not opposed, however, to enslaving Africans, or rather transferring these slaves from African to American masters, for this is all that is generally done. They were slaves before; they only exchange an idolatrous, barbarous master, who has power to kill them when he pleases, for a civilized and generally Christian master, who will feed and clothe them well, treat them humanely, and afford them an opportunity to hear and receive the gospel. The exchange for them is so happy, that the slave here is soon elevated immeasurably above what his African master was. I cannot, therefore, object to an institution whose results are so good. The type of slavery here is much more mild, humane and just than in Africa. But, then, if the slave trade is wrong, as I have admitted, you ask if the slaves brought over by it are not held in unlawful bondage? I answer *No*, for the following reasons, at which I have already hinted: 1st. The slave trade did not *reduce* them to bondage. They were in a bondage, not of their own chosing, before. They were made slaves by the decree of heaven, and the providence of God brought about the execution of that decree. I have already stated, that, according to the calculations of the most intelligent travelers, three-fourths of the African people are in slavery to the other one-fourth. Then, if the slave trade has transferred men and women from a cruel and inhuman master to a civilized, Christian and humane one, it has done them no wrong, but a great favor. If man devised it in his cupidity, 'God meant it for good.' If the Yankee Congressmen did refuse to let the Southern representatives repeal the slave trade laws, because Yankee vessels were growing rich by it, Divine providence overruled their selfishness, for the moral and temporal welfare of the Africans brought over. 2d. As the condition of the descendants of Ham is one of slavery under the Divine decree, it is right for those holding them in bondage to soften the rigors of this vassalage as much as their condition will admit. Indeed, is it not the part of philanthropy to do so, and especially of Christian philanthropy? If I, a slave-holder, have a neighbor who treats his slaves cruelly, it is a debt I owe to humanity to endeavor to correct the evils in that master's treatment; and if I fail, I may endeavor to have the ownership of those slaves transferred, in a lawful manner, to a better master. Now, if the Africans would sell their own slaves to us, and not make war upon one another to secure a greater number, it would be our duty to carry on the slave trade, for the benefit of the enslaved. It would be right to transfer the ownership to a people who would appreciate the responsibilities resting upon masters, and who would understand and sympathise with the condition and wants of the slaves. The wrongs then which have been connected with the slave trade did not belong to it, any further than the temptation it held out to the cupidity of the barbarous tribes of Africa. It purchased the slaves at a price agreed upon by the master, and then transferred them to American owners at a price agreed upon. Whether the master in Africa came into the possession of his slaves lawfully or not, may be as difficult a question to settle, as whether Jacob obtained his birthright justly. One thing we know : both were in accordance with the Divine purpose, and both were brought about by the Divine providence. The Hebrews, on the eve of their departure from Egypt, *borrowed* jewels from their neighbors ; the Jews drove out and reduced to vassalage by force the inhabitants of the land of Canaan. How can these things be justified ? Both acts were done in obedience to the Divine will, and were, therefore, right. Long before these acts were committed, God had said · 'Canaan shall be a servant of servants to Shem and Japheth.' Who should begin to bring them under this bondage, when or how, was not revealed. It was left for Divine providence to develop these. It began with the Jews in Joshua's time, if not in Abraham's day, and continued till their dispersion, as a punishment for the rejection of the Messiah. The door has again been opened by the same Divine hand—and who shall say that hand erred in so doing ? As well might Jacob have said providence erred in sending Joseph into Egypt, or Jesse to have complained against the Almighty because David was persecuted by Saul. 'My ways are not as your ways; neither are my thoughts as your thoughts saith the Lord, for as the heavens are higher than the earth, so are my ways higher than your ways and my thoughts than your thoughts.'

"It would be fortunate for the Africans if they all had Southern masters. Their condition would be much better in every respect. They would be treated better, physically : better clothed, better fed, better cared for. Their minds would be better developed, and their moral condition unspeakably better."

"But you have not got to the kernel of my nut yet," said the Doctor. "If slavery is wrong in the United States, it is wrong in Africa. Though the African masters may have held their slaves for twenty centuries, does that make it right ? The first master *reduced* the first slave from freedom to servitude ; he therefore did wrong, for no man has a right to reduce another to slavery. Now, the question is: Does the long continuance of slavery justify the act? does it remove the wrong? does it make a wrong right?"

"Well, sir, I understand you," said Mr. T. "You have made a man of straw, and desire me to fight him. You have supposed a case which does not exist, and asserted a fact, as you have many times before, which you cannot prove. You have asserted that the first master reduced a *freeman* to *servitude*. But I have proved, by Divine authority, that God reduced one-third of the descendants of Noah to slavery by his own decree. It was not man that made the decree, it was the Creator. It was not man that reduced the freeman and made the first slave, it was the Almighty—the glorious Maker and Supreme Ruler of the Universe. Were Canaan's descendants ever free after God said they should be servants?—had they any rights to freedom after he took them away? If slavery had its origin in error, then your complaint must be laid against your *Maker*, not against us. I refer you to Him. Read the 9th chapter of Genesis again, for I find your memory is very treacherous. Now, then, sir, your nut is cracked, and, like everything else you have borrowed from Dr. Wayland, is found to contain nothing. The sophistry of Dr. Wayland is well adapted to bolster up a cause the strength of which is water, and the foundation thereof sand. He has no truth on this subject which he can produce, he therefore approximates as near the semblance of it as possible; he has no logic, he therefore substitutes sophistry, which answers his purpose just as well with the Northern mind."

"I am very glad he mentioned it, uncle," said Nellie, "for I am sure if an Abolitionist had offered that as an argument against slavery to me, I could not have replied to it. It really seems that you have the Bible on your side sufficiently to refute every argument upon which the Abolitionists rely. I wish Dr. Wayland or Senator Sumner was here, or some other one of the more public men of distinction at the North; not that Dr. Pratt is not as well posted as any of them, but they are more accustomed to discussions on this subject, and *might* think of some argument that will escape him. I am exceedingly anxious to have the whole argument exhausted, the subject thoroughly analyzed. I feel confident my good uncle is able to meet the whole sandhedrim of Abolitionists."

"Dr. Pratt has prepared and preached many sermons on the subject at home, where he had all the Abolition authorities and speeches before him; he has not forgotten the arguments which fired his auditory with indignation against slave-holders. Here he has Dr. Wayland's discussion with Dr. Fuller, and I see he is familiar with the writings of Sumner and Channing, and I presume he has read everything on that subject which has been given to the public— and, saving his presence, he is better posted than any Northern man with whom I have met. So you have no occasion to fear, my Nellie, but what all the strong Abolition arguments—if there are any such— will be presented. The Doctor shall have a fair chance, and as much time as he wants.

"If you have no further remarks, Doctor, will you be kind enough to turn to 1 Timothy vi : 1–5, and give us the Greek of the word translated servants."

"*Douloi*, sir," remarked the Doctor, curtly.

"'Let as many *slaves* as are under the yoke, count their own masters worthy of all honor, that the name of God and his doctrine be not blasphemed: and they that have believing masters, let them not despise them, because they are brethren; but rather do them service, because they are faithful and beloved, partakers of the benefit. These things teach and exhort. If any man teach otherwise, and consent not to wholesome words, even the words of our Lord Jesus Christ, and to the doctrine which is according to godliness: he is proud knowing nothing, but doting about questions and strifes of words, whereof cometh envy, strife, railing, evil surmisings, perverse disputings of men of corrupt minds and destitute of the truth, supposing that gain is godliness; from such withdraw thyself.'

"The following truths," said Mr. T., "are deducible from the above quotation: 1st. That slaves are to esteem their masters worthy of all honor. This refers to heathen masters, as you will discover by a casual reading of the passage. A Christian slave was not to be puffed by his conversion, so as to look down with disrespect or even indifference upon his idolatrous master. He was not to disregard his commands because he was without the knowledge of God, and in the way of error, but he was to esteem him worthy of all honor. Abolitionists would teach them to look upon such a master as a merciless tyrant, a reprobate, a man-stealer, a heartless and remorseless oppressor. But Paul says: 'Count them *worthy* of all honor.' A heathen, idolatrous master, is worthy to be honored by his slave. What a striking contrast between the advice of modern Abolitionists and primitive Christians! 2d. The reason assigned why slaves should thus honor their masters, is, that the name of God and his doctrine be not blasphemed.' Now notice this reason. The '*doc-*

T

*trine'* of God *requires* that slaves honor their masters. Doctrine means teaching. You remember it comes from the latin *docco* to teach. Then the teachings of God are blasphemed by the disesteem of a slave to his master. Doctor, did you ever teach a fugitive slave thus to blaspheme? However, I withdraw the question, it is one of too great delicacy to urge; but many ministers in New England have. 'The *name* of God' is also blasphemed in the same way. 'Name of God' is generally understood to mean 'authority of God.' It may mean that here. The heathen master has a theoretical knowledge of the religion of his slave, and knows it requires of all its disciples to live a holy, blameless, humble, innocent life; but if his slave becomes proud, disrespectful, disobedient, his master despises his religion, to which he attributes these results, and the master and slave are thereby both made blasphemers—the latter by his disobedience, the former by the example of the latter. 3d. If both the master and the slave are Christians, then Paul says: 'Let them (the slaves) not despise them because they are brethren; but rather, (i. e., much more) do them service, because they are *faithful* and *beloved*, partakers of the benefit.' Here are the two—the master and the slave—both in bondage to Christ, both freed men by the blood of atonement, brethren beloved, both partakers of the heavenly calling and benefit. But is this a reason why the slave should elevate himself to a political and social equality? No, let them *much more* do them service. It is a strong additional reason for obedience and love. What! a master beloved by a slave? So says Paul, and he calls him *faithful* also, conceives of him as a lovely character, one deserving the love of others, wearing the ornament of a Christian character unspotted by the world. You or Dr. Wayland would have said, 'and they that are believing masters let them emancipate their slaves, let them not be guilty of the enormous sin of slavery,' so you see a new dialect has been introduced into the Church since the days of Paul. 4th. 'These things teach and exhort.' Here is an inspired command to the minister of the gospel to instruct the slaves to obedience to every class of masters—to honor their masters—to do willing service to them—to cherish affection for them. When the slaves are taught their duties in these respects, the minister must exhort them to the faithful discharge of these obligations. But, Doctor, you Abolition preachers would not obey this Divine injunction, would you? You have not; but, on the contrary, you have most palpably violated it, by urging them to resistance of the master's authority. When a slave violates these precepts and flees to you for protection and concealment, instead of telling him as the angel did Hagar, 'Return to thy mistress,' or, as Paul, 'Count your master worthy of all honor, and do him service,' you take him by the hand and tell him, 'You did right, sir; I congratulate you on your escape from slavery.' You will hide him or pay his way to Canada, and if perchance the master find him in your borders, you raise a mob, and protect him against the rights of the master, the judgment of the law, the Constitution of the land, and the mandate of heaven. How strangely the conduct of Abolitionists appears (when compared with their professions of superior piety,) with the instructions of heaven. 5th. Here is a vivid, life-like description of you Abolitionists, as given by the Holy Spirit, through Paul. It is a graphic picture, a living likeness. Paul could not have made it more complete and perfect if he had lived in the nineteenth century, and been a regular auditor of your fanatical speakers, and a daily reader of the *Tribune*. Hear it, look at it, and may God help you to understand and apply it. 'If any man teach otherwise, (that is just what you and every other Abolitionist is doing,) and consent not to wholesome words, (this is what you have refused to do, you do not consent to, but oppose these wholesome words on slavery) even the words of our Lord Jesus Christ, and to the doctrine which is according to godliness. (You reject the words of Christ, you reject the godly doctrine, by rejecting the above instructions to slaves.) He is proud (marginal reading 'a fool') knowing nothing, but doting about questions and strifes of words, whereof cometh envy, strife, railing, evil surmisings, perverse disputings of men of corrupt minds, and destitute of the truth, supposing that gain is godliness.' Will you bear with me a moment, Dr. Pratt, while I point out a few of the well drawn features of this picture.

"1st. 'Proud, knowing nothing.' 'He raves,' says Dr. Doddridge. 'He has a dreadful mental distemper, and is brain sick. Bigoted— in Southern parlance, has the swell-head, or as Job would say, thinks he is the man and wisdom will die with him. To come directly to the point, he is a fanatic. He knows nothing, and yet his pride induces him to think he knows more than any one else. He looks with contempt upon those who oppose his views, and those who differ from him are considered stupid dolts. He is too wise in his own esteem to need further instruction, and is too ignorant to discover his own deficiencies.'

"2d. 'Doting about questions.' Makes a hobby of one idea. Dotes with fondness upon it; views others as fools who disagree with him. He is 'silly and insane' about his 'question.' Talking, he speaks of it; writing, he discusses it; sleeping, he dreams of it. Everything else is insignificant compared to it. If he is a public speaker, it is his theme; if a preacher, it seasons his sermons; if a legislator, he makes laws for it. He endeavors to stir up others to see and think with him. Now, was not that a master stroke of Paul's pencil? But it was guided by unerring wisdom.

"3d. 'Whereof cometh envy, strife, evil surmisings, perverse disputings,' &c. Here are the ugly features of this most striking face. But if you wish to see how correctly they are drawn, go to the capitol when Congress is in session. Go to a religious convocation of Northern and Southern Christians. Go to the Metropolitan Theatre—go anywhere that the voice of an Abolition orator is heard, and you will see that this sketch was taken by the unerring pencil of Divine Inspiration, and you cannot fail to recognize the original. You will see the 'envy and strife,' you will hear the 'evil surmisings and *perverse disputings*.' You will say, these are those who 'consent not to wholesome words, even the words of our Lord Jesus Christ,' for if any man have not the spirit of Christ, he is none of his, and the 'wisdom that is from above is first pure, then peaceable, gentle, easily to be entreated, full of love and good fruits, without partiality, and without hypocrisy.' But, alas! none of these are to be seen in Abolition meetings and discussions. I tell you, Dr. Pratt, abolitionism in its present form is an offence against God, the Bible, religion, the peace of the Christian world, and against common sense, and the more enlightened experience of the age. I would tremble, sir, at being obnoxious to the charges here laid against those who oppose the Divine teachings on the subject of slavery. Do you observe here, that Paul calls this instruction on slavery, the 'words of the Lord Jesus Christ?'—that in order to enforce the precept he gives the highest moral and religious authority known to the world, the King of kings and the Lord of lords? And yet you, Dr. Pratt, and Dr. Wayland, and others who profess to honor the authority of Christ, array yourselves in opposition to Him, who spake as never man spake. How can you come in such direct and violent conflict with the authority of heaven. How dare you be so presumptuous, so impious? Why, sir, it is a fearful position. Christ commands—you give a counter-command. He enacts—you repeal. He speaks with divine authority—you stop your ears. He says slaves must obey their masters—you say they ought not. God says they shall *serve*—you say they shall not. Christ says these things teach and exhort—you say

I will teach just the opposite. Well has the Apostle said, "*From such withdraw thyself.*"

"It is time we had obeyed this divine injunction, for it is *authoritative*, because positive. Already have two christian denominations withdrawn from you, and they did but obey this command of the Apostle. Soon will follow a more complete, and to the North, a more disastrous separation. When the bonds of this political Union shall have been severed, and the upheaved state of society and business consequent thereupon, shall have settled down, you will find that your Samson is shorn of his strength, your government tame, imbecile, effete, or else you will become a military despotism. Already is 'Ichabod' written upon its temple of liberty, and the 'Rope of Sand,' as the Constitution was once called, has been rent asunder by the ruthless hands of fanatical abolitionists. The compact has already been broken, and we are released."

"You speak with a great deal of assurance, Mr. Thompson," said the Doctor, as if he was just aroused from some profound reverie. "I cannot reply to you now. I have much to say—you seem to have had all your own way this evening, and I have 'given you rope.' I would reply now, but Mrs. Thompson is feeble, and it might not be best for her to sit up longer, so I will not tax her patience. As I am anxious for all present to hear what I have to say in reply, I will defer my answer until to-morrow evening."

The party retired to their rooms—Mr. Mortimer having taken leave at the conclusion of Dr. P's remarks. Mrs. Norton was very anxious to hear what her pastor had to say in reply, for her faith in the rectitude of abolitionism was very much shaken; she began to fear it was a sin, and one of such magnitude that she dare not commit with indifference. She had previously felt very little interest in the discussion, thinking there was no *very great* sin in slavery, or her brother would have seen it; and that there must be some errors which made its abolition right, else so many wise and good men at the North would not have advocated it, or perhaps it was a question not settled at all in the Scriptures, and therefore men entertain different views about it. But she had never been able to see very clearly either the right or wrong about it. But now that Jesus had taught it, that the inspired limner had given so graphic and appalling a description of the opposers of slavery, she felt if this was true, if her brother had made no mistake in his interpretation of this Scripture—the matter was no longer one of indifference—she must decide—she, too, like her daughter, must come out from among them and separate herself, or she would be a party to their wrongs.

Nellie was delighted. She felt grateful that she had seen her error, and had avowed her change of sentiment. Her uncle's explanations were as clear to her mind as a sunbeam.

She was astonished that her pastor should feel disposed to reply at all. She had never studied his character. She knew not how strongly pride of opinion and pride of position sometimes influence even christians against their conscientious convictions. She knew not how difficult it would be for Dr. Pratt to say, " We of the North are wrong after all, and you of the South are right, but I was ignorant of this fact till convinced by a Georgia slaveholder." Ah! it was too much—the Doctor could make no such admission.

But our readers must desire to hear what Dr. Pratt had to say in reply. Be patient, for time and tide no more hasten than they " wait" for the accommodation of the inquisitive and impatient.

## CHAPTER XIII.

*Music—Embarrassing Position—Success—Doctor Pratt's Gasconade—Mr. Thompson's Reply—A True Picture of Northern Cruelty—Abolition Preachers omit a part of the Gospel—Cannot Preach it at all—Infidelity of Abolitionism.*

Mr. Mortimer came over about four o'clock, P. M., in pursuance of an invitation from Nellie to enjoy a musical treat which she had promised him. He never failed to fill his engagements with her, for they were obligations, the performance of which was most pleasing. Her music was in exquisite taste—her voice soft, sweet and melodious; but he imagined that in conversation she possessed greater power to charm and fascinate.

He very soon proposed a promenade in the flower yard, though long since had the frosts of winter left the shrubbery entirely bereft of its adornments of leaf and flower. Yet one was by his side more delicate, more beautiful and lovely than any which had bloomed, as he imagined, outside of Paradise. Her words were sweeter music to him than the harp or piano, the forest songster, the chiming of sacred bells, or the chanting of holy songs. He was conscious of an affinity between them, which, when he was absent from her, made him long to be in her presence again. Though he had said much to her before, he had never fully unfolded his feelings, nor was he certain that his own deep, ardent affection was reciprocated. He had no reason to doubt her partiality for his society, but no positive declaration had ever been made by either party. This occasion he had selected for the purpose of coming to a definite understanding. He plucked the frost bitten rose buds, rolled them in his hands, and crushed them between his fingers, which were cold and bloodless. His heart palpitated with unusual rapidity—his throat became unaccountably dry, and the powers of speech strangely forsook him. What was the matter? Am I sick? he thought, no I have no headache, no fever, no symptoms of disease. "But this is a very awkward and foolish position. I *will* speak."

But the supper bell is ringing, and we must not eavesdrop the young lovers. They linger, and are in a low conversation. The spell is broken, the dumb is speaking, the patient has recovered, and the future must develop whether Mr. Mortimer was successful. Nellie's face is flushed, and she has no relish for tea, while Mr. M. is unusually vivacious.

But the reader is waiting with impatience to hear Dr. Pratt, who has the floor. In his hand he holds a small bit of paper, which must be either the skeleton of his speech or a memorandum of the points of his argument. We may begin to tremble, for Jupiter stands forth in his majesty, with the wand of power in his hand.

"The time has come when self-respect, philanthropy and patriotism demand that I should be heard in defense of my principles. Duty calls, and I respond with pleasure. I will no longer prove recreant to the high trust which I feel is reposed in me of vindicating the purity of abolitionists and the rights of man. The character of the former have been aspersed, while I have sat silently by; were they present I would ask their forgiveness. But by whom aspersed? Who has become the self-appointed judge to sit in trial on the motives of a highly enlightened and eminently christian people? *Who* has become the expounder of divine and heavenly truth, and a teacher of correct morals and religion? *A slaveholder*—one who lives in the daily violation of the most palpable principles and spirit of our holy religion—one who binds men in the chains of bondage—one who coerces men and women against their will to labor for his benefit— one who totally disregards the rights of others—one who comes in contact with the intelligence of the age, and in conflict with the religious convictions of the civilized world—one who has the presumption (excuse the word) to say that abolitionism is fanaticism; that such goodly men as Wayland, Channing, Beecher and Barnes are fanatics; that such statesmen as Sumner, Lovejoy, Seward, Wilmot, in the United States, and the wisdom of the English Cabinet, are knaves. One born at the North, reared in our schools, rocked in the lap of pious horrors for the inhumanity of slavery, and then, *and then*, proved a recreant to the early instructions of truth! Such is the man who would lecture abolitionists on good morals and the divinely inspired word—a man who endorses an institution that bears on its face a perpetual fraud, and embodies in its essential elements the most flagrant wrongs—wrongs which are 'so transcendent, so loathsome, so direful,' that they must be encountered *wherever they can be reached*, and the battle must be continued, without truce or compromise, until the field is entirely won. *Slavery*—the very word is a reproach to our dialect; it should be stricken from use; it is a stigma upon the civilization of the age—a burning disgrace to our christianity. What evils have followed in its train? Rather may I ask, to what evils has it not given rise? Are there tears in this lovely, sunny land?—they are the tears of slaves. Are there sighs and groanings at the North?—they are on account of this moral pollution that hangs as an incubus upon society. Do wives and husbands weep over an inhuman separation from each other? Slavery must bear the curse. Are parents and children ruthlessly torn asunder?—the iron hand and heart of slavery have crushed and broken these loving spirits. Do humanity and religion weep over the indulgence of the most brutal passions that ever disgraced our race?—it is because slavery has given rise to the indulgence of these unhallowed propensities. Are the streams of human life made bitter and its paths set with thorns?—these are but the natural fruits of the evil genius of slavery. Are there wranglings in the halls of our national legislature?—slavery has broken its peace and sundered its bonds of union. Are the peace and harmony of our churches invaded? Are the friends of religion at enmity with each other? What has done all this? Who has dared to invade the sacred sanctuary, the Holy of Holies? The emissaries of satan embodied in slavery. It has placed its polluted hand upon the consecrated vessels, and has the presumption of Uzziah to offer holy sacrifices upon its divine altars; then turning to the true and appointed priests of the Most High, would lecture them on moral and religious propriety, and give them exegeses of the Divine word.

Now, Mr. Thompson, you have a bird's eye view of the evils of slavery and the presumption of slaveholders. Do you say that an inspired Apostle endorses and enforces this institution? Dare you say that the immaculate Son of God fostered slavery? The thought is presumption—its expression blasphemy. Slavery always has, and always must, resort to the most palpable perversions of Scripture to sustain itself. Then, sir, tell me not that slavery is right. It is not true. I would not believe it though one rose from the dead to testify to it."

Mrs. Norton was elated as her pastor proceeded, and felt sure he was demolishing every position her brother had taken. She felt well satisfied when he was done that human wisdom could do no more, and that human ambition could desire no more. She fully expected her brother would yield. What could he say in reply?

"Are you through?" quietly asked Mr. T.

"I am, sir," was the Doctor's emphatic reply, with an air of satisfaction, which was rather amusing, as it seemed to say "I have triumphed."

"I have no *reply*," said Mr. T. "to make to your fulmination. I must be contented with a very modest little criticism, which I hope you will receive kindly. I shall offer nothing in defense of myself for presuming to teach you. It is the duty of those holding the truth to give it to those who are in error, whether they will hear or forbear. With such honorable company as Washington, Calhoun, Clay, Madison, Jackson, Berrien, Crawford, etc.; with such pious associates as Abraham, Isaac and Jacob, David, Solomon and Elisha, Bascomb, Thornwell and Fuller, I am not reproached by being called a slaveholder. I have been greatly disappointed, Doctor, in your reply, as you consider it. I thought you would show that my interpretation of the Scriptures was wrong, that the text meant something else. I supposed you would bring up some *argument* to prove abolitionism right, but you made no effort to do so, and I think displayed much wisdom by the omission. A good lawyer sees his weak points before his opponent does, and never alludes to them, lest his antagonist should take advantage of them. You are wise and crafty. You assert much, and do not fail in your proofs, because *you attempt none.* I must say of your speech, however, that it is eminently *characteristic*. You are a representative character. You illustrate abolitionism. You would have the word *slavery* blotted out from our language. What would you insert in its place in the New Testament? "It is a stigma upon the civilization of the age and a burning disgrace to our christianity," you say. Why, Paul, why were you so unfortunate in the selection of a word, which has become a stigma upon civilization? How much more so for you to put it into the Divine word. But answers Paul: "The Holy Spirit gave me the word, and told me to write it." But did you not know it would be offensive to the delicate sensibilities of this age, and that much complaint would be made against it? "Yes," says Paul, "I knew that those who would 'not consent to wholesome words, even the words of our Lord Jesus Christ,' which He gave me, would always be 'doting about questions and strifes of words'; but they are only the 'perverse disputings of men of corrupt minds, who are destitute of the truth.' But, Paul, cannot this word *slavery* be blotted out from the revelation? 'If any man shall take away from the *words* of the book of this prophecy, God shall take away His part out of the book of life, and out of the holy city, and from the things which are written in this book.' Then I guess, Doctor, we had better not meddle with this word. We had better have the stigma upon our civilization than to have our part taken out of the book of life. We cannot very well get it out of our language, so long as we use that old fashioned book called the Bible, and as our sainted parents have told us it came from heaven, and as their dying testimony bore witness to its heavenly comforts and immutable truth, it might be well for us to respect even its *words*, as these are the signs of its inspired thoughts. I confess myself at a loss, Doctor, for your speech is hard to find. It passes out of mind. One cannot very well hold it. I think though you said something about the evils of slavery, what we Southerners call the *abuses* of the institution. I promised to be frank and ingenuous in this discussion, no matter what it costs of feeling. I will keep my word. Slavery has its *abuses* as well as every other relation in life. Some cruel, heartless masters, destitute of proper moral feelings, sometimes separate husband and wife; and the same evil, by similar characters, is done to parents and children. There are cruel masters as well as cruel husbands and parents; there are tyrannical masters as well as kings and princes. But you do not say 'the evils of marriage or of the parental relation,' you do not say 'the evils of power,' but the *abuses* of marriage, the *abuses* of the parental relation, the *abuses* of power. So we say the *abuses* of slavery. These abuses in slavery, like those of marriage and power, are the exceptions, not the rule. That they ought not to exist, that they are contrary to the precepts and genius of christianity, I most freely admit; that they should be corrected, is the firm conviction and earnest desire of our people generally; that they have been greatly diminished for the last few years, until they are scarcely to be found in our land at the present time, is the observation of every close observer. Every master is held responsible, both by law and public sentiment, for the mild and proper treatment of his slaves, for furnishing them with food, clothing and religious privileges; that we are accountable to God for the manner in which we treat those whom He has placed in bondage under us, is a fact believed by all among us, save those who may reject the Divine revelation. There is not a master of moral standing in all the land who would not contribute his influence to the correction of every abuse of slavery. We know what these abuses are; you and your abolition fraternity do not. We are willing to be instructed on this subject by each other, but not by those who deny the moral and Scriptural validity of the institution. We understand our responsibilities, and assume them with the same confidence of our ability to discharge the duties connected with them that we cherish in the other relations of life. We feel able to think and act for ourselves without the officious intermeddling of abolitionists. While Southerners are willing to aid one another in correcting every abuse of slavery, they will resist with their whole moral, mental and physical powers any and every attempt to break its chains. The existence and use of an institution and its abuse are two widely different things, as unlike as white and black, light and darkness. Marriage is of God, and is therefore good, but its abuse is wide-spread and ruins thousands, 'but must marriage on this account be abolished?' 'No,' said Mr. Mortimer, 'not yet I hope.' All smiled but Nellie, who blushed deeply. Mr. T. proceeded: 'Governments are indispensable to the well-being of society, but rulers are sometimes tyrants and usurpers. Shall governments be abolished on this account? The parental relation is greatly abused. A heartless mother or brutal father may treat their children with shocking inhumanity. Shall this institution of heaven be abolished on account of these occasional abuses? We may safely say there is no position of trust or power in which fallible man has been placed but what has, by some, been abused. Shall man, on this account, never again be entrusted with positions of honor or power? Surely you would not thus disintegrate human society! No, you would not do this; but, as a member of that society, you would labor to correct the evils, and thus benefit your race. This seems to be the plan marked out by the Divine Providence for the South, and we are following the guiding hand and doing the work thus assigned to us. But let us *alone*, and we will accomplish it. All abolition interference but stays the hand of reformation. Correct the evils that exist among you at the North, for they are fearful, and we will attend as best we may to those at the South. Take the beam out of your own eye first, and then you can see more clearly the mote that is in ours."

"To show," said Nellie, "there are cruelties not less abhorrent at the North than any which can possibly exist at the South, I propose, if you all will permit me, to read a few extracts from a book written by a Philadelphia lady, who knew personally the facts of which she writes. Speaking of the leading abolition characters, male and female, with whom she was acquainted, she says: 'They make a great noise in the world, and create for themselves the reputation of philanthropists. These persons are generally small and mean in all their operations. The sight of a widow struggling through the world with her fatherless children cannot awaken their pity. The picture of misery presented by the forlorn state of those helpless children, who are taken into the houses of our citizens and treated with a degree of cruelty that would appear apochryphal to those who have not been eye-witnesses to it, has no effect to call forth their sympathy. The wretched class of sewing girls, who form so large a portion of our cities, who toil from early morning till late at night, for the miserable pittance that but just suffices to keep soul and body together, who go down to the grave while yet but very children, or, what is far worse, live on, if living it may be called, to a premature and imbecile old age, *shut out from every enjoyment of life*, debarred from all the innocent recreations of youth, aye, debarred even from those bright *hopes* which come to the happy, these slaves, *these very slaves* of the *North*, find neither friendship nor humanity amongst these abolitionists; but, on the contrary, these noble beings, these friends of the oppressed and down trodden slave, employ the poor sewing girl, beat her down in her price, make her work till as near mid-night as possible, and then make her wait for her wages for weeks and sometimes for months after she has earned them.

"I know a poor girl, a dress-maker, who worked at her trade until four weeks before her death, wearily dragging herself about to her customers, and then sitting down in her lonely garret to put together the finery that was to adorn them. She was a christian, a member of the Episcopal Church, and had a name and a soul as pure as the untrodden snow. She was in a consumption, and when she found herself growing very weak, she sent for my mother and myself, and we hastened to her and performed every little office of friendship that was in our power. One day she said to me, 'Lizzie, I have a request to make of you.' 'Name it Bridget,' said I. 'I want you to take this little bill to Miss ———, in Girard street; tell her how ill I am, and that I really need the money, and ask her to please settle it. I have already gone there several times, and she has always put me off. . .'. : . . She was dressed in a handsome silk dress, and had on quite a profusion of jewelry. I handed her the bill, and told her that poor Bridget was very ill and could not possibly live but a few weeks, and begged her to pay it. She spoke quite saucily, and seemed to think it a very insulting thing to her dignity to be dunned in that way. I left the matter in her hands, and I am ready to prove that poor Bridget went to her grave in Ronaldson's burying ground without ever receiving one penny of the money. There is not a lady in the whole Southern country that could have been capable of such an act."

"Nor has a slave ever died under such circumstances of want," said Mr. Thompson.

"A poor woman," continued Nellie, "with a husband bed-ridden for months, she feeble, and at the time in bed, with six children crying for bread, sent a little account to a wealthy lady in Philadelphia, who lived in elegant style. When poor little Ellen Harly arrived, the woman of wealth was surrounded by some visitors. Sending for the lady into another room, Ellen modestly and bashfully told her errand. The reply was characteristic : ' And is this what you had the impertinence to bring me from my company for, to hear this miserable story about a sick father and mother and a whole troop of starving brats?' The old tale to move people's pity, but it won't do, I can tell you. You ought to be taken up as vagrants. If I was not very charitable, I should send you to prison at once—however, I won't be hard with you—here is a *half dollar*, come back to-morrow and I will pay you the rest, and remember to tell your mother that I shall never employ such a low bred person to sew for me again. I find it quite insufferable."

"Now," said Nellie, "have a little patience while I present some instances of cruelty in Northern masters and mistresses, which I presume cannot find a parallel in the South.

"This same little Ellen Harly was the daughter of a gentleman who sat out in life as a New York merchant, with as bright prospects in business, and with as pure and angelic a wife as ever graced the fashionable circles of the city. But her too generous husband lost all by security. Being reduced in health by consumption, till he was unable to give his personal attention to any business, and having been forsaken in the day of his adversity by the numerous heartless friends who in former years had thronged his parlor, his wife sold her jewels and obtained money enough to pay their expenses to Philadelphia. Here they were reduced to such straits that, as their children grew large enough, they were compelled to put them out for their food and clothing. This was the fate of dear little Ellen, who was placed with a Mr. Wilson, about twelve miles from the city. The sensitive mother's heart shrank within her as she clasped the dear daughter to her bosom before committing her to the man who had promised she should be treated as a child in his family.

"When once domiciled in the family, she was made to iron and wash; she scrubbed the house, and did an amazing amount of chores of every description. She drove the cows home at night, carried in the wood, and often had to split it. She carried all the water from the spring, a full quarter of a mile. Her food was of the coarsest and most scanty kind imaginable.

" When, after an absence of at least a year, she returned home to her mother, she was very much in the condition of pious Job of Scripture memory, when he was forced to scrape himself with a potsherd. She stared vacantly, and sometimes wildly upon every body; sometimes seemed absent minded, and again fierce as a tiger. The startling truth burst upon the poor heart broken mother, that Ellen had lost her reason, but how or wherefore she could not tell. One day when the light of reason had for some hours lit up poor Ellen's face, her mother resolved to question her particularly about her home in the country. 'Ellen,' said she, did Mrs. Wilson ever whip you when you lived with her?' 'O yes, every day,' answered the girl. 'What did she whip you with?' 'The cowhide sometimes, sometimes the wall.' 'How do you mean the wall, Ellen?' 'O, she beat my head against the wall till I had such a queer feeling in it, and I could see sparks of fire in my eyes. Then Mr. Wilson used to kick me all about the room.' 'What did you do to deserve such treatment, Ellen? You must have been very saucy to them, Ellen, and very bad?' 'O, no, mamma, I was not saucy. I think they thought me stupid, and indeed I didn't know how to do any thing right just as I was told, for I had never worked so hard before; but I wasn't bad.' Here Ellen began to sob and cry as if her heart would break, but at the moment one armed Jim, a drunken neighbor, came reeling up the court, singing a rollicking song, and Ellen, starting up with a wild burst of laughter, ran out to see him, and in her face one could perceive no gleam of reason left. A few days after, in a wild delirium of the brain, Ellen left the house, and was not missed by her parents till near nightfall. Every search for the poor demented child was fruitless. A day or two afterwards Mr. Harley read the following in one of the morning papers, which told the sad sequel of poor Ellen. Judge of the feelings of the poor mother's heart as her husband read—

" ' Found drowned !—The body of a little girl was found yesterday morning floating in the river Schuylkill, by a party of boatmen. The child was about ten years of age, had on a faded calico dress and linsey woolsey petticoat. In her pocket was a handkerchief, thimble and fine tooth comb. The coroner held an inquest on the body, and the jury rendered a verdict of accidental drowning. The body has been taken to the green house, where it awaits the recognition of friends.'

"Such is the result of the cruelty of Northern masters to their poor slaves. You have read of poor little Lily, who was whipped by her rich mistress, in a Northern city, until she fainted, and was then borne to the garret and locked up in the room with two skeletons to frighten her into terms, and made to stay there for weeks, while her food was bread and water. You may also have read of the wrongs and cruel treatment of little Harry, for a trifling offense. He says of his master:

" ' He ordered me to undress. I did so. He told the men to tie me up to a limb of the tree with some strong cord they had brought with them. This they soon accomplished, and then I felt the hard and heavy blows of the cowhide cutting and bruising my flesh, and seeming to be grinding my bones to powder. I held out as long as I could, but at last I cried for mercy. I implored his pity, still the blows descended, and at each repetition laid open the quivering flesh. In the midst of this agony consciousness forsook me, and I knew not what happened to me for hours afterwards. When, however, I at last opened my eyes, I found I was laid in my own garret, but there was no one near me. I felt an intense burning thirst. There was no water at hand. I tried to rise from the bed, but my bruised and mangled body would not permit me. I writhed in agony. . . . . . . I heard a noise on the stairs of a heavy step ascending. The next moment my master entered the room. He held a lemon in his hand, cut in two. For what purpose he had brought it, I soon learned. He turned me over on my side, and with a malicious leer on his face he squeezed the juice into the open cuts on my back. O God! O my mother! can you imagine the torture he inflicted upon me. I felt the cold shivering of agonized despair run over me. I implored him to have mercy upon me, as he hoped to find mercy with God; but no, he pursued his purpose till he had satisfied himself, and then left me, deaf to my cries for water, deaf to everything but the cruel promptings of his iron like heart.'

"These are no fancy sketches," added Nellie. "They are written by a pious and intelligent lady of Philadelphia, who vouches for the truth of them before the Searcher of hearts. Such is the refined cruelty of Northern philanthropists! who are heart sick at the inhumanity of Southern slaveholders. Perhaps it would be best for us Northern people to abolish slavery at home, or, at least, discontinue its abuses. Our *example* might do more for the South than our precepts have as yet accomplished. These Southerners will not be so apt to heed our efforts while we preach one thing and practice another. Nor will they hear us as long as we misapprehend them. They know we are ignorant of many of the things whereof we affirm, and it is not strange that they refuse to be taught by us. The abuses above alluded to were perpetrated by prominent abolitionists, who would give a thousand dollars each per annum for the abolition of slavery."

Nellie ceased speaking, and for a time no one seemed disposed to speak. Soon, however, Dr. Pratt broke the silence by saying, "Mr. Thompson, you are frequently twitting me with a failure to produce Scripture or argument against slavery. I shall beg leave to dissent from the admission of Dr. Wayland, "that there is no *precept* in the New Testament against slavery," and prove to you there is. I remember being in Baltimore a few years ago at a christian convocation, and to have heard a Southern minister, perhaps Dr. Johnston, of South Carolina, ask one of our most celebrated divines, "What he considered to be the strongest Scripture in the Bible against slavery." Taking the New Testament in his hand, he turned to 1 Cor. vii : 21, and read: "Art thou called being a servant? Care not for it; but if thou mayest be made free, *use it rather.*" I hold, sir, that here is an inspired preference expressed for the freedom of the slave. It is best, "Use it rather," it is for his development as a christian, and therefore will promote his efficiency, and consequently is for the glory of his Savior. If all these good results are to follow the emancipation of a christian slave, then every christian master is under obligation to liberate his christian slave."

"Your quotation," said Mr. Thompson, "without the context, would seem to bear the construction you give it. If the master proposes to free his slave, and the slave is advised to accept it, there must be some reason for the advice which made the condition of freedom preferable. But let us go back and read the context, beginning at the 17th verse: "But as God hath distributed to every man, as the Lord hath called every one, so let him walk. And so I ordain in all the churches. Is any man called being circumcised? let him not become uncircumcised. Is any called in uncircumcision? let not be circumcised.... *Let every man abide in the same calling wherein he was called.*" Here, Doctor, is a key furnished by the inspired author of this language by which to reach his meaning. The Jew was called being a Jew; let him not desire to be a gentile. The gentile was called being a gentile; let him not at his conversion desire to be a Jew. The master was called being a master, and the slave was called being a slave. Then let neither of these be discontented with his condition, but "abide in the *same* calling wherein they were called." With this interpretation agrees Dr. Alford, who was himself an abolitionist. The early Fathers, as they are called, believed this passage favored slavery. Chrysostom says: "If thou art called as a slave care nothing for it; nay, although thou canst become free, yet serve rather, for the believing slave is yet free in the Lord, and the free man a slave of Christ." Your construction is of modern date, and owes its origin to abolitionism. Indeed, it seems to conflict with the great idea which occupied the mind of the Apostle when he wrote, to wit: That the gospel of Christ was not to unsettle the relations of human society. There is not the slightest intimation to the master that it is his duty to liberate his slave, not even a preference for it is hinted at, nor is the slave to *seek* his liberty. If, then, this is your strongest Scripture, and your best argument, your cause is indeed a weak one. Do you derive authority from this text for the organization of abolition societies for sending out abolition emissaries and tracts, and for stirring up insurrectionary feelings in the minds of wicked and discontented slaves? But according to this "strongest Scripture," none but christian slaves would be entitled even to accept freedom, if tendered; nor does your construction seem to impose any obligation whatever, even on christian masters to liberate their "called" slaves. So that the very most you can make of this passage is, that if a christian master should think it best for his pious slave to be free, and voluntarily offer him his freedom, that it would be well for the slave to accept it. Such things have frequently been done in the South. A slave is converted, exhibits a deep sense of his obligations to his race to preach to them the gospel, feels called to bear the news of salvation to his father-land. His master is made acquainted with his convictions and desires, and feeling a deep sympathy in the same good work, sets him at liberty, and pays his expenses across the water, having first given him a generous outfit, and then contributes annually to the support of his pious missionary. Under such circumstances, if a slave may "be made free," I would say with all my heart, "Use it rather." Nor would any pious Southern christian dissent from this view.

Your view of this passage is not universally conceded by Biblical critics, even among abolitionists. Conybeare and Howson, the former "Late Fellow of Trinity College, Cambridge," and the latter "Principal of the Collegiate Institution, Liverpool," both learned critics and translators, give the passage in examination this version: "Wast thou in slavery at the time of thy calling? Care not for it. Nay, though thou have the power to gain thy freedom, seek rather to remain content." In the foot note these men say: "The Greek here is ambiguous, and might be so rendered as to give directly opposite precepts; but the version given in the text, (which is that advocated by Chrysostom, Meyer and DeWette,) agrees best with the *Kai* and *also with the context.*"

Here, then, are two abolition witnesses, at least, who testify that your pillar of abolitionism is a strong column in supporting slavery.

Now, Doctor, I wish to call your attention to Paul's instruction to Titus. Chapter ii: 9–10: "Exhort servants (*douloi*) to be obedient unto their own masters, and to please them well in all things; not answering again; not purloining, but showing all good fidelity, that *they may adorn the doctrine of God our Savior in all things.*"

Titus, as you know, was a young minister, who was just entering upon the great work to which he was called. Paul was giving him a charge as to the matter and manner of his sermons and exhortations. Under the inspiration of the Holy Spirit, he tells him to "Exhort slaves to be obedient unto their own masters, and to please them well in all things." Now would it not have a better moral effect for you Northern preachers to study Paul to Timothy and Titus a little more, and the writings of Wayland, Channing, and the class who so unhesitatingly oppose the teachings of inspiration, a little less. Would it not be safe for religion to preach just what God says, or must we "add to and take from" the Divine law, in order to perfect it? Do you think, Doctor, you would be willing to teach to my slaves and others in the South the doctrines here taught? Would you be willing to tell them, as a minister of Christ, that they could not " adorn the doctrine of God our Savior," without obedience to their masters, and unless they "strove to please them well in all things? Could you do this, dare you do it, without coming in conflict with your abolition principles?"

The Doctor sat silently looking on the floor for a moment, and then raised his head as if he would speak. Slowly turning his gaze on Mr. Thompson, he finally replied: "Why not? I do not see that it materially interferes with my principles. It only teaches, as Dr. Wayland has said, patience, fidelity, meekness and charity—duties which are obligatory on christians towards all men, and of course towards masters. And I will also add with Dr. W. that it is to be observed that the Apostles are in every case careful not to utter a syllable by which they concede the right of the master, but they always add a reason for these precepts, viz: the relation in which the slave stands to Christ."

"It only teaches, you think," said Mr. T., "patience, meekness, fidelity and charity. But does it not teach *obedience* to masters? It says, 'obey your masters.' Does it mean something else? But the Apostles are careful 'not to utter a syllable by which they concede the right of the master.' Though it is sinful to disobey, so that by disobedience the servant reproaches the doctrine of God our Savior; and their obedience is of so great importance that the unerring wisdom of a holy God sent oft-repeated messages, injunctions and commandments requiring positive and uncomplaining obedience and acquiescence to the master's behests; yet ' not one syllable is uttered conceding the master's right.' I am reluctant, Doctor, to accuse you and Dr. Wayland of mental obtuseness, but really something is wrong. What is it? Where shall I find it? To what shall I attribute it?"

" The Unitarian says : ' The divinity of Christ is not taught in the Bible.' The Universalist says future punishment is not' to be found there; the Roman Catholic says there is a purgatory to be found there; the Jew says the Messiah has not yet come, that there is no *divine* evidence of it; the Atheist says there is no God. You say all these err, and I most cordially agree with you in that opinion, but the unreasonableness of these errors are not less apparent than that of yours. I will, however, call your attention to this fact again when we come to consider the Epistle of Paul to Philemon. But I cannot leave this subject, Doctor, without saying *that so completely antagonistic are the teachings of the Bible to those of abolitionists, that you cannot preach the whole gospel of the Son of God. Your pulpits will never again have a pure gospel—your hearers will never be blessed with ministerial instructions on the whole of revelation.* Mark what I have said, and let God and His word bear witness to its truth or falsehood."

"Well, husband, it is getting rather late," said Mrs. Thompson, "and I feel fatigued. If the company will excuse me as an invalid, I will retire."

"Certainly, wife, and we will suspend till to-morrow evening. Mr. Mortimer, you will return again."

"Thank you, sir. I desire to hear you through. I am very much interested."

Mr. Mortimer handed Nellie to the piano. All having retired, she felt less restraint in singing a song, at his request, which breathed the sentiments of a heart pure and loving for the one who stood by her side. At a late hour, Nellie retired to her room. She was really happy. No misgivings—no shrinking back. Here were two congenial hearts, united already in a bond of pure, unselfish love. No mercenary motives, no social policy, no worldly element had kindled the virtuous fire that burned within.

"And then that hope, that fiery hope,
Oh! she awak'd, such happy dreams,
And gave her soul such tempting scope
For all its dearest, fondest schemes."

## CHAPTER XIV.

*A Complete Endorsement of Slavery by Inspired Example and Precept—Dr. Barnes in Error.*

MR. MORTIMER returned to his home, entered his solitary room, stood before a large mirror surveying himself for a moment, soliloquising as follows: "Yes, I am the same identical man I was before, though really I have a different sensation about me. I wonder what Nellie, so pure, so angelic, could have promised herself in consenting to become Mrs. Mortimer? She could not have promised herself a handsome husband, or one very engaging in conversation, nor one very intelligent. Well, she loved me, and love "thinketh no evil and hideth a multitude of faults." I am a perfect blunderer, an unmitigated bungler. Did ever anybody feel so embarrassed and appear so awkward as I did? But it is all over, and I was successful, yes, successful in winning the noblest heart of the noblest, purest, most fascinating, graceful angel out of Paradise. Who so happy as I? None, positively none. But this is only the happiness of hope, of anticipation; how much more delightful will be the reality. Nothing shall ever prevent the realization of such a beautiful and bright prospect, unless heaven reverses our purpose; but heaven is propitious, and therefore the sequel will be a joyous reality.

> "Auspicious *hope*, in thy sweet garden grow
> Wreaths for each toil, a charm for every woe:
> Won by their sweets, in nature's languid hour,
> The way-worn pilgrim seeks thy summer bower;
> There, as the wild bee, murmurs on the wing,
> What peaceful dreams thy handmaid spirits bring!
> What viewless forms th' Æolian organs play,
> And sweep the furrowed lines of anxious thought away.
> Conjugal hope! thy passion kindling power,
> How bright, how strong in youth's untroubled hour."

"Massa, I 'clare you sleep all day, I 'bleave ef I let you," said aunt Hannah as she shook the bed whereon her young master was soundly sleeping. Mr. M. opened his eyes, and was surprised to find he had slept till past nine o'clock. Why did you not wake me earlier, aunt Hannah?" "Why, you see, master, you comes home late, and

I hates to 'sturb you 'fore you gits your nap out. I 'speck that young Miss over at Miss Thompson's, what keep you up so late, I never see you stay out so late 'fore. I 'spect some'n twixt you and that gal, aint they mas. You gwine to git us a mistis? I hope she be good, but I know you wouldn't git no other sort." Her Master assured her that Miss Nellie Norton was a perfect Helena in beauty, a Minerva in wisdom, a Dorcas in kindness, and an angel in everything else.

But the reader is anxious to listen again to the discussion of slavery. So we will pass over in silence all the joyous anticipations of the two young loving hearts in which they indulged during the day, as they contemplated meeting again at evening. It was an auspicious discussion for them; they prized it highly, and hoped it might continue till Nellie's visit South terminated.

Mr. M. entered just as the family were all seated in the parlor after tea.

"You stated last evening," said Mr. Thompson to Dr. Pratt, "that the Apostles are, in every case, careful not to utter a syllable by which they concede the *right* of the Master." This opinion you obtain from Dr. Wayland. I propose to prove, both by the example and precepts of Paul, that Dr. W. and yourself are in error. 1. *By Example.* Onesimus was the slave of Philemon, a wicked, discontented, unprofitable servant. He ran away from his master, and sought refuge in the city of Rome. By some means he attended the preaching of Paul there, and was converted. Now what was the Apostle to do? If Philemon had no right to Onesimus, then Paul was under no obligation whatever to send him back. If he sent him back, knowing the master had no right to him, he was guilty of a violation of the rights of a fellow-man; he *reduced* a free man to slavery; his pro slavery sentiments predominated over his sense of justice. He outraged the inalienable rights of a freeman. His master, perhaps, knew nothing of his whereabouts; it could have been well concealed from him. But Paul was a minister of Jesus Christ, and must "teach all things whatsoever Christ had commanded;" he must do right. The once unprofitable slave, now an humble convert to the teachings of the gospel, was penitent for his past transgressions. Being bought with the blood of Christ, he must now "glorify Him in His body and spirit." He now felt that his master had a *right* to his services. Both moved by the same purpose to obey God according to His word—the one to show his repentance by worthy fruits, and the other to seek to soften the pious heart of an outraged master. Paul tells Onesimus he must return to his master; the servant acquiesces cheerfully. Whereupon Paul writes this masterly epistle to Philemon, in which he "makes a strong, prudent, pathetic, affectionate appeal" to him in behalf of the slave, basing his plea upon the repentance of the fugitive.

Now Paul thought that the master did or did not have a right to this slave. If he did not, then he was no longer a slave, but a free man; but if he was free, then by sending him back Paul reduced a free man to slavery. This you cannot deny. But that an *inspired* Apostle would thus violate the obligations of man to man, we do not believe. Then it follows that the Apostle did, mentally at least, concede the right of the master; and animated by the manly purpose of observing and enforcing that right, he sends home the runaway. Then, sir, you have an apostolic example, which stands as a perpetual rebuke to all anti-fugitive slave laws, and one by which heaven daily speaks to you abolitionists in accents of truth, solemnly warning you against your errors. Paul's example is as good testimony as a precept; he stands forth as a witness whose faith is proved by his works."

"But, Mr. Thompson," said the Doctor, "You do not mean to say that Onesimus was certainly a slave? Dr. Barnes says: 'All that is necessarily implied in it is, that he was in some way the servant of Philemon, whether *hired* or *bought*, cannot be shown.' Moreover, Dr. Barnes says that the word *doulos* denotes servant of any kind, and it should never be assumed that those to whom it is applied were slaves."

"Do you endorse these views of Dr. Barnes, Mr. Pratt?"

"Why not? I am sure he is a very popular note writer and expositor, and this he could not be if he were not a scholar."

"Have you ever found a single place in Greek literature where *doulos* means anything but a slave? I appeal to you as a gentleman, and as a scholar, to answer me categorically, and, if you have, to produce the authority, and I will at least agree that Dr. Barnes may be excused for so absurd an assertion."

"I have not, sir; but Dr. Barnes may have seen what I have not. Our great and good men should never hazard opinions, for they might lead others astray. I therefore infer that Dr. Barnes said what he knew to be true."

"You may have noticed it, as a remarkable fact, at least I have, that Dr. Barnes makes no effort whatever to prove the truth of many of his reckless assertions. In this case, what I have said of him is verified. You must take his *ipse dixit*, because he is Dr. Barnes, the distinguished note writer of Philadelphia; it is too great a condescension on his part to stop to make proof; it is presumption in any one to call in question his learning and veracity. It seems that you have awarded to him all he asked; you have believed it because he asserted it, but Paul has declared the contrary, on slavery, to be true, in half a dozen places, but you do not believe him. Dr. Barnes is better authority with you than Paul. Great men, and sometimes a man who has some reputation for goodness, may become reckless in their declarations; especially is this true when endeavoring to build up a favorite dogma, and if they do not err intentionally they may in judgment, so that our only safety is to form our own conclusions from a fair, candid, impartial and thorough investigation for ourselves. All men are fallible in judgment, and all writers have some preconceived opinions which bias their minds, and lead far towards forming the conclusions at which they arrive. Dr. Barnes' assertion is simply the result of this preconceived prejudice against slavery. He, perhaps, believes what he says; he may be honest. I would not judge him harshly; but it is certainly strange that, coming in conflict with the almost universally expressed opinion of the learned and wise, he leaves his bare statement to stand solitary and alone, without a word of testimony to prove it. It is not strange that he did not produce proof; this he could not do, but it is strange that he made the declaration. But with abolitionists, he stands unimpeached and unimpeachable, and this is all he desires. Now let us put in proof the opinions of learned men, none of whom are slaveholders, but some, and perhaps most of whom, are or were abolitionists, and see whether Dr. Barnes' opinion of Onesimus are current among the learned. He says: "All that is necessarily implied in it (*doulos*) is that he was in some way the servant of Philemon, whether *hired or bought cannot be shown*." On the other hand, Coneybeare and Howson, Englishmen, and doubtless abolitionists, but as scholars say, "the fugitive Asiatic *slave* Onesimus." In speaking of the *right* of Philemon to his slave, they say of Paul: "He would not transgress the law, nor *violate the rights* of Philemon by acting in this matter without his consent."

Bloomfield says: "Slave Onesimus had absconded, and having come to Rome, had been converted to the christian faith and baptized by Paul. In order to repair the injury done to his master, he was anxious to return to him, and Paul wrote this letter to entreat Philemon to pardon his offense."

McKnight says: "Onesimus, a *slave*, having run away from his master," after his conversion "being sensible of his fault in running away, wished to repair that injury by returning to him."

Dr. Clark says: "Onesimus, a *slave*, had, on some pretence, run away from his master, &c."

Dr. Scott says: "Onesimus, a *slave* of Philemon, Paul judged it proper to send him back to his master."

These proofs are sufficient to show the presumption of Dr. Barnes in asserting as not true the universal opinion of great and learned men, without giving his reasons.

Now, sir, there is another fact which I wish you to notice in this epistle, which contrasts as strangely with the feelings and customs of the North as do the Bible and abolitionism. I refer to the tender affection and christian fellowship expressed by the Apostle for slaveholders. I say this stands in singular contrast with Northern feeling and custom. Let me proceed, very briefly, to exhibit this difference.

Your Dr. Barnes, in his "Church and Slavery," says: "Is the *voluntary burning of a few widows* on the funeral pile, either as an obstruction to the gospel, or as *actual wrong*, to be compared with this (slavery) system? Is the swinging on hooks, or the painful torture of the body in Hindoo devotion, an obstruction to the gospel at all to be compared in extent, or *in enormity*, with American slavery?"

Christ says of a slaveholder: "I have not found so great faith, no not in Israel."

Paul, under inspiration, says of a slaveholder: "Hearing of thy love and faith which thou hast towards the Lord and toward all saints, that the communication of thy faith may be effectual by the acknowledging of every good thing which is in you in Christ Jesus. For we have great joy and consolation in thy love, because the bowels of the saints are refreshed by the brother."

Here is a brief contrast; it might be greatly enlarged, but this is enough for the present.

I have frequently alluded to the infidel tendencies of abolitionism. I will quote only two extracts in confirmation of what I have said. Dr. Barnes, in the work just alluded to, says: "We must give up the point that the New Testament defends slavery, or we must give up a very large—and an increasingly large—portion of the people of this land to infidelity; for they neither can, nor *ought* to be convinced that a book which sanctions slavery is from God. I believe that this must and *should be so*, and that there are great principles in 'our nature, as God has made us, which can never be set aside by *any authority* of a *pretended revelation;* and that if a book professing to be a revelation from God, by any fair interpretation, defended slavery, or placed it on the same basis as the relation of husband and wife, parent and child, guardian and ward, such a book neither *ought* to be, nor could be, received by mankind as a divine revelation." How strangely this sounds from the lips of one who has written an exposition of these words: "Let as many servants (slaves) as are under the yoke count their own masters worthy of all honor, that the name of God and his doctrine be not blasphemed." This is not the *germ* of infidelity; it is its first fruit. It is not distilled as the gentle dew; it is a bold stream from an impure fountain. It is not a hasty expression uttered from the impulse of the moment by an excited debatant; it is the calm, deliberate language of an aged man *in his study,* writing on serious and solemn subjects. *It is the funeral knell of a pure christianity in abolitiondom.*

My other extract shall be from Mr. Wright, taken from his speech before the anti-slavery society in Boston in 1850. It should be borne in mind that his auditory was composed largely of professed christians, whose sentiments, we may presume, were reflected by the speaker. Here is a specimen of Mr. Wright's piety: " Down with your Bible! down with your political parties! down, down with your God that sanctions slavery! The God of Moses Stewart, the Andover God, the God of Wm. H. Rogers, which is worshipped in the Winter street Church, is a monster, composed of oppression, fraud, injustice, pollution, and every crime in the shape of slavery. To such a God, I am an Atheist!"

You do not fail to discover in both these extracts that their authors would not hesitate to give up the Bible for abolitionism. The decision is already made and proclaimed. The infidelity is deep rooted and incurable. Mr. Wright, I presume, would be glad of an excuse to abandon the Bible, and to blaspheme its blessed Author. Dr. Barnes has some pride of opinion on the subject, having been committed to its advocacy previous to the present excited state of the controversy on slavery; he is, however, evidently preparing the way for a public abandonment of the Divine Revelation, if it can be proven to teach slavery.

" Such leaders—and these are *representative characters*—will soon carry a people into the deepest, darkest depths of infidelity. Its black shades are already gathering around you; its midnight darkness will soon enshroud you. This angel of the world of woe, this destroying enemy of individuals and nations, that inaugurated the reign of terror and baptized France in a river of blood, is making fearful inroads at the North. Having stolen the livery of heaven, he has ascended your pulpits; he occupies your theological chairs; he has gained high official positions in your Churches; he teaches in your Sabbath Schools; he prints books and newspapers, professedly religious; in a word, he occupies all the positions of moral influence in your country, and he touches nothing that does not retain his baneful sentiments. He has not yet avowed his rejection of the Bible; he will not, he dare not at once and suddenly unmask himself; it would frustrate his designs. He begins with a denial that it teaches certain truths which are patent to the most superficial reader, and then asserts that if it did teach these obvious truths, it would, and ought to be, rejected. This subtle form of infidelity is the general helper of the clergy. He furnishes them with pathetic appeals founded on fiction, but addressed as truth to human sympathies. He casts the drapery of eloquence and plausibility over the deformity of his own principles to conceal them from the public eye. ' Whose coming is after the working of Satan, with all power and signs, and lying wonders, and with all deceivableness of unrighteousness in them that perish, because they received not the love of the truth.'

"You may think this is gasconade, but I assure you, Doctor, the subject is one of deep and momentous seriousness. New England gave me birth; around its scenes, hallowed in memory, all my early recollections cling with undying fondness. It is the home of many loved ones, who are bone of my bone and flesh of my flesh. I could never boast over the moral or religious fall of any people, much less the land of my fathers. I say with painful apprehensions and unfeigned sorrow, that without a reform in the views of your leading men, you are as certain to become an infidel people as that Theodore Parker has rejected the Bible. The same reason that led him into infidelity, will make the rest so, viz: because the Bible is a proslavery book.

"But I have suffered myself to be so absorbed in the thought of your danger, that I had almost forgotten to return to the *contrast*.

"Northern Christians and Churches have declared a non-fellowship with Southern Christians and Churches, on account of slavery. Our most able and godly men sometimes spend their summers in New England. They are almost universally excluded from your pulpits and communion tables. I do not complain of it, because I think it would be esteemed as a special benefit, privilege, or comfort, to commune with a semi-infidel people, but simply to show how different your treatment of slave-holders is to that which they received at the hands of the Apostles.

"The Apostles received slave-holders into the Churches. They gave them special instruction how to treat their slaves, but uttered not a single word about emancipating them. Paul says to the slave-holders—who were members of the Churches—in Ephesus: 'And ye masters, do the same thing unto them, forbearing, threatening, knowing that your master also is in heaven; neither is there respect of persons with him.' Now, who were these masters? Turn to the address in the Epistle i: 1. 'To the *saints* which are at Ephesus, and to the *faithful* in Christ Jesus.' In verse 15, the Apostle says: 'After I heard of your faith in the Lord Jesus, and love unto all the saints.' In verse 19 of vi. chapter he requests them to pray for him. Note how affectionately Paul writes to these slaveholders, how much love he bears to them, how much Christian confidence and fellowship he expresses for them, when he says: 'Pray for me.' In the 4th chapter he gives much advice, rebukes many sins, and warns them against many evils which he mentions, but never once alludes to slavery as one of them. I here repeat, what I have before said, that in the long catalogue of sins denounced in the whole Bible, slavery is not mentioned among them once. *I challenge the Abolition fraternity of the world* to show one single sentiment in this Divine Book of morals and religion, given to us by a sinless and infinitely wise, just and holy God, which by any fair and legitimate construction, can be made to condemn slavery. 'It is God that justifieth, who is he that condemneth?' Again, in speaking of the spiritual union which existed between these slave-holding Christians and their Savior, Paul says: 'We (i. e., himself and they) are members of his body, of his flesh, and of his bones.' In the days of Paul, slave-holders were united to Christ, but in Dr. Barnes' day they are too bad to be members of his mystical body. Then they were 'beloved in Christ Jesus.' Now they are worse than the heathen who 'burn the widows on the funeral pile.' Then they were 'dearly beloved.' Now they are excluded as unworthy of a place in the catalogue with those cruel barbarians who, in their idolatrous devotion, 'swing on hooks,' or inflict other 'painful torture on the body.' Then they were 'fellow-helpers of the truth.' Now it is asked, 'What would be the advantage of substituting a religion where such views and purposes (as slave-holders entertain) are avowed, for those systems which now actually prevail in heathen lands.' Then slave-holders were entrusted with high official positions in the Churches. Now, Dr. Barnes says 'the duellist, the horse-racer, the bull-fighter, should be left unrebuked till slavery is anathematized! Christ said: 'I have not found so great faith, no not in Israel,' as was exercised by the centurian slaveholder. Now, Dr. B. says 'he is guilty of an enormous system of injustice and wrong.' Now if Christ and Paul recognized them by such endearing appellations; if they committed such high and holy trusts to them; if the Apostle accepted them as 'co-laborers, fellow-helpers,' why should not you? Have you discovered wrong which Jesus overlooked, or are you purer, better, more "separate, from sinners" than He? Is slavery more sinful now than then; has moral odium attached to it since those days? If so, by whom? From what source do you derive your information? What book have you accepted as your code of morals and religion on this subject? Have you, like Joe Smith, found a new revelation, which says that slavery is wrong, the 'sum of all villainies,' that you must withdraw from slaveholders all religious and moral fellowship, and denounce them and the institution? Oh yes; you have found the revelation! Not under a rock, where Joe Smith found his, but it came like Minerva; it was the offspring of a brain, not that of Jupiter, no nor of any of the gods, but of those 'whom the gods would destroy.' Were Paul here, he would not accept it as coming from above; he would call it 'another gospel,' and say of him that preached it, 'let him be accursed.'

"Paul, in writing to his two young brethren in the ministry, is not silent on the all-absorbing topic of slavery. But what are his instructions to them? Did he say exclude slave-holders from any participation in the privileges of the Churches? Did he tell them to have no fellowship with such? This would have been your advice; Dr. Barnes would have said so. But Paul did not; for this would have condemned his own practice. His position is just the reverse of yours and Dr. B.'s. He advises slave-holders to 'withdraw from' (have no fellowship with) Abolitionists. Do you doubt it? Do you demand proof? Then you shall have it? He instructs Timothy as follows: 'Let as many slaves (douloi) as are under the yoke, count their own masters worthy of all honor, that the name of God and his doctrine be not blasphemed: and they that have believing masters, let them not despise them, because they are brethren, but rather do them service, because they are faithful and beloved, partakers of the benefit. *These things teach and exhort. If any man teach* OTHERWISE, *and* consent not to wholesome words, even the words of our Lord Jesus Christ, and to the doctrine which is according to godliness. . . . *From such withdraw thyself.*" No sane man can give any other construction to this scripture, than that it *teaches slaves to obey their masters as a religious duty.* To enforce this duty by 'teaching and exhortation' is to 'consent to sound words, even the words of the Lord Jesus Christ, and to the doctrine which is according to godliness.' But who ' teaches otherwise'? You, Dr. Pratt, and your co-laborers, who are endeavoring to inculcate a wide-spread spirit of insubordination among the slaves of the South. That you do not, that you cannot, that you *dare* not, encourage slaves to obey their masters from obligations of moral right, is too apparent to require proof. An Abolitionist can no more do so, than an Atheist can preach the gospel of Christ. You 'consent' to it? No, sir, you *oppose* it with all your mental and moral influence. Then what is our duty? What does God *require* of us? He gives us no discretion in the matter; it is a positive injunction and imperative command, '*From such withdraw thyself.*' This command is from the ' King Eternal, Immortal, Invisible, the only wise God.' Can we, dare we disobey Him? We have dared to do so; too long have we 'leaned to mercy's side; ' and as a punishment for it, Providence has brought us into reproach among you, that we may be *driven* out, as were the Israelites from Egypt. Had we effected a separation, moral, religious, social and political, twenty-five years ago, the South would now have been the greatest nation in the world, as it is destined to be at some future day, if we are but true to our God and to ourselves. When the last link that binds us to the North is broken, when the last Southern star shall be plucked from your national galaxy, and slavery and the South left to the destiny marked out for them by the Hand which guides the universe, her career, under Providence, will revolutionize the morbid sensibilities of the world on the moral validity of slavery. The world is wrong, and the South must set it right; the world is in error, and is dependent upon the South for ' the truth, the whole truth,' unmixed with the alloy of mistaken and misguided humanity. When left to herself, her prosperity will be without a parallel. Her moral and religious, her social and educational interest will outstrip, in their advancement, any national progress known to history. She possesses greater undeveloped resources of mind and material than any nation upon earth. The development of these elements of a great nation has been kept in abeyance by our continued union with a people to whom we have tamely yielded the monopolies of the government.

"You have cried 'give, give,' and we have given, till, as a child spoiled by over-indulgence, there is no possibility of satisfying you. You have organized a powerful system of opposition to our peculiar institution, and many among us have timidly asked if we were not wrong, while they hesitated to go forward. A few of our politicians have pursued a temporizing policy. The same spirit has naturally affected the educational and religious interests of the South. But few have had the courage and disposition to go to the Fountain of Light—but few have searched the scriptures. The masses did not know of the rich legacy bequeathed to us in our Father's will, and therefore but few have had the moral fortitude to come out boldly against the reiterated sentence of condemnation passed upon us by the civilized world, and to plant themselves upon the Divine foundation and *justify themselves*. We have stultified ourselves by the vacillating policy of the past. Henceforth we will repel, with the sword of *Truth*, every attack made upon us by Abolitionists. Sufficiently long have you fettered us, and hindered our national progress. The deceitful Delilah has betrayed her Samson, till his spirit is aroused—he will arise in his might and shake himself; then may the Philistines begin to tremble. But we can never prosper without the Divine benediction; this we cannot obtain till we obey the inspired injunction, 'From such withdraw thyself.' This we will soon do. Like Pharaoh, you are doubling our tasks and increasing our burdens; you are galling our necks under the yoke. We have borne the burdens patiently; we have seemed to love our bondage; you thought we did, or that our tame, unmanly spirits would continue to bear as the ox the chafing load. But not so; soon will the cry go up to heaven, and the God of Moses will bring deliverance in that day. Pharaoh had his Moses, George the Third his Washington, and those who would attempt to interpose between God and the fulfilment of his command, when we shall 'withdraw from you,' 'may profit by their example.' It will be done; it *must* be done, for heaven has decreed it. God has commanded, who shall annul?

How strange, then, that abolitionists should say to slaveholders, "you shall not preach in our pulpits, nor sit at our communion tables; we have no fraternity with you, stand aside, we are holier than thou!" Why, sir, you are reversing heaven's order. Your practice and presumption, pardon the expression, in this respect, as in many others, have placed you quite in advance of God's instruction. You have done a work of supererogation. Who hath required this at your hands? But it is well. God intended there should be no confraternity between us, and as we would not sever the tie, He has permitted you to do it. The disciples could never have crucified their Lord, that they might obtain life through His death. His enemies were to do this. The generous South felt it was selfish to sunder a bond which would benefit them, but ruin you. You have spared them this pain. We have obeyed you when you said, "*stand aside*, for we are holier than thou."

"We are not alone in this view," said Mr. Pratt. "The civilized world is opposed to you. The good and wise of every land are against slavery and the South. England, France, Germany, and indeed wherever letters, religion and civilization have gone, slavery has been frowned upon. You stand isolated and alone, with the world against you. Not a voice is raised in your behalf, save by Spain. And yet you say we are wrong and you are right. Can all the rest of mankind be wrong and you alone right? Can so many good and wise men of earth be blind to the truth? Do not people possess sufficient penetration and research to discover truth, but you slaveholders? The proposition is preposterous and presumptuous. But you are too bigoted in your own views, and too deeply *interested* to listen to reason. The universal voice of mankind is enough, it would seem, to convince you. But you say, that voice is untrue. How, then, can we convince you? 'In the multitude of counselors there is safety,' says Solomon. We present a multitude, indeed; but you refuse to hear us. I will therefore simply announce to you a fact, which you are at liberty to believe or not as you may see proper; it is this: *Slavery is doomed*. Sooner or later it will be numbered among the extinct relics of a past barbarism. It cannot always stand before the intelligent and moral frown of christendom."

"Slavery," said Mr. Thompson, "is not the only subject upon which majorities agree in their opposition. England and France, and most of the nations of the world, agree most heartily in opposing republics. Are they, therefore, wrong? An overwhelming majority of the so-called christian world is opposed to protestantism; is it therefore wrong? Nine-tenths of the world is opposed to christianity; but is christianity therefore wrong? The *multitude* cried, away with Him, crucify Him, crucify Him! Were the multitude therefore right, and ought Christ to have been crucified simply because they all united in this cry? Bring the religion of the Bible, which is the foundation of the righteous, to your test. There are eleven or twelve hundred million inhabitants on the earth; out of that number there are not more than twelve million of christians, or one in one hundred who receive the Bible as a revelation from God. Is the Bible therefore a fable because not accepted by so large a majority? There are seven or eight hundred million of idolaters in the world, largely more than half the human family; is idolatry therefore right? In our own land, where we boast of our civilization and christianity, there are not more than one in eight who practically accepts the Bible; then is that *one* wrong because the eight are practically against him? The multitude is not to be implicitly trusted on moral subjects; their examinations and investigations are generally very superficial, and their conclusions often erroneous. In truths revealed by heaven, every man is responsible for the formation of his own opinion, unbiased by what others may say or believe. "To the law and to the testimony" should and must be the motto of every mind. The opinions of the North, of England, France and Germany in opposition to slavery, do not alter or effect the teachings of the Bible on this subject. The Bible is a pro-slavery Bible, and God is a pro-slavery God, notwithstanding all you say to the contrary. We judge for ourselves—it is our duty to do so—we are responsible to God for the opinions we thus form, and before high heaven we are solemnly and conscientiously convinced that slavery is of Him, and therefore right. If right, it is not doomed; for if God be for us, who can be against us? Its battles are God's, its victories will be His, for He will defend it from all the rude attacks of infidelity, whether from pseudo-christians or outspoken infidels. The battle is not to the strong; victory belongeth unto the Lord. But if you are so confident the institution will be destroyed, why not take the advice which the learned Gamaliel gave to the council of the Jews? "Refrain from these men, and let them alone; for if this counsel or this work be of men, it will come to nought; but if it be of God, ye cannot overthrow it, lest haply ye be found to fight against God:" You may be convinced once for all, Doctor, that "railing accusations," abusive words, bitter denunciations, vain glorious boasting, and all that class of weapons, so popular at the North, will never affect the Southern mind, unless it be to awaken contempt for those who attempt to carry their point by such puerile methods. You might shame a child out of doing what was right, if you were so disposed; sarcasm and ridicule may so affect a simple minded person that he may swerve from a good purpose, but you must understand that we are neither children nor simpletons, but men who know the right and dare practice and defend it, indifferent as to the cost or consequences. David says: "When mine enemies and my foes came upon me to eat up my flesh, they stumbled and fell." So it will be with the enemies of slavery. Take one example across the water. You are aware that Bishop Colenso, of the English Episcopal Church, has issued a volume denying the authenticity and inspiration of the Pentateuch. In the preface to that treatise he acquaints us with the steps by which he was led to embrace the skeptical views embodied in it. Not the least of these steps was the fact that he found Hebrew slavery inconsistent with *his sense of justice*. There is nothing surprising in this. The Scriptures give no countenance to the humanitarian views of the age; and where these tendencies are mistaken for "instincts of piety," the Scriptures must be repudiated. When anti-slaveryism looks at Judea in the times of the fathers, with the eyes which have so long scowled on the South in our times, the result is avowed (or at least palpable) infidelity. The infidelity does not then come into being; it simply drops its mask.

The downfall of a people may be dated from the time they repudiate *truth*; this you have done; your blows against the South will therefore be like those of a man growing weaker every moment of his conflict, by the loss of blood, until his strokes are scarcely felt. On the other hand, "righteousness exalteth a nation," as we adhere to truth our strength will increase, and we will become stronger and stronger in the never-failing power of the Omnipotent One. Slavery is "doomed" whenever the Bible is destroyed and God dethroned, not before, for here is his foundation. But I had like to have forgotten to give you the inspired *precept* recognizing the master's right in his slave. But this I must postpone for the present, for I see Nellie is gaping. To-morrow is Christmas. I believe, Doctor, you have been invited by my servants to preach to them in the afternoon. Mr. Mortimer, you must come over and take a Christmas dinner with us. The fatted calf has been killed, and we are going to have a general feast. The unusual industry and fidelity of my servants entitle them to an extra entertainment, which I have promised to them." Mr. Mortimer promised to return again to-morrow, and the party all retired to their rooms.

## CHAPTER XV.

*What Dr. Pratt Heard and his Reflections thereon—Christmas Presents—Negro Plays—Miss Murray's Sentiments—Dr. Pratt's Sermon and its Consequences.*

After retiring to his room, Dr. Pratt listened for some time to the hymns and prayers of the servants, who had congregated for that purpose at one of their houses. There was a pathos and fervor about these exercises that were to the Doctor very remarkable, and what seemed strange to their distant listener was, that they did not grow weary in well doing; for at midnight, when all the family were sleeping soundly, these pious negro chants broke upon the still air with unwonted melody and freshness. "And these are the oppressed and down-trodden, the miserable and hopeless slaves of Southern tyranny," soliloquised the Doctor as he closed his window to the sound. That there is piety and fervor of heart in these negroes, even a sceptic could not deny. To say they are not happy would be a positive slander upon them. How favorably their condition contrasts with their wild, uncivilized brethren across the water! What a blessing that they were taught a Savior's name! But if they are so pious and happy in slavery, how much more so would they be if in the enjoyment of freedom! Surely, liberty would be a great blessing to them! I wonder my excellent christian host has never been moved to the noble deed of emancipation by this thought; for I really believe if he saw as I do, the benefit of freedom to his slaves, no motive of selfishness would prevent their liberation from bondage. He says, and I believe thinks, that they would be less pious and happy if free. This cannot be true, because it is unnatural. And still I can safely admit, here in my own dark chamber, that I have never known nor heard of such piety and uniform religion among them at the North or anywhere else in a state of freedom. This is strange and unaccountable to me. I do not, I cannot comprehend it. Why is it? Is Thompson correct when he says slavery is their normal state? Does God, on that account, make even the hated institution a blessing to them? But these are Southern thoughts, and shall find no lodgment in my heart. Slavery is wrong, even if the negro is better and happier in its chains. So the Doctor shut out from his mind the light which was beginning to dawn upon it, and quieted his conscience which began to be somewhat awakened, by courting the embrace of the "sweet restorer," till he could rally his sterner will, at a time when the evidences of the happiness of slaves had somewhat faded from his memory.

As the first rays of the gray morning arose to gild the eastern sky, a servant entered with soft and noiseless tread to kindle a fire in the bed chamber of Mr. Thompson. The master had been lying for some time in pious meditation, prayer and thanksgivings for the blessings of a merciful Providence during the past year, and for the hope of salvation through that Redeemer, the anniversary of whose natal day was once more dawning upon the world. He heard many footsteps around the house, and occasionally low and indistinct talking in the yard. He understood its meaning. He arose and dressed himself hurriedly, and gently shaking his wife, took down a key and left the room. As he made his appearance, fifty voices cried out all at once, "Christmas gift! Christmas gift! Christmas gift!" till the welkin was made to ring with the enthusiasm of the clamor. All in the house were aroused. Dr. Pratt shuddered and drew the cover tightly over his head, and for a few moments indulged horrible thoughts of insurrection, fire and blood; but all being quiet, he ventured to rise, and gently pushing open a blind saw the yard literally covered with negroes, little and big, old and young, male and female, and Mr. Thompson standing in their midst. What Mr. T. was saying the Doctor could not distinctly hear, but he soon saw a separation take place; the females retreated toward the house, while Mr. T. with a lighted candle advanced to a small store house in the yard. A box was drawn to the door and opened, and Dr. P. soon divined the object of this strange gathering of the negroes. Mr. Thompson held up a coat, and looking at the mark, called out a name, when the one called advanced, hat in hand, and bowing and scraping his foot, received with a glad smile and a grateful "thanky, master," the Christmas gift. This was repeated till every one had received a coat, or pair of pants, or hat, or some other Sunday garment, which filled up the measure of his desire. At the house a similar scene was transpiring. Mrs. Thompson was surrounded by the female servants, each of whom received some highly gratifying testimonial of the kind and generous heart of the mistress. All returned to their homes, well satisfied, cheerful and happy, each esteeming his own present the best; it was to them indeed a "Merry Christmas."

About ten o'clock Dr. Pratt proposed to Nellie to walk over to the negro cabins to see how the colored people spend Christmas.

Alice, who was familiar with all the scenes of country negro life, accompanied them. Approaching their cabins, they saw a large number in the yard, dressed in their most gaudy Christmas attire. Their movements were as unique as was the head dress of a few of them. They were drawn up in two parallel lines, about ten feet apart. One stood outside the ranks, who proved to be the leader of the play, and therefore had no connection with the "rank and file." In military parlance, he was the commandant of the post. His orders were issued in verse adapted to a measure, and melody with which all were equally familiar, but they were not the less implicitly obeyed because sung instead of spoken. The chorus, which was sung by all, was the signal for action. The movement consisted in locking arms, swinging round and moving to the foot of the line, all in time to the music. If the reader desires a better description, he can just witness the play called Twistification by our genteel young ladies and gentlemen, and with the exception of the song, which accompanies all the holiday pleasures of the negro, they will see the exact counterpart of what Dr. Pratt witnessed. Several other performances, bearing some similarity, but affording to the negroes a pleasing variety, were witnessed by the spectators. The Doctor was disgusted at these "crude poems," as he termed them, and at the child-like simplicity of the grown colored people. He was not aware that in many instances these "crude poems" were improvised, and that the refrain alone was supposed to be known by the audience. To Nellie there was something so novel, that even the simplicity possessed the power to fascinate and attract her for an hour and a half, in spite of all the Doctor's importunities to leave. "Just look there, Doctor," she said. " See those happy faces, hear those cheerful voices, Mr. Pratt; these are the oppressed, down-trodden and miserable slaves, who groan beneath the burdens of involuntary servitude, and writhe in the galling chains of vassalage. Though they could not help their condition if they would, yet, after all, I believe they are voluntary slaves. What better freedom do they want than this? to what good purpose would they apply it?

From the joyous faces, the glee and mirth, the fun and frolic, the unrestrained hilarity of these negroes, I verily believe the language of every heart is:

> "I was born for rejoicing, a 'summer child' truly,
> And kindred I claim with each wild joyous thing;
> The light frolic breeze, or the streamlet unruly,
> Or a cloud at its play, or a bird on the wing.'

Now, Mr. Pratt, don't you think they are happy? Are you not most agreeably surprised in this respect, and do you not believe if all our Northern people were to see just what you and I see, they would be greatly softened in the bitterness of their opposition toward slavery? Don't answer me as an abolitionist in controversy with my uncle, but as my friend, expressing simply the truth."

"My opposition to slavery takes higher ground than simply the condition of the enslaved. The universal equality of the race, as taught in the Declaration of Independence, is its basis."

"I did hope," replied Nellie, "to have received a direct answer to my question." The Doctor was silent, and she said no more. The Doctor seemed sour and ill-tempered as they walked away, while Nellie and Alice chatted gleefully of the odd and ridiculous songs to which they had just listened. They both agreed that "Jinin the ingine" deserved a place in the public prints, provided its original composer could be found and his name accompany it. He certainly deserved a niche in the temple of fame. Pity a poet of such original genius should pass away unknown to the literary world. Would not N. P. Willis embalm his name in the essence of poetry, or Mr. Thackary immortalize it by criticism, or Dickens make him hero of some charming tale? The girls thus amused themselves till their morose escort had well nigh dispersed the mental cloud that obscured his social sun. Feeling no disposition to awaken a train of unpleasant reflections, further to disquiet the Doctor's thoughts, and knowing it was about the time Mr. Mortimer was expected, Nellie proposed a return to the house. She found Mr. M. seated in the parlor, with Miss Murray's travels in his hand, conversing with Mrs Norton, who now looked with peculiar interest upon her future son-in-law. On the arrival of Nellie, her mother made an excuse and left the room. The two loving hearts being all alone, one would suppose the hour to have been given to expressions of the tender affections of the heart, or the blissful lot which they both anticipated in the future; but Nellie's mind was *enthused* with the subject of slavery. Having spent the early morning in reading Miss Murray, and having just witnessed some new evidences of negro happiness, she was much disposed to speak from the abundance of her heart on this new subject.

"Mr. Mortimer, did you ever read Miss Murray's travels in the United States? I see you have it in your hand."

"I have not had the pleasure of seeing it before."

"Would you be entertained by a few extracts from it, giving her views on slavery?"

"Certainly. I would be very glad to hear them."

Nellie opened at page 206 and read: "Slavery may not be the best system of labor, but it is the best for the negro in this country. If it be true of the English soldier and sailor, that his condition has been ameliorated in the last fifty years, it is quite as true of the negro. Slavery is that system which exchanges subsistence for work, which secures a life maintenance from the master to the slave, and gives a life labor from the slave to the master. Slavery is the negro system of labor; he is lazy and improvident; slavery makes him work, and insures him a home, food and clothing; it provides for sickness, infancy and old age, allows no tampering or skulking, and knows no pauperism. All cruelty is an abuse; does not belong to the institution; is contrary to law; may be punished, prevented, and removed. If slavery is subject to abuses, it has its compensations also: it establishes permanent and therefore kind relations between labor and capital. It does away with what Stewart Mill calls 'the widening and embittering feud between labor and capital.' It draws close the relation between master and servant; it is not an engagement for days or weeks, but for life. The most wretched feature in hiring labor is the isolated, miserable creature who has no home, no work, no food, and in whom no one is particularly interested. Slavery does for the negro what European schemers in vain attempt to do for the hireling. On every plantation the master is a poor law commissioner, to provide food, clothing, medicine, houses, for his people. He is a police officer to prevent idleness, drunkenness, theft, or disorder; there is, therefore, no starvation among slaves, and comparatively few crimes. The poet tells us there are worse things in the world than hard labor, 'Withouten that would come a heavier bale'; and so there are worse things for the negro than slavery in a Christian land. Archbishop Hughes, in his visit to Cuba, asked Africans if they wished to return to their native country; the answer was always *No*. If the negro is happier here than in his own land, can we say that slavery is an evil to him? Slaves and masters do not quarrel with their circumstances; is it not hard that the stranger should interfere to make both discontented? All Christians believe that the affairs of this world are directed by God for wise and good purposes. The arrival of the negro in America makes no exception to that rule. . . . . There has been malignant abuse lavished upon the slave holders of America by writers in this country and in England; they consider abuses as the necessary condition of slavery, and a cruel master as its fair representation. They have no knowledge of the thing abused—they substitute an ideal for a reality. They have shown as little regard for truth and common sense as if we were to gather up all the atrocities committed in Great Britain by husbands and wives, parents and children, masters and servants, and denounce these several relations in life in consequence of these abuses. . . . To attempt to establish the hiring plan with Africans is as wise as to attempt to establish the constitutional government of England in Ashantee or Dahomey. Carlyle says the world will not permit Cuffy to lie on his back and eat pumpkins forever, in a country intended by Providence to produce coffee, sugar and spices for the use of all mankind, and that he must one of these days resume his work for Brother Jonathan or some other master. The blacks in Hayti have only changed masters; they are the slaves of a black chief as in Africa. The pagan mummeries have been resumed—they are engaged in petty wars instead of peaceful labors. The Emperor has his standing army, and is anxious, as more important potentates, to employ it in the legitimate business of cutting throats. The African cannot originate a civilization of his own; from the slave civilized and instructed by slavery can any regeneration of the African continent be alone looked for.'"

On page 212, Miss M. says: "I find that the term 'slave' is rarely made use of in the South. The blacks are called 'our servants,' or more commonly 'our people.' We must remember that when slaves are to be disposed of, people in this country do not consider they are literally buying *men*, but *services*, and what we hear of are the abuses, not the laws of the system. Should a master ill treat a slave, the law protects the latter; and I am inclined to believe cases of such treatment are rare. If a slave violates the law, a judge sends to his master, and says, 'This is your servant, if you do not punish him, I must.' Of course the culprit much prefers to be corrected by his own master, by whom all extenuating circumstances are understood, and allowed for; and he is usually left in his hands."

Again, on page 215, she says: "I have observed a noble, generous, gentlemanly spirit in this part of the Union. I feel assured that if the Southern proprietors, as a class, had found reason to believe that the institution of slavery was prejudicial either to the Christian or temporal interests of the blacks, they have chivalry enough in their composition to have cast aside mere motives of private interest; but they knew, as we did not know—that was the difference. They have a right to accuse us of ignorance and conceit, and they are more forbearing than we had any claim to expect."

On page 219, she says: "I now see the great error we have committed is in assuming that the African race is equal in capacity with the European, and that under similar circumstances it is capable of equal, moral, and intellectual culture. The history of Egypt, of Rome, of the English, French and Spanish Colonies, and the experience of American slavery, prove the reverse. No separate African civilization has sprung up from centuries of contact. St. Domingo has relapsed into barbarism, except in the case of some of the towns. The other emancipated colonies, not excepting Jamaica, are retrograding fast in the face of a white population, and notwithstanding Government influence: in the United States, spite of more than a hundred years of white association, though they have been made rather superior to their brethren in Africa in intellect and moral character, they remain—and ever will remain—inferior to the whites. I believe—and must not hesitate to express my belief—the negro race is incapable of self-government; and I suspect its present condition in the United States is practically the best that the character of the negro admits of. It is for their happiness and interest to remain in tutelage. . . . . The most practical mode of improving a semi-barbarous race is to place it in the proportion of one to two in the midst of a civilized people. The system of slavery has been blamed for the ignorance and vices of the Africans. Are they less ignorant or more virtuous where slavery does not exist?"

On page 221, writing from a plantation in South-eastern Georgia, she says: "I forgot to mention that there are from three to four hundred negroes on this estate. Mr. and Mrs. Cooper have no white servants; their family consists of six sons and two daughters. I should not like to inhabit a lonely part of Ireland, or even Scotland, surrounded only by three hundred Celts. I believe there is not a soldier or policeman nearer than Savannah, a distance of sixty miles. Surely, this speaks volumes for the contentment of the slave population. When I think of the misery and barbarism of the peasantry of Kentail, and other parts of Scotland, (putting aside that of Ireland), and look at the people here, it is hardly possible not to blush at the recollection of all the hard words I have heard applied to the slave-holder of the South. Why, the very pig-sties of the negroes are better than some Celtic hovels I have seen. Mr.

Cooper is under some difficulty about a negro family he took in trust to manumit from the produce of their own labor. The people are. averse to being freed, and especially to being sent to Africa. It certainly seems a cruelty to force them to accept that which they consider no boon. I believe this is a dilemma by no means rare."

"Now, sir, what do you say of Miss Murray?"

"That she is a lady of accurate observation, sound judgment, great moral honesty, and what is better, if possible, a truthful woman. I am much obliged to you for the extracts, they are well expressed, and contain facts which her people ought to consider and accept. She has done what but few foreigners have ever done before—given justice to the South and to slave-holders."

As Mr. Mortimer was about changing the subject to one more congenial with his heart, and one, too, not at all objectionable to Nellie, they were summoned to the dining-room to partake of the sumptuous and elegant Christmas dinner prepared by Mrs. Thompson.

Dinner being over, at the appointed hour, Dr. Pratt, with the family, repaired to the Church to fulfil his engagement in preaching to the colored people. Nellie and Mr. Mortimer alone preferred to remain at home. The Doctor's text may be read in Luke ii: 10–11, Behold I bring you good tidings of great joy, which shall be to all people. For unto you is born this day, in the city of David, a Savior which is Christ the Lord. His theme was this: "Salvation through Christ Jesus, to a fallen world, is good tidings of great joy. He first showed the need of a Savior. Man was guilty, and therefore justly condemned by the righteous law. 2d. That he was unable by any act of his own to free himself from that condemnation. 3d. That Christ's atonement accomplished what neither man nor the law could do, for He was made unto us wisdom and righteousness and sanctification and redemption. The propositions were logically proven, and the sermon well elaborated, and to a more cultivated auditory would perhaps have had a fine effect, but the preacher possessed no powers of adaptation to the uneducated persons before him. Very many of them, however, knew Christ experimentally, and felt his love soothe their hearts like an emollient to an aching wound. They knew he was talking about Jesus, and though his thoughts were too profound, his reasonings too abstruse, and many of his words were as Hebrew to them, yet they had heard the text and knew what it meant, and like the deaf woman who always would go to church, they "had a great many sweet and happy thoughts about the Saviour." So, upon the whole, they enjoyed the meeting very much.

It was understood that the Doctor was going to leave them in a few days to return to his Northern home. So "Uncle Jesse," when called on to close the meeting, proposed that the "brother come down from the pulpit, as the brothers and sisters wanted to shake hands with him for the last time." Brother Dick was called off to sing while the parting hand was given. He looked round to see if the members were present who could sing the song which he considered appropriate for the occasion. Being satisfied on that subject, he, with his choir, sang the following; each line of which was repeated three times, with an air, enthusiasm and melody which must be heard to be fully appreciated:

> "Christ was born in Bethlehem,
> And in the manger stayed;
> The Jews they crucified him,
> And nailed him to the tree.
> They put him in the sepulchre,
> And over him rolled the stone;
> Down came the angels
> And off of him rolled the stone.
> Christ he rose triumphant
> To conquer death and hell.
> Mary she came a weeping
> To see her lovely Lord—
> Shout! shout! the victory!
> I'm on my journey home."

While they were singing this unique song, with a pathos peculiar to our colored people, they marched up in a confused crowd to take leave of the Doctor, each extending the hand to every other white person in the house, and then to each other. After the benediction was pronounced, a circle of the colored sisters about the centre of the house, each holding the other by the hands, sang the following song, marking time with their feet, bodies, and uplifted arms:

> "Shout children, for I ain't got weary yet;
> My Lord called me and I must go,
> For I ain't got weary yet.
> When I touch one string the whole heavens ring,
> For I ain't got weary yet.
> There's a long white robe in heaven for me,
> For I ain't got weary yet.
> That long white robe I'm bound to wear,
> For I ain't got weary yet.
> There's a starry crown in heaven for me.
> For I ain't got weary yet.
> There's golden slippers in heaven for me.
> For I ain't got weary yet.
> Those golden slippers I'm bound to wear,
> For I ain't got weary yet."

They emphasized with voice and gesture, "I ain't got *weary yet*," and shrieked at the top of their voices, "That starry crown I'm *bound* to wear," "Those golden slippers I'm *bound* to wear." The enthusiasm became wild and noisy, and some of the circle, who were young, and therefore more impulsive than the rest, became almost frantic with excitement. Here and there an old sister might be seen standing at a short distance from the happy circle of singers, with folded arms and closed eyes, rocking to and fro, humming in a sing-song manner, like some of the less informed preachers of a half century ago delivered their sermons.

The Doctor and Mr. Thompson and family left these happy people to enjoy themselves as long as they chose, and in their own way. The Doctor made some remarks on the peculiarity of negro character, and Mr. Thompson thought these peculiarities were natural and providential, adapting them to the position assigned them.

The reader is perhaps growing impatient to see the "conclusion of the whole matter." I will not, therefore, stop here, even to describe the more than happy interview between Nellie and Mr. Mortimer, suffice it to say they both wore smiling faces, and seemed quite as cheerful and happy as at any former period—perhaps it was the happiest Christmas of their lives—but of this, more anon.

## CHAPTER XVI.

*The Right of Masters Proved by Positive Precept—The Dining Party—Dr. Pratt Goes North—What befell him in Charleston—Mr. Mortimer Visits the North—Nellie returns with him—An Agreeable Surprise.*

Although it was Christmas night, it was agreed that they would have a little social conversation on slavery, by way of recapitulation, and to conclude the discussion. The Doctor's health seemed much better and he was rapidly improving, and had made up his mind to leave in a few days for Savannah, *en route* for home.

"Well, Doctor," said Mr. Thompson, "as you are shortly to leave us, and will probably be busy making your arrangements, I will first recapitulate, so far as I can remember, my arguments on slavery, hoping that when you return home you will fully examine them in the light of revelation, with an impartial mind, to see whether I am right, and I trust you may be brought to see your error and renounce it."

First. It has been proved that God instituted slavery by subjecting the descendants of Ham to those of Shem and Japheth. Second. That this slavery was made perpetual by the positive enactment of heaven. That man is therefore not responsible either for the origin or continuance of the institution. The divine law, both in the Old and New Testaments, gives the relation of slavery its full sanction. There is no law to condemn; there is much to approve and regulate the institution. Even Dr. Wayland admits there is no precept against slavery. But there are prohibitions against all wrong—therefore slavery is not wrong, for "where there is no law there is no transgression." Third. The Holy Spirit positively enjoins obedience on the part of slaves to their masters, thus giving the seal of the divine approbation to this relation. Fourth. It has been shown that the Jews in Palestine, and slaveholders in the South, enslave the same people. Fifth. Masters are taught how to treat their slaves, but instruction on this point would have been omitted if the relation had been wrong, for the Bible no where teaches us how to do a wrong. No where in the gospel is a man taught how to treat his second, third and fourth wives. Poligamy is a sin, and therefore is not regulated by inspiration; the sin is rebuked, but no duties connected with it are mentioned. Sixth. The Apostles admitted slaveholders and their slaves to church membership, without requiring a dissolution of the relation. But they did require them to abandon their sins and iniquities; therefore slavery was not considered to be a sin by these inspired men of God. Seventh. The Apostles required slaveholders to withdraw from abolitionists as incorrigible opposers of the teachings of Christ, and as disturbers of the peace and quiet of the churches. Eighth. That abolitionists cannot preach the whole gospel. They do not believe that "All Scripture is given by inspiration of God, and that it is profitable for doctrine, for reproof, for correction, for instruction in righteousness. They therefore omit that portion of it which commands slaves to be obedient to their masters.

Lastly. It has been shown that abolitionism unavoidably tends to infidelity; that abolitionists are now taking positions which embody the worst forms of infidelity ever known to the world. Having joined the church and obtained control of the pulpit, press, theological chairs and publishing houses—in a word, having obtained control over the moral and religious sentiments of the North, their influence is potent and irresistible for the destruction of truth and righteousness.

I have now one thought more, and my work is done.

You quoted and endorsed Dr. Wayland's language .that "the Apostles are in every case careful not to utter a syllable by which they *concede the right* of the master." I have already proved that by implication and by example they did concede this right. I now propose to fulfill my promise by proving very briefly that this right is conceded by positive precept.

In speaking of his desire to retain Onesimus in his service, that he might minister to him, Paul says, in Philemon 13-14: "Whom I would have retained with me, that in thy stead he might have ministered unto me in the bonds of the gospel. *But without thy mind would I do nothing.*" Why did not this great Apostle keep this runaway slave? He evidently needed his services, and greatly desired them. If he did not admit the right of Philemon, then he would have violated none in retaining the slave. According to the Northern sentiment, which gave rise to the anti-fugitive slave law, he was and of..right ought to be free. His master never had any right to hold him in slavery; he was guilty of man stealing when he bought him, and any act of the slave which released him from this unjust ownership of a covetous tyrant should be hailed with joy by all the good, and aided by all the lovers of liberty. But this inspired man of God took a different view of it. "You are entitled to your slave, brother Philemon. I want him, would like very much to keep him, I need his services while I am here in bonds, but he is yours and I cannot keep him without your permission. I have as much right to take your provisions, your furniture, or any other property you possess. He has long been unprofitable to you on account of the wicked and abandoned life he has led, but now he is a converted man, feels his wrong, has repented it, recognizes his obligations to you, and desires to return. I, too, feel it my duty to return him to you. I send this letter by him, asking that in consideration of his repentance and reformation, you will receive him, and forgiving the past, will treat him kindly." You will, perhaps, think this a Southern view. I will therefore refer you to the opinions of great and good men across the Atlantic, who have not generally been accused of favoring slavery.

Coneybeare and Howson. "He (Paul) wished to keep him

(Onesimus) at Rome, and employ him in the services of the gospel. Yet he would not *transgress the law*, nor *violate the rights of Philemon*, by acting in this matter without his consent."

Here is the testimony of two emancipationists to the fact that Paul would not "violate the rights of Philemon." Then he had rights, else Paul could not have violated them. These rights the Apostle "conceded" in sending his slave, for if he had sent him only as a helper of the gospel, any other brother might have done as well, and Onesimus would have been detained, inasmuch as the Apostle was so desirous to have his setvices

MacNight. " Without knowing thy mind, *whose slave he is*, I would do nothing to encourage him to stay with me."

Doddridge says in his paraphrase : Whom indeed I was desirous to have kept near me, that he might have officiated for thee, and in thy stead have attended upon me in the bonds I suffer for the sake of the gospel. . . . . But I would do nothing in this affair without thy *express consent.*

Matthew Henry says: Paul herein, notwithstanding his apostolic power, would show what regard he had to *civil rights*, which christianity does by no means suspend or weaken, but rather confirm and strengthen. Onesimus, he knew, was Philemon's servant, and therefore without his consent not to be detained from him.

Other authorities might be cited, but these are enough to prove that wise and good men of other times believed that the Apostles did concede the right of masters. The opinion of Dr. Wayland is of modern origin. None of the fathers agree with him; none of that host of learned and devout theologians of the two last centuries concur in his views. His own prolific brain, in its terrible conflict with truth, gave birth to this subterfuge, in order that he might present at least a plausible pretext for his persevering and incorrigible opposition to slavery. Better men than he, men of erudition and mental acumen, who have been willing to be taught by inspiration and receive without cavil its holy instructions, have discovered much truth in favor of slavery, the existence of which your Dr. W. denies.

" It is true," replied the Doctor, " that Paul *seems* to concede the right of Philemon in the language you quoted, but he and his christian brother were upon most intimate terms of friendship and fraternity, and he sent Onesimus back to prevent a rupture of those ties, and not as an act of justice—the latter it could not have been."

"It was either an act of justice, or it was an act of injustice," said Mr. Thompson. Onesimus was either a freeman or a slave, i. e., he was either the property of Philemon or he was not; if he were, then it was an act of justice to send him back; if he were not, it was an act of injustice to send him to Philemon. If he were a freeman, Paul outraged the rights of a fellow being; if he were a slave, he did simply an act of justice, which was due to Philemon, as well as to that holy system of moral honesty and pure religion, of which he was a representative. If Onesimus was a freeman, he had always been one, unless he had been manumitted, of which there is not the shadow of evidence. If he had always been free, then Paul was mistaken about the injustice he had done his master, since he had never been in a relation which demanded any service to Philemon. Paul sent him back in the capacity of a slave. Did he do so out of deference to the *feelings* or to the *rights* of Philemon? If to the *feelings*, then he was guilty of reducing a freeman to bondage that he might retain the friendship of a man who was guilty of the "sum of all villainies." But would Paul, that great Apostle, whose immutable adherence to right had brought upon him the bitterest persecutions, and for which he was then in bonds; that Paul, who had given up all things for Christ, and counted them not loss, but gain; that he, who had forsaken all his worldly gains, honor, kindred and nation—in a word, everything, for truth and righteousness—that he, who had stood before the Sanhedrim and hazarded all for the sake of righteousness, who, in chains, reproved the wickedness of Felix in such eloquent terms that the heathen prince trembled at the recital of his crimes and their consequences—he who, with a moral heroism, almost without a parallel in the great achievements of christianity, stood before the bloody tyrant Nero, and pleaded the cause of despised christianity, and triumphed in swaying the mind of that most cruel of all the Cæsars—that this Paul should be guilty of an act of injustice to prevent the rupture of fraternal ties between himself and our simple-minded christian brother! Why, Doctor, the idea is preposterous! But did Onesimus go back to save the feelings of Philemon? Was his regard for one who had held him in unjust bondage so tender as that? Did he voluntarily yield himself up from a state of lawful freedom to one of perpetual bondage, just to please Philemon? If so, then, Doctor, learn a lesson of kindness. Dear, good Paul knew his brother Philemon had been guilty of a great wrong in holding Onesimus in slavery. The slave had escaped and gone several hundred miles to Rome; the Apostle finds him there, and after his conversion receives him into the church. Then he says : Now, come, Onesimus, your master and I are good friends and brethren ; we love each other very much, and I intend to perpetuate that friendship at any cost. I am aware of the sin of slavery, and know your master did wrong in holding you in that relation ; but, come, you must go back ; I love him and must keep his love ; go back, and let him continue to outrage your inalienable rights. Now, was he not very kind? Doctor, do you abolitionists feel so towards us slaveholders of the South ? If not, I would entreat you to learn affection and courtesy from this inspired Tarsian. Avoid the errors growing out of Paul's want of decision and firmness, but imitate the excellent virtue of amity, which you think controlled his action in sending back this runaway slave.

You cannot deny that all the facts in the history of this case go to prove beyond all question, that Onesimus was lawfully the slave of Philemon, and that Paul sent him back in response to the demands of justice : had he done otherwise, it would have been an outrage upon the rights of the master, such as you Northern people unblushingly perpetrate daily, in the name of our blessed christianity, against the rights of Southern slaveholders. But the day of retribution comes on apace, when you will no longer " cry peace, peace," but when for all these violations of human rights, and this setting at nought the revealed will of God, you will see in anguish the swift destruction as it comes upon you."

" How could those inspired of God to instruct man as to the duties which he owes to his fellow-beings ' concede the right ' of one man to hold another in involuntary servitude against his will, entailing on him all the evils of this horrible system ? " replied the Doctor, for the want of something more apropos.

" How one inspired man did concede this right I have already shown you," said Mr. T., " but ye believe me not."

The " evils of this horrible system " have as much real existence as the ghost of Banquo that gave such alarm to Macbeth. The latter had murdered the former, and he imagined he saw his ghost, and was greatly alarmed. You of the North first introduced slavery and the slave trade : when you found it unprofitable you sold them into Southern slavery, into his " horrible system." Do your consciences torture you for it ? Do you see the ghost ? Does it harrass your minds and disturb your dreams ? Are you trying to atone for your former cupidity by adopting this mode of denying your great sin, if slavery be a sin ? But, seriously, involuntary servitude is not necessarily against the will of those who serve. The contentment and happiness of our servants afford the most gratifying evidences of their willingness to serve. It is a singular fact, and one worthy of note, that African slaves have never voluntarily attempted to throw off the yoke of bondage. When any attempt of the sort has been made by insurrections, unprincipled white men have always been the instigators.

God has given the master a right to the labor of the slave, and no man should interfere with it. He has also given certain rules for the government of the master in his treatment of the slave. The obligations are reciprocal. The servant should be faithful at all times and under all circumstances, both to the good and to the froward. The master should "do justly and love mercy" in his treatment to his slaves, doing as he would be done by, "under subsisting relations." To conclude, God has forged the chains of slavery, and riveted them upon the descendants of Ham and Canaan. He has formed the relations of master and slave, and united them together now. "What God hath joined together let not man put asunder."

"When do you think of returning home, Doctor?" said Mrs. Norton.

"In a few days, ma'am; just as soon as I can arrange for the trip."

"I am almost tempted to go with you, I am so anxious to see husband," said Mrs. Norton.

"O, no, mother, you cannot go *now;* for, however anxious we may be to see father, and he to see us, I know he would not have us return before spring," said Nellie.

As the conversation was not exclusively social, the reader is not anxious to know what was said.

Two days after, Mr. Mortimer gave a dining to Dr. Pratt, to which Mr. Thompson and family were also invited. It was something new for so many fashionable ladies to be seen at this bachelor establishment, for although Mrs. Thompson frequently went over in company with her husband, yet it could not be said to be a place of resort for the ladies of the community. The servants gazed with wonder, while their ivory teeth shone through their ebony lips like the silver lining upon the dark cloud.

Their crackery and unique appearance somewhat amused the tidily dressed maids of Mrs. Thompson. She had inculcated more or less taste in her servants, by bringing them into perpetual contact with her own unexceptionable neatness. But the dining passed off delightfully, leaving pleasant recollections to be treasured in after days. Nellie looked round, and observed very closely everything about the house. There was some furniture, but no arrangement. There were carpets, but they were threadbare; the bureau was dusty; the plastering of the house was cracked, smoky and full of cobwebs; everything indicated a want of attention. Only here and there was a rosebush in the yard; no flowers, no taste. "O how uninviting; but there is a warm heart and a noble spirit that presides over this chaos, and which will, with the aid of my guiding hand, bring order and neatness out of this wreck and confusion."

A few days after, Dr. Pratt bade adieu to his Southern friends. At Savannah he took the train for Charleston to reach a steamer, whose Captain was an old and particular friend, and from whom he hoped to receive some favor in the way of a free passage. A sad occurrence, however, befell the Doctor while in Charleston, which his friends have never noised abroad, and which is here alluded to only as an incident characteristic of his faith. As it will be considered a virtue rather than a failing by his Northern brethren and congregation, and as he has decided never to visit the South again, it may be a kindness to give it publicity. At the hotel in which he took lodgings in Charleston, there was a very neat, genteel mulatto boy of about seventeen summers. As the Doctor had to stay over about three days waiting for the steamer to sail, he became very conversant with the boy Ned. Among other topics of conversation was that of slavery. Though naturally contented and happy, the Doctor found him quite pliant under his representations of the blessings of freedom. So being emboldened by his successful attempts to impress the boy, he asked him why he had never made his escape on a steamer. He stated to him that many had done so, and succeeded in making good their escape, and added: "You can do so, too, if you will. I will give you any assistance in my power."

"But I's got no cap but dis," said Ned, "and dey will see de hotel sign and take me up. Den I's got no fine close to wear when·I gets to New York."

"I will loan you my silk velvet cap, and when you get to New York we will buy you some good clothes to wear. Will you go?"

"O, yes, sir, dat I will. You'll fix me up fine, won't you? Give me boots and a fur hat like your'n, and git me a heap of nice things, and then I can do as I please and won't have no work to do. Hoop! that 'll be great, hurrah for Ned." The boy went off into ecstacies, and the Doctor lapsed back into a serious mood over the sad disappointment that was to blight these happy anticipations of the simple minded boy on his arrival at New York.

Late in the afternoon the Doctor walked down to the steamer, which was to sail the next morning at ten o'clock, and, sauntering round, selected the place where Ned was to conceal himself. After tea he gave Ned the cap, and told him where to hide, and that he must stay in his concealment till they arrived in New York, and that he would come every day and feed him.

Before the sun arose, Ned was on the steamer and safely ensconced in his hiding place. But Hamp, the colored supervisor of the servants at the hotel, soon missed Ned, and having made "diligent search" for him, returned without "tidings." The fact was immediately reported to the landlord. He very soon suspected that his boy had been seduced, and was endeavoring to make his escape. The truth was his suspicions had been somewhat excited previously, on account of the great attention and unusual time which Ned had devoted to Dr. P's room. He looked over his register to see who was at his house, and finding no one from the North but Dr. Pratt, he felt convinced that he was the author of the mischief. So sending immediately for a lawyer, he advised with him as to the best course to ascertain the guilty party and obtain redress. He was advised to have Dr. Pratt arrested, and to take out a search warrant for the steamer, both of which he did at once.

The Doctor was immediately brought before the municipal court having jurisdiction of such cases. He pleaded not guilty. While the landlord was proceeding with the testimony, proving that he was the only man at his house from the free States, that Ned waited on him, and that he always over stayed his time when in his room, and that he had dropped some hints to the other waiters, the mystery of which was now solved by the circumstances, and while the Doctor was growing very serious, as his vivid imagination pictured a guard house with iron bars, himself looking from the inside, and perhaps something unspeakably worse in the not distant future. While all this was taking place, the officers sent to search the steamer, returned, bringing Ned with them. The appearance of the boy awakened some merriment with all save the Doctor and his angry landlord. The peaked head of Ned running up to a point on top was inclosed down to his eyes by the cap which sat so gracefully on the intellectual cranium of the Doctor of Divinity. Ned's optics were much less than two new moons, but were certainly dilated to an unusual extent by the excitement of his novel situation. "Whose cap is that on your head?" cried the landlord, rather unamiably.

"This here man's," cried Ned, pointing to Dr. Pratt.

"How did you come by it," reiterated the enraged landlord.

"I hope the Court will call the gentleman to order; his questions are irrelevant; negro testimony is not good in court against a white man," said the counsel for the defendant. Dr. Pratt looked better, a ray of hope dawned upon his darkened future. Negro inequality was right, at least, in this instance.

"The Court cannot permit any questions addressed to Ned; he cannot be a witness in the trial of this case."

"Is this your cap, Mr. Pratt?" asked the landlord.

"I had one like it, sir; it may be in my trunk, or the boy may have stolen it. I did not give—"

"Stop, Mr. Pratt," said his counsel. "I appeal once more to the Court, and ask that the prosecutor may not be permitted to ask questions of my client. A man cannot be forced to give testimony against himself. I hope the Court will not take into consideration any admission which has been made by my client."

"That Yankee rogue gave that cap to Ned to hire him to run away with him. You ought to be rode on a rail, lynched and driven out of town."

"Order! order!" said the Court. "The Court will not permit any such remarks by prosecutors or others to defendants on trial. I will strictly enforce order, and punish any further violations of the rules of the Court."

"May it please your honor," said Dr. Pratt, "I am a stranger in your midst; I have not an acquaintance in your city, save Capt. C , who is to sail in one hour from this time, (looking at his watch.) Will the Court do me the favor to send for him that I may prove my character?" The Doctor was much agitated, but firm.

The Captain having heard that his friend was accused of attempting to steal the boy, had concluded to come up and render him any assistance in his power. He entered just after the Doctor had taken his seat.

"If the Court will give Capt. C. an opportunity to make any statements he may see proper in regard to my character, I will be obliged to it, and receive the same as a kindness," said Dr P.

"Capt C. has permission to do so," said the Court.

"I know Dr. Pratt to be the pastor of a large, wealthy and intelligent congregation in the State of Massachusetts. I have known him for a dozen years or more, and during that time he has enjoyed the confidence of his flock," said the Captain.

"Isn't he an abolitionist," thundered the landlord.

"Order! order!" cried his counsel.

"It is a proper question," replied the Court, "but not very properly asked."

"I believe he has never been accused of favoring slavery, but still I never thought him so unreasonable as to be guilty of such a crime as that of which he is accused."

"Do you purpose leaving on the steamer this morning, Mr. Pratt?" asked the Court.

"Yes, if permitted, and will bid adieu to the South forever."

"There are two reasons why the Court will acquit the defendant: 1. It is a golden old maxim of the law that 'ninety and nine guilty men had better go free than that one innocent man should suffer.' The circumstances throw deep suspicion on the character of the prisoner, but do not demonstrate his guilt. 2. He is a citizen of another State, and on his way hither, and cannot by any possibility commit a similar offense again, even admitting him to be guilty in the present case. The end of punishment is the prevention of crime—the end being obtained in this case without the infliction of punishment, it is ordered that the prisoner be released."

The Doctor made a grateful bow to the Court, locked arms with the Captain, and with a wiser head, left for the steamer in great haste.

On the breaking out of the present war, Dr. Pratt became a chaplain for a Massachusetts Regiment. On the morning of the 22d of July he left Washington City to reach his congregation in camps, and in due time arrived at Centreville, when the first noise that saluted his ears was the wild clatter of the panic-stricken army as they fled before the impetuous pursuit of the Southern soldiers. Visions of Charleston flitted athwart the excited imagination of the sage Doctor, and mounting his horse he gave evidence of his ability to lead the most dashing and reckless cavalry. He had read that Scripture which says of danger: "Only with thine eyes shalt thou behold; . . . . it shall not come nigh thee," and he labored successfully to secure its fulfillment. On being twitted by a brother chaplain a few days afterwards for his speed, his apt reply was characteristic of the wholesome lesson he had learned from past dangers. "The prudent man foreseeth the evil and hideth himself."

The Doctor sagely concluded after this that it was predestined that he should remain at home with his congregation and family, giving aid and comfort to his country by inflammatory speeches in favor of the glorious Union, the Stars and Stripes, and against the

South. He has filled his mission well and secured the highest commendation from his master Abraham.

On the first of May, Nellie and her mother left their affectionate kindred with mingled feelings of pleasure and pain. Nellie sang, "Homeward Bound," as the steamer gently rocked upon the undulating bosom of the deep; but visions bright and far cheered the heart and filled up the measure of hope as she thought of the noble and loved one behind, who was soon to follow her. Safely at home once more, Nellie lost no time in beginning her preparations for the tenth of July, on which occasion she was to assume another name and character, and leave for a Northern tour. She found time, however, to read and answer a letter from a Southern correspondent once a week. Her pastor was greatly displeased with the match, and tried by operating on the mind of her father to break it off. Mr. Norton, however, was a prudent man and a doting father. Nellie was his idol; he confided greatly, too, in her judgment, and positively refused to say a word against the consummation of her desires. Mr. Norton had spent several years of his earlier manhood in Virginia, and did not approve of Dr. Pratt's bitter opposition to slavery.

On the 28th of June Mr. Mortimer left Savannah for New York, where he spent several days before leaving for New England, and where, on the 5th of July, he was met by the Rev. J. L. from Georgia, the pastor of his negroes—whose expenses he had proposed to pay if he would take the trip, suggesting that it might prove beneficial to his health. The truth was Nellie and Mr. Mortimer had both agreed before she left, and after the late misfortune at Charleston that they must have some one who could unite them in the holy ties of marriage, and she left it with Mr. M. to make the arrangement.

The tenth was a bright and beautiful day, and at eleven o'clock Mr. Mortimer and his Southern parson made their appearance at Col. Norton's, where, a few moments afterwards, the two loving hearts solemnly covenanted to perform all the duties of husband and wife required of them by the laws of God and man until they should be separated by death. Cordial congratulations, happy smiles, tears of affected joy and regret made up the scene which for a few moments transpired:

        Yet happy they, the happiest of their kind,
        Whom gentler stars unite, and in one fate
        Their hearts, their fortunes, and their beings blend.
        'Tis not the coarser tie of human laws,

> Unnatural oft, and foreign to the mind,
> That binds their peace, but harmony itself
> Attuning all their passions into love.
> Where friendship full exerts her softest power,
> Perfect esteem enlivened by desire—
> Ineffable, and sympathy of soul;
> Thought meeting thought, and will preventing will,
> With boundless confidence: for nought but love
> Can answer love and render bliss secure "

Saratoga Springs, the Falls of Niagara, and the city of Quebec, were visited by the bridal party. In due time their faces were turned homeward. Stopping for a few days in New England to gaze once more upon the loved scenes of her early childhood, and to bid a last farewell to friends and kindred—on the first of October Nellie left the dear home of her early happy days to share the pleasures and divide the sorrows of her honored husband in the Empire State of the South.

On arriving at her new home, she was greeted by her uncle, and aunt with joyous spirits and loving hearts. A change striking and delightful had come over the appearance of the bachelor's premises. The house had been neatly painted, the rooms newly plastered, the threadbare carpets had given place to new, soft, rich Brussels. The furniture was all new, beautiful and stylish. Sofas, chairs, ottomans, what-nots, &c., all just from the great emporium of Northern commerce, and of the latest style, adorned the mansion, and proved the loving forethought and tender regard of Mr. Mortimer. Nellie threw her arms around her noble husband, and thanked him from a warm and affectionate heart for these new tokens of his love.

Being installed as mistress of the premises, Nellie sat about an organization and systematic arrangement of the family and household interests. Taking her aunt as the model, it need not be stated that she succeeded beyond the expectations of her most sanguine friends.

Her home is now the asylum of the sick and wounded soldier of the Southern army; he always finds a cordial welcome, and a generous hand to supply his wants, or to soothe his sufferings.

Her noble husband wields a trenchant blade in favor of Southern rights, and has on many battle fields taught the foe to quail before his invincible courage.

&c.

www.ingramcontent.com/pod-product-compliance
Lightning Source LLC
Chambersburg PA
CBHW020856230426
43666CB00008B/1210